GANG LIFE IN TWO CITIES

An Insider's Journey   Robert J. Durán

Columbia University Press   New York

Columbia University Press
Publishers Since 1893
New York   Chichester, West Sussex
cup.columbia.edu
Copyright © 2013 Columbia University Press
All rights reserved
Library of Congress Cataloging-in-Publication Data
Durán, Robert J.
     Gang life in two cities : an insider's journey / Robert J. Durán.
          p. cm.
     Includes bibliographical references and index.
     ISBN 978-0-231-15866-4 (cloth : alk. paper)—ISBN 978-0-231-15867-1 (pbk. : alk.
paper)—ISBN 978-0-231-53096-5 (e-book)
     1. Gangs—Colorado—Denver.   2. Gangs—Utah—Ogden.   I. Title.
HV6439.U7D463 2012
364.106'60978883—dc23

                                                                    2012024433

⊗

Columbia University Press books are printed on permanent and durable acid-free paper.
This book is printed on paper with recycled content.
Printed in the United States of America
c 10 9 8 7 6 5 4 3 2 1
p 10 9 8 7 6 5 4 3 2

COVER PHOTO AND FRONTISPIECE: Robert J. Durán
COVER DESIGN: Milenda Nan Ok Lee

References to Internet Web sites (URLs) were accurate at the time of writing. Neither the author nor Columbia University Press is responsible for URLs that may have expired or changed since the manuscript was prepared.

To the *barrios* of Denver and Ogden where the Chicana/o dreams for a better future

PERSEVERE!

To *mi familia* who has always been there for me: Dad (José), Mom (Leeann), Andrew, Richard, Christopher, Angela, Jody, Anthony, and Mario

To Charlene *por vida* and our four wonderful children: Jazmine, Doroteo, Jocelyn, and Justice

Contents

Acknowledgments

I am tremendously thankful to many individuals for helping this book see the light of day. For the production of the book I am sincerely grateful to Lauren Dockett, the past editor at Columbia University Press, for seeing the potential in my original book proposal and providing me the support to produce this work. I thank Roy Thomas, the senior manuscript editor, for continuing this momentum and Anita O'Brien for making the writing shine. The initial and secondary reviews from two scholars were extremely helpful. I am grateful to the Racial Democracy, Crime and Justice–Network for allowing me opportunities in 2007 and 2011 to work on the ideas and material for this book, as well as for the mentorship, encouragement, and peer reviews from Ruth Peterson, Lauren Krivo, Steven Lopez, James Diego Vigil, Scott Decker, and Avelardo Valdez.

Thanks go to individuals at New Mexico State University (NMSU), including Cynthia Bejarano for encouraging me to express my voice; my best homie Carlos Posadas for his constant friendship and support along with the initial idea to submit my book proposal to Columbia University Press; and Tom Winfree for supporting me and providing excellent discussions regarding the gang literature. Thanks also to the participants at NMSU's Teaching Academy Publish and Flourish workshop for providing additional attention and peer review feedback to help improve the writing process. Much love to NMSU and my colleagues in the Department of Criminal Justice for providing me a home after the completion of my dissertation. Moreover much appreciation to my friends and colleagues of the newly emerging Latino/a criminologists: Alice Cepeda, Vera Lopez, Cid Martinez, Ramiro Martinez, Wilson Palacios, Anthony Peguero, Edwardo Portillos, John Rodriguez, Nancy

Rodriguez, Victor Rios, Xuan Santos, Mike Tapia, Martin Urbina, and María Vélez. Thanks to those who paved the way: Alfredo Mirandé, Joan Moore, Felix Padilla, Luis Rodriguez, Martín Sánchez-Jankowski, and James Diego Vigil.

Although *Gang Life in Two Cities* is an original manuscript, my analysis has benefited from peer reviews received from prior publications. A section of chapter 2 appeared in *Journal of Contemporary Ethnography* 38(2):143–68 and *Social Justice: A Journal of Crime, Conflict and World Order* 36(1):82–101. A section of chapter 3 originally appeared in *Enduring Legacies: Ethnic Histories and Cultures of Colorado*, edited by Arturo Aldama, Reiland Rabaka, Daryl Maeda, and Elisa Facio for the University Press of Colorado. A section of chapter 5 originally appeared in *Latino Studies* 8(3):373–98. Several sections of my article in *Aztlán: A Journal of Chicano Studies* 34(2):99–134 are included in the introduction and in chapters 6, 7, and 8. Each of these publications received guidance and feedback from editors and reviewers who strengthened my arguments. I received funding support during my doctoral study at the University of Colorado from the Society for the Study of Social Problem's Racial/Ethnic Minority Graduate Scholarship, Becker Fellowship, Hispanic Scholarship Fund, and Beverly Sears Grant. The money received from these sources enabled me to successfully complete the dissertation. The College of Arts and Sciences Stan Fulton Endowed Chair contributed proceeds toward the completion of this book.

I truly appreciate my faculty mentors in the Department of Sociology at Weber State University, who inspired me with the passion to become a sociologist. During graduate school Patti Adler trained me in ethnography. She pushed me to get into my settings, develop an analytical framework, and improve my writing. Patti mentored me on how to complete graduate school, become a better teacher, and develop a trajectory to help prepare for promotion and tenure at NMSU. I also thank Arturo Aldama, Joanne Belknap, and Joan Moore for their continuous encouragement in developing my dissertation and providing mentorship after I left Colorado.

Although the production and research mentorship helped me to craft this book, such a project requires my utmost appreciation for the barrio and its inspiring residents. It was in the barrio where homeboys and homegirls, activists, cops, lawyers, teachers, and members of the community allowed me access to their lives to learn more about gangs. I hope this work captures your voices and provides an avenue for much needed solutions in the post–civil rights era. I use pseudonyms for most of the individuals and groups I interviewed. The names of gangs and events are maintained for historical specificity unless it reduces the anonymity of an individual; in these cases the gang name is omitted. To my key partners, you are deeply appreciated in my life and in the creation of this book. One of my key partners gave me permission to thank him directly: Ernesto Vigil. Ernesto was my mentor who transformed my consciousness about gangs by emphasizing the importance of history and the role of the Crusade for Justice in changing the city of Denver.

My family deserves the most gratitude as they went through the good and bad times in my life. They provided me with the drive and encouragement to push myself beyond the limits to be a better person. I thank Charlene Shroulote and our four children—Jazmine, Doroteo, Jocelyn, and Justice—for loving me. Moreover, Charlene has supported my life and its various transitions since I was 16 and definitely deserves my utmost thanks for everything that she has helped me accomplish. Her constructive criticism has helped develop many of the points made in this book and throughout my life. My life has also benefited from the tremendous support and love from the Durán family—my parents, brothers, sisters, aunts, uncles, nephews, nieces, and entire extended family—and from my second family—Mary Jane, Otis Sr., Johnny, Francine, Otis Jr., and their extended family. Finally, I could never have completed such a project without acknowledging and appreciating all the prayers and support given to me from my mom, dad, Father Pat, and the Abbey of Our Lady of the Holy Trinity.

GANG LIFE IN TWO CITIES

Introduction

It is late on a Saturday night in 1993 at the home of a Mexican American gang member in West Ogden, a racially and economically segregated section of Ogden, Utah.[1] I am 16 years old. The occasion is a party following that night's successful attack on members of a rival group. At the request of a young woman, the gang has gone to the house of an enemy group and beaten up the occupants—a fight I participated in, though I am not a member of the gang. The mood is celebratory as people recount the bravery, loyalty, and fighting skills they displayed during the attack. There is a discussion about whether it was a mistake to shout the gang's name at the victims of the beat-down, and talk turns to the question of whether anyone will snitch on the gang.

Suddenly attention is focused on me: I am the only person in the house who is not a member. A tall man walks in my direction and confronts me. Do I want to join? The room becomes silent. Angry glances are thrown in my direction, while my friend Rudy protests that I am not a threat to the gang. I try to sink into the wall, but I have only two options: I can fight and be accepted into the gang, or I can be attacked while attempting to leave. Either way I get roughed up, but if I leave I make enemies instead of friends and I will be seen as a coward.

After a brief delay I walk into the center of the room, set down my quart of beer, throw up my hands, and say, "Let's go!" Everyone in the room becomes excited about another opportunity to fight. The house owner says, "Let's take it outside so we don't get blood all over." We walk outside and the gang leaders surround me. I look at the person in front of me and begin throwing punches. A barrage of fists and feet come at me from all angles, and everything turns into a chaotic blur. After what seems like an eternity, someone says, "Okay, okay, that is good."

I feel like I stepped out of the eye of a tornado. Someone tells me I can go inside and wash my face off. I walk inside and look into the mirror. My face and body are beaten and bruised. I cup my hands as I pour water over my face and smile happily when I realize that I did not lose any teeth. I came out okay. When I step outside I am greeted welcomingly. The mood is once again celebratory as I am told about some of the gang's rules and hand signs. I am now a member.

Getting jumped into a gang was not an expected outcome for my life. I was living in Ogden, and if you asked any of the gang experts around the country they would have limited information available to comprehend gang activity in the state of Utah. This was not Boston, Chicago, Los Angeles, or New York; it was a conservative and highly religious state where everything was perceived as better than the ghetto neighborhoods that existed across the country. My homies and I were going through struggles that appeared to have no relevance to most people. We were not going to college. We were headed to the penitentiary. Some of us were headed to the cemetery. Gang members were portrayed as demons on the nightly news and in the local newspaper. Many individuals simply considered us as "wannabees" because the perception was that gangs existed in other places, but definitely not in Utah. If anything, being seen as mediocre made us represent the gang more strongly and attempt to prove by our behavior that this lifestyle was real.

When individual gang members from Los Angeles or Chicago moved to Ogden, the local gangs challenged them to join a local gang or face immediate opposition. Many out-of-town gangsters chose to join local gangs, but some were able to remain separate. Several members of a well-known Los Angeles gang were able to resist and recruit local residents into their gang. The growth of this gang and its determination to establish a local presence developed into the largest gang feud in the city. Gangs in Ogden have been periodically fighting since the early 1980s; however, since the early 1990s reoccurring homicides and an increased number of shootings have reminded those involved with gangs that this lifestyle brought real consequences.

As a young man of Mexican and indigenous descent on my father's side and Scottish and Czech background on my mother's side, I grew up identifying as Mexican and associating with primarily black and Latino youth. My own gang involvement brought me to a point in my life where living as a gangster was my complete identity. I traveled a long road to get to the point where I could become a researcher. My curiosity about how and why gangs operated was driven by a search for solutions. College was my ticket to a better future, and my entire passion involved the study of gangs. This path made me appreciate how former and even active gang members could play a powerful role in reducing gang violence. Such a transformation did not happen overnight but grew in competition with the argument of gangs as criminals.

Gangs as Criminals

The argument of gangs as criminals originated from a variety of sources and has increasingly developed since the 1980s. The nightly news and television shows such as *Gangland* (History Channel) portray violent, criminal images of how gangs are organized syndicates designed to make money or prey on the innocent. Law enforcement generally argues that gangs are becoming more dangerous and violent and continually growing in size. Gang members are depicted as remorseless individuals who do not care about whom they hurt and the reasons why. The U.S. Department of Justice has begun exploring transnational ties as resources devoted toward gang suppression have become a major source of revenue for many communities across the United States (Diaz 2009).

The research on gangs has often countered and argued against the media and law enforcement view of gangs, but researchers are not immune to sharing a similar opinion that crime or illegal activities are the defining characteristic, arguing that illegal activities are the key difference between gangs and other social groups. The most popular subset of the literature, starting in the 1950s and 1960s, presents gangs as defying middle-class norms by exhibiting behavior that is "malicious," "negativistic," and "nonutilitarian," with no real purpose—acts committed just "for the hell of it" (Cohen 1955). Gang members were considered emotionally disordered and pathological individuals whose paranoia about the actions of enemy gangs leads them to perceive society as discriminatory (Yablonsky 1962, 1997). Gang members were believed to have lower intelligence (Short and Strodtbeck 1965), suffer problems in proving their manhood (Bloch and Niederhoffer 1958), and maintain a class-specific culture oppositional to middle-class norms (Miller 1958). Many researchers in this tradition before the 1970s maintained a classist, sexist, and prejudicial view of gang members.

In the 1970s the argument became more sophisticated. Malcolm Klein evaluated two gang intervention programs in Los Angeles and developed the following definition of gangs:

> Any denotable adolescent group of youngsters who (a) are generally perceived as a distinct aggregation by others in their neighborhood, (b) recognize themselves as a denotable group (almost invariably with a group name), and (c) have been involved in a sufficient number of delinquent incidents to call forth a consistent negative response from neighborhood residents and/or enforcement agencies. (1971:13)

In creating this working definition, Klein saw gangs as antisocial and a group apart. During his forty years of studying gangs (Klein 2007), Klein would become one of the most influential gang researchers. His definition was copied so many times that by the publication of his 2006 book with Cheryl Maxson, five of the six major definitions of gangs mentioned crime. Klein has been central in the creation of Eurogang, a group of scholars who study gangs in the United States and Europe (Decker and Weerman 2005), which I joined in 2007. The working group reached a consensus that the definition of street gangs worldwide should be "any durable, street-oriented youth group whose own identity includes involvement in illegal activity" (Klein 2007). Despite my admiration for Klein and many of his collaborators, I feel that the inclusion of illegal activity in the definition has not allowed for a separation between the scholarly view of gangs and the law enforcement and media view.

The "gangs as criminal" argument has received support, however, as self-report surveys began finding that gang members were more violent (and criminal) than non–gang members (Battin et al. 1998; Bjerregaard and Smith 1993; Curry, Ball, and Decker 1996; Esbensen and Huizinga 1993; Miller 1982; Thornberry 1998). The ongoing survey research that has often found gangs and crime to be synonymous has grown in the last two decades. Major funding for these research projects has often been provided by federal agencies that have helped the "gangs as criminal" argument become the scholarly mainstream (Decker and Van Winkle 1996; Howell 2012; Miller 2001; Spergel 1995).

A small number of gang researchers have not agreed with this argument and have instead argued that such patterns reflect "moral panics" (McCorkle and Miethe 2002; Zatz 1987) or social movements (Brotherton and Barrios 2004; Hagedorn 2008). This has encouraged the development of a counter–gang paradigm. I agree with a slightly modified version of Brotherton and Barrios's (2004:23) definition of gangs:

> A group formed largely by youth and adults of marginalized social class [or racial and ethnic groups] which aims to provide its members with a resistant identity, an opportunity to be individually and collectively empowered, a voice to speak back to and challenge the dominant culture, a refuge from the stresses and strains of barrio or ghetto life, and a spiritual enclave within which its own sacred rituals can be generated and practiced.

Developing a Counter–Gang Paradigm

Based on my experiences and research, I realized there are two major deficiencies in the gang literature that revolve around methodology and theory. First, in terms of methodology, there are still significant challenges for determining what we know and how we go about discovering this information. Most gang researchers have faced difficulties of standpoint or gaining access to gangs, and this obstacle has prevented them from comparing and contrasting their findings in different locations. Second, in terms of theory, the explanations provided about why gangs are formed and how they function have changed little since the 1970s when the "gangs as criminal" argument became popular. Only a small number of gang researchers have considered racial and ethnic bias as a central component for understanding the origin, continuation, and criminalization of gangs. Exploring the role racial oppression has played in the development of gangs and society's response allows us insight into how gangs can be transformed by incorporating the political consciousness and activism from prior points in history. This book will move beyond these two obstacles by arguing for a counter–gang paradigm that builds on the systematic process for how we acquire knowledge and then explain the observed patterns.

How Do We Acquire Knowledge?

Measurement issues of validity are the first important concern in creating a counter–gang paradigm. The foundation of gang research is rooted in an ethnographic methodology, but that has recently been overtaken by a detached quantitative analysis based on surveys and law enforcement claims. Each methodology can offer insight into gangs: the ethnographic data-gathering approach attempts to gain access to members' lives through interviews and fieldwork to understand how they see this lifestyle. Sanyika Shakur, also known as "Monster Kody," an original gangster from the Eight Trey Gangster Crips, argued, "There are no other gang experts except participants" (1993:xiii). Ethnographers attempt to learn the gang member perspective in their own social environment. Quantitative studies, on the other hand, do not require the researcher to speak to gang members directly but rather seek information indirectly, using questionnaires and surveys. Large data sets separate the researcher from the individual through coded variables and levels of significance. These studies are good at including large numbers of people and then comparing them with others across the country. Gang research has benefited from quantitative studies, but the scholarly discipline has never reached a point where direct participatory research is no longer needed. My argument is that to truly understand gang life, researchers needs to place themselves close to the participants—to walk in their shoes and see the world as they do (Jorgensen 1989), and to give their stories a voice so that others can understand the challenges they face on a daily basis. *Gang Life in Two Cities* is based upon this premise.

Gaining access and information directly from gang members has never been easy for researchers. My review of Howell's (2008) bibliography revealed that more than a thousand researchers have studied gangs since 1927, yet fewer than forty have actually devoted a year or more to associating with gang members, and less than a dozen have spent a substantial part of their lives eradicating gang violence (see table 1 for an overview of these researchers). Adler and Adler (1987) argued that there are a variety of types of membership roles when conducting ethnographic research: the greatest level of commitment on the part of the researcher involves the complete membership role. One variant of the complete membership role is gaining access opportunistically, which Reimer (1977) outlined as using the sociological imagination and turning it inward to reflect on the researchers' unique historical and biographical experiences. My research on gangs began opportunistically by using an ex–gang member status that kept me networked into those engaged in this lifestyle. In only one previous study of gangs has a researcher taken an active stance to become a member (Sánchez-Jankowski 1991).

TABLE 1
Gang Researchers Who Have Used Ethnography or Field Research Methods

Researcher	Charac-teristics	Site	Methods and Focus	Time Period
Barrios, Luis	L, M	New York	Field observation of Latin Kings	1996–99
Brotherton, David C.	W, M	New York, California	Field observation of Latin Kings	1994–99
Campbell, Anne	W, F	New York	Participant observer, three women in different groups	1979–81
Chin, Ko-Lin	A, M	New York	Grant, research team, Chinese gangs	1992
Cureton, Steven R.	B, M	Los Angeles	Ethnography with Hoover Crips	Two months 1999, 2000
Dawley, David	W, M	Chicago	Community organizer, Vice Lords	1967–69
Decker, Scott H.	W, M	St. Louis	Grant, with separate field researcher	Three years
Durán, Robert J.	L, M	Denver, Ogden, southern New Mexico, El Paso	Ethnography, primarily Latino gangs	2001–06; 2007–12
Fishman, Laura T.	B, F	Chicago	Detached workers, Vice Queens—black females	1960–63
Fleisher, Mark S.	W, M	Kansas City, Mo.	Participant observation, Fremont Hustlers	1995–97
Garot, Robert	W, M	Los Angeles	Alternative inner-city school, primarily black and Latino youth	1997–2001
Hagedorn, John M.	W, M	Milwaukee	Grant, focus on top dogs, former gang member fieldworker	1985–86, 1991–92, 1994
Horowitz, Ruth	W, F	Chicago	Grants, participant observation, Lions	1971–74, 1977
Hunt, Geoffrey	W, M	San Francisco	Grant, male and female gang members	1991–93
Joe-Laidler, Karen	A, F	San Francisco	Grant, male and female gang members	1991–93
Klein, Malcolm	W, M	Los Angeles	Grant, detached worker programs	1962–68
Mendoza-Denton, Norma	L, F	Silicon Valley, Calif.	Latina youth gangs	1993–97
Miller, Jody	W, F	Columbus; St. Louis	Grant, young women, mostly black	1995–97

TABLE 1
(*continued*)

Researcher	Charac-teristics	Site	Methods and Focus	Time Period
Miller, Walter B.	W, M	Boston	Evaluation special youth program,	1954–57
Moore, Joan	W, F	Los Angeles	Grant, collaborative	1974–75, 1984–85
Padilla, Felix	L, M	Chicago	Diamonds, Puerto Rican	1989–90
Phillips, Susan A.	W, F	Los Angeles	Graffiti, tattoos	1995–96, 2003
Portillos, Edwardo	L, M	Phoenix	Primarily Latino/a gang members	1995
Quicker, John	W, M	Los Angeles	Chicana gangs	Mid-1970s and research in progress
Sánchez-Jankowski, Martín	L, M	New York, Boston, Los Angeles	Gang members, variety of races and ethnicities	1978–88
Sanders, William B.	W, M	San Diego	Police and gang unit cases	1978
Short, James F.	W, M	Chicago	Grant, detached workers with one white and six black gangs	1959–62
Spergel, Irving	W, M	New York	Participant observation and field interviews	1959–60
Taylor, Carl	B, M	Detroit	Owner of private investigative/security company, research team	1980–86
Thrasher, Frederic	W, M	Chicago	Field observation	Early 1920s
Valdez, Avelardo	L, M	San Antonio	Grant, mixed-gender research team, female gang members	1995–98
Venkatesh, Sudhir	I, M	Chicago	Black Kings, Robert Taylor Homes	1992–1994
Vigil, James Diego	L, M	Los Angeles	Grant, primarily Latino gangs	1976–78, 1992–95
Whyte, William F.	W, M	Boston	Corner boys and college boys	1937–40
Yablonsky, Lewis	W, M	New York	Director of crime prevention program	1953–58

Source: This list was compiled from articles, books, and faculty websites.

Note: The characteristics examined here include race and ethnicity (Asian, black, Indian, Latino, and white) and gender (female and male). Other characteristics of interest include age, role in the setting, and background, but I am unable to complete this information for all researchers at this time.

To my knowledge, I am one of a small number of former gang members who have gone on to attain a doctoral degree, and one of the few to conduct an ethnographic study of gangs as the primary researcher.[2] Many ethnographic researchers attempt to nurture gang insiders to develop their studies (Brotherton and Barrios 2004; Campbell 1984; Cureton 2008; Decker and Van Winkle 1996; Fishman 1995; Fleisher 1998; Garot 2010; Hagedorn 1988; Horowitz 1983; Moore 1978, 1991; Padilla 1992; Valdez 2007; Venkatesh 2008; Vigil 1988, 2002, 2007; Whyte 1943). However, these researchers often personally lack the social networks to go deeper into this social life. Researchers often do not share important characteristics with the populations they study in terms of age, ethnicity, gender, race, and urban background. Such personal characteristics are important for ethnography because the researcher is the tool by which data are gathered. Ethnographic research can take us closer to the reality of gang life than any other methodology can because of the researchers' time commitment and higher levels of data validity, but all these studies face different forms of obstruction in developing the analysis and gaining access to natural field observations. Being a former gang member supported my study of gangs in two ways: (1) by increasing my networks and access to the lives of members and associates, and (2) by enhancing my analysis of patterns of behavior, survival struggles, and levels of state-sponsored opposition.

My second contribution to the study of gangs in this book is the incorporation of comparative gang research. Malcolm Klein (2005:135) contends that "gang research would be far more productive if it were based on comparisons." According to Klein, two central themes missing in the literature are comparisons across history and across location. Moreover, studying gangs in more than one location can provide the objective distance and analysis that C. Wright Mills argued for. Mills explained the importance of incorporating both history and comparison to understand the essential conditions: "If we do not take a fuller range into our study, we often condemn ourselves to shallow and misleading results" (1959:148). Comparison between cities and the incorporation of history allowed me to explore similarities and differences in gang culture and especially the response to gangs.

Ethnographic and field studies of gangs have primarily focused on one city and usually a small number of gangs. Although most traditional studies focused on four large cities, more cities have been added since the 1980s, including Columbus, Detroit, Kansas City, Milwaukee,

Phoenix, St. Louis, San Antonio, and San Francisco (Decker and Van Winkle 1996; Fleisher 1998; Hagedorn 1998; Hunt, Joe-Laidler, and Evans 2002; Miller 2001; Taylor 1990; Valdez 2007; Zatz and Portillos 2000). Only a few researchers have conducted ethnographic or field research in multiple sites (Brotherton 1996; Brotherton and Barrios 2004; Fleisher 1998; Gemert and Fleisher 2005; Hagedorn 1988, 2008; Miller 2001; Sánchez-Jankowski 1991). Quantitative studies have been somewhat stronger in comparative research, as shown by the multicity and longitudinal studies conducted in Denver, Colorado; Rochester, New York; and Seattle, Washington (Battin et al. 1998; Esbensen and Huizinga 1993; Thornberry et al. 2003). The problem with these studies is that time-intensive attention is never developed or pursued to validate self-report claims.

My research adds to the comparative study of gangs by exploring the differences between traditional and emergent gang cities (Decker and Van Winkle 1996; Klein and Maxson 2006; Spergel and Curry 1993; Thornberry et al. 2003). Traditional gang cities, also referred to as chronic gang cities (Spergel and Curry 1993; Klein and Maxson 2006), are described as large metropolitan areas where gangs have existed for decades. Emergent gang cities are smaller to midsize cities with gangs that emerged during or after the 1980s. The distinction between emergent and traditional cities can be tested to some extent by the comparison between Denver and Ogden. On the surface these two gang-influenced cities are quite different—"traditional" versus "emergent." However, as we will see in the next several chapters, the actual experiences of gang members of Mexican descent are very similar in both cities. These experiences include encountering the criminal justice system, negotiating the line between associate and member, and learning the core values of the gang. This thus raises a question: if lived experiences of gang members are similar, of what value is the distinction?

Solving this conceptual argument requires moving the argument from traditional and emergent toward a framework of racial oppression. There are clear differences in the community response to gangs based on the time frame in which gangs were first considered a threat, which is often related to racial and ethnic minority population increases. For example, El Paso, Texas, is considered to have had a gang presence since the 1920s, but the response to and magnification of gang issues in this community have definitely not been as punitive or pushed to the level of moral panic as in Denver and Ogden.[3]

How to Explain What We Know?

The second reason for creating a counter–gang paradigm is to provide an analysis of the structural impact of race and ethnic bias in the form of racial oppression. Gang members have been primarily characterized as male (97 percent), poor (85 percent), and comprising the following racial and ethnic groups: Latino (47 percent), black (38 percent), and rarely white (8 percent) (National Gang Center 2009). Both Latinos and blacks are three times as prevalent on gang lists compared with their proportion of the population in the United States, whereas whites are underrepresented by twelve times. The power to socially construct or create the conditions for 85 percent of the listed gang members as Latino and black requires discussion. Gang research in the early 1900s in the United States described members who were primarily European (Thrasher 1927; Whyte 1944). Gangs were seen as supporting the various rackets in the city and offering youth an opportunity to move into politics (Hagedorn 2008; Whyte 1944). Thrasher (1927) argued that white gangs could be transformed into prosocial groups such as Boy Scouts. As European ethnic groups became increasingly assimilated into the wider U.S. culture, most of their gangs faded away. For the most part researchers before the 1950s came across as sympathetic to the plight of gang members and did not overdramatize violence or cultural fears with theory. In the mid-1950s and continuing to the present, gangs have been primarily characterized as nonwhite, immigrant, violent, criminal, remorseless, and more dangerous than the past. The failures of the post–civil rights era to alter the racial landscape ushered in a time frame in which eradicating inequality was seen as unfair. Color-blind and common-sense racism became the accepted ideologies for the promotion of the white racial frame (Bonilla-Silva 2003; Feagin 2010; Haney López 1996, 2003). Code words provided rhetoric in which the conversation shifted to race-neutral ideas such as "criminals," "drug dealers," "gang members," and "illegals," but the suppression was focused on people of color.

The ongoing segregation of people of color from whites allowed for certain neighborhoods to create the conditions for a barrio internal colony: indigenous populations dominated by foreigners (Barrera, Muñoz, and Ornelas 1972; Blauner 1972). Placing gangs of Mexican descent into a colonization framework contributes to a theoretical understanding of the barrio experience and how it differs from the experience of the white numerical majority (Acuña 1998, 2000; Almaguer 1971; Barrera 1979; Barrera, Muñoz, and Ornelas 1972; Blauner 1972; Freire 1970; Memmi 1965; Mirandé 1985; Vigil 1999). Barrera describes colonialism as "a structured relationship of domination and subordination, where the dominant and subordinate groups are defined along ethnic and/or racial lines, and where the relationship is established and maintained to serve the interests of all or part of the dominant group" (1979:193). This racial hierarchy offers both material and psychic benefits to whites and thus ensures that racism remains difficult to eradicate (Delgado and Stefancic 2001, 2005). Along with suppression by the criminal justice system and poor living conditions, firearm production and the attractiveness of the gang image led many into unfortunate outcomes, which only enhanced a colonial design of indigenous self-destruction and self-hate.

An analysis of race and ethnic relations is essential to understanding gangs. I argue that if one wants to learn about gangs, one should first learn the history of race and ethnic relations in the community of interest and explore how contemporary patterns maintain this inequality. Both Latinos and blacks have experienced inequality within the historical experience of the United States. Each racial and ethnic group has encountered a different racialized history within each state; I will outline racial projects in the states of Colorado and Utah. Almaguer (1994:212) argued that "Race is fundamentally a sociohistorical category that is historically contingent."

Gangs in Denver and Ogden originated out of forms of poverty and second-class treatment where the dominant groups varied based on the organization used to attain white supremacy. In Colorado the Ku Klux Klan held dominance in the early 1920s, and many of its leaders maintained positions of power into the 1940s. This dominant framework of being in opposition to blacks, Catholics, foreigners, and Jews created an Anglo identity of maintaining traditional Protestant values. Gangs in Denver were seen as a zoot suit migration from Los Angeles after riots there in 1943. In Utah members of the Church of Jesus Christ of Latter-day Saints (LDS) fleeing persecution brought their religious beliefs to the territory that later became a state. Political and social power was built within the state by Mormon settlers who lived separately from Native American tribes. The railroad ushered in a new wave of residents who were different in religion and national ancestry. These groups served as labor but often faced intense discrimination.

The colonial experience determined what social rights were granted and outlined the life chances for those considered nonwhite. Colonization structured the life chances for youth of color in several ways: (1) by providing reasons for joining neighborhood groups created for physical and psychological protection; (2) by creating the conditions that encourage gang rivalries; and (3) by allowing the dominant majority to frame gang behavior and create a suppression response. Socially disempowered racial and ethnic groups have created gangs as a source of empowerment and social control. Ignoring the current and past experiences of racial and ethnic oppression hides the significance placed on the social construction of race and keeps racism masked and perceived as an illusion, yet it is issues of race, class, and identity that fuel gang membership.

The fourth contribution offered in developing a counter–gang paradigm involves understanding how gangs developed from racial oppression and thus require a social movement response that includes forms of empowerment through civil rights. During the 1960s a variety of organizations were created to attain equality and political power (e.g., the Black Panther Party, Brown Berets, Crusade for Justice, Student Nonviolent Coordinating Committee, and US organization), thus challenging the social conditions that pushed individuals toward gang membership. During this time gang membership became unpopular, and barrio and urban youth found greater opportunities and ways to channel their energy through nonviolent and self-defense-oriented organizations. As these groups faded away in the post–civil rights era, gang membership once again became popular.

Gangs developed as socially disempowered youth who were primarily segregated into certain sections of the city because of ancestry, poverty, and different religious and cultural beliefs created groups that were first described as gangs by the dominant group. Gangs essentially served as forms of protection. The labeling created a self-fulfilling prophecy as groups adopted names to build on the increased attention. Gangs as a perceived and actual form of empowerment were then converted by the state into legitimized forms for future criminalization.

The literature on gangs has rarely developed the argument of how gangs have been transformed by social movements or how the utilization of grassroots empowerment can fundamentally alter gangs (exceptions include Brotherton and Barrios 2004; Dawley 1973; Hagedorn 2008; Hayden 2004; Montejano 2010; Moore 1978; Vigil 1999). These authors argue how gang member transformation occurred in prison or in the community by emphasizing cultural pride and the incorporation of people with past or present gang ties. Esteva Martínez (2003) found gang members actively involved in decreasing violence and working with outside organizations for intervention. Hayden (2004) discovered similar patterns of current and former gang members working to create peace treaties and programs that provide alternatives to gangs. Rodriguez (1994), Ruiz (1997), Shakur (1993), and Williams (2007) highlight former gang member involvement in shaping and changing the path from self-destruction to alternative realities of challenging second-class treatment.

James F. Short (1997:204) argued, "Each city has its own special history, and what works in one city might not work in another. There is no substitute for local knowledge, including both up-to-date information and an appreciation of history." Residents of Denver and Ogden have responded differently to forms of inequality. In Denver the long history of activism by black, Chicano, Native American, and white community residents has created a resistance movement. One group that significantly influenced contemporary advocacy groups was the Crusade for Justice, which was one of the most organized and powerful Chicano organizations during the 1960s and 1970s (Vigil 1999). Contemporary advocacy groups in Denver have attempted to emulate the successes of previous forms of activism. In Ogden the voices of black and Latino residents have been silenced owing to the dominant group's ability to suppress opposition and demonize minority groups as criminals, leaving the barrio discredited and further marginalized. Poor, non-Mormon whites to some degree also have an ambiguous standing in the community. The result is a growing level of division and lack of communication to create needed change.

Based on my research and involvement in the Chicano community, I propose that advocacy groups utilize nonviolent civil rights tactics to push for greater participation of people of color in education, employment, and politics and to counter the stereotypes by which racial and ethnic minority groups are portrayed. This book argues that the central reasons for gangs are racial oppression and colonization. Challenging these forms of inequality and arguing on behalf of a counter–gang paradigm have often been met with criticism from mainstream researchers. Change is not easy, but looking at gangs from a different angle can provide solutions, if this is what the state really desires. A counter–gang paradigm requires less infatuation with crime and more attention to how structural inequality legitimately oppresses racial and ethnic minorities. A counter–paradigm advocates attempts to live and work with those involved in this lifestyle to develop solutions, for those who are closest to gangs may in fact offer some of the best solutions. Hayden (2004:137) captures one of David Brotherton's interviews with King Tone to describe reformation within the barrio:

> So either me and the ghetto make it together, or me and the ghetto die together. And I think that if more people would take that concept into the street and the schools and everything, there wouldn't be a ghetto. Because the Kings are starting to recognize that it isn't a ghetto, it's home. All you gotta do is not shoot each other, not sell drugs, and walk each other's kids to school. You just make this no more ghetto. So that's where I'm at. I want to beat this ghetto.

This book emphasizes the important role cultural activists and current and former gang members can play in transforming gangs. By capturing the stories of those involved in this lifestyle and discovering the issues they encounter, we can take one step closer to much needed solutions— not only for gangs but for empowerment of the entire barrio.

Organization of the Book

Gang Life in Two Cities begins chronologically with my research and moves into thematic themes that capture the gang experience in both Denver and Ogden. At the beginning of each chapter I incorporate the storytelling style perfected by critical race theory to help introduce readers to my access into the social world of gangs. Delgado and Stefancic (2001:39–41) argue that "One premise of the new legal storytellers is that members of the country's dominant racial group cannot easily grasp what it is to be nonwhite. . . . Engaging stories can help us understand what life is like for others, and invite the reader into a new and unfamiliar world." "Naming one's own reality" has been a powerful form of storytelling and counter-storytelling used to critique and challenge dominant paradigms.

Chapter 1 describes my transition from active gang member to pursuit of an interest in why gangs exist. The chapter explores my entrée into the social world of gangs in a complete membership role by which I could gather interviews and field observations. It discusses ethnography as a methodology and how it attempts to gain entrance into the lives of others. I explain my involvement in gangs in two different cities and share the voices of those I met and worked with as key partners. Such an analysis of my methods seeks to create greater reflexivity by which to outline the data presented in subsequent chapters.

In chapter 2 I explore the war on gangs that developed in the post–civil rights era. The war on gangs utilizes the gang suppression model of law enforcement, which is increasingly being developed in correctional institutions. Aggressive policing, legitimized by the label of "gang," developed in the two cities during the 1990s and became the primary strategy for suppressing the black and Latino community. Such an initiative increased the changes that urban youth of color would serve time in the penitentiary. The chapter begins with a police stop of suspected gang members that resulted in a community member's confrontation with the gang unit. The gang label has been used to profile large numbers of black and Latino youth for increased police contact and subsequent negative treatment. My interviews with gang-involved individuals and law enforcement personnel are supplemented with field observations of over two hundred police stops while working with People Observing the Police. I argue that gang suppression contributed to the longevity of gangs and enhanced negative relationships for gang members with the police and rival gangs.

Chapter 3 begins with a description of gangs in Denver. I start with a story of hanging-out with D-loc as he outlines the neighborhood divisions for gangs. D-loc was the director of a gang-intervention group focused on reducing violence, which was instrumental in developing my networks with gang-involved individuals. Then I move into the history of gangs, outlining how the participation of the dominant group with the Ku Klux Klan during the early 1920s shaped race relations within this city. Next I explain the gang activity in Denver during the 1940s and 1950s and how it began to decline in the 1970s, only to remerge with renewed energy during the mid- to late 1980s. Finally I analyze the developments in gang enforcement in the 1990s and 2000s that influenced the outcomes for those involved in gangs. This chapter builds the argument of racialized oppression and its impact on the development of gangs and how social movements seeking to alter these conditions had the potential to transform gang continuance.

In chapter 4 I provide a historical overview of being Latino, non-white, and non-Mormon and living in Utah. The opening story shares my entry into Ogden as an ethnographic researcher and explores the changes occurring with my gang-involved friends. The urban violence continued to serve as a point for policy makers to launch new initiatives for combating gangs. To help understand the transition points of gang development in Ogden as opposed to Denver, a historical overview of Utah is provided. The Wasatch Front, a metropolitan region in northern Utah that contains 80 percent of the state's population, is evaluated to explore the role of race and religion in forming a context where gangs emerged. Ogden, the railroad junction city, connected a more diverse set of residents into an area where crime, vice, and toughness had experienced a longer history of encouraging new social adaptations for the Latino community. Included are interviews with and descriptions of Latino residents who lived in the area as early as the 1920s. This chapter explains the role gangs have played in the city and how the historical response to demonizing racial and ethnic minorities along with immigrants has suppressed social activism but encouraged the gang label to enhance control of marginalized groups by intertwining the power of nativism, race, and religion.

Chapter 5 explores a socially created response to racialized oppression in the form of gangs and how youth encountering structural obstacles struggle to negotiate the line between staying an associate and becoming a gang member. The chapter begins with my ethnographic fieldwork, which used not only firsthand observation of Latino barrios but comparisons with neighborhoods with the highest concentration of white people. Such observations developed an analysis of contemporary race and ethnic relations in two states where the general climate is to view racial and ethnic discrimination as an artifact of the past. The structural challenges in the barrio formed a pattern of unreceptive schools, poor neighborhoods, and families encountering difficulties in learning how to manage these obstacles. Youth in the barrio chose to reduce victimization by seeking friendship and creating a social support group that brought status. Generational descent divided the Latino gangs, as did socially constructed separations of race and neighborhood. An organizational typology of gangs is developed to explore these adaptations.

Chapter 6 examines the core ideals of the gang. Only a small number of youth have chosen gangs in the post–civil rights era as the form of recourse against accepting inferior treatment. I begin with a story of getting jumped by a gang with my two brothers and how my inability to negotiate a nonviolent outcome posed a direct difficulty in altering the gang experience. This chapter analyzes the internal dynamics of the gang that makes gang intervention complicated. The core ideals are the glue that holds together gangs of Mexican descent in both cities. The group pressure to act a certain way and maintain these values brings a mixture of excitement and suffering. Although many gang members strive to uphold these standards, only a few can truly accomplish these goals. These ideals include displaying loyalty, responding courageously to external threats, promoting and defending gang status, and maintaining a stoic attitude toward gang life. Gangs continue to exist despite a long history of prevention, intervention, and suppression, none of which has altered the structural inequality of racism.

Chapter 7 offers solutions to gang activity based on a racial oppression and anticolonial model. The chapter begins with the Area Support for All People (ASAP) group struggling to provide alternative ways of acting and thinking. Key among these social movements were the Crusade for Justice in Denver and the Spanish-Speaking Organization for Community Integrity and Opportunity (SOCIO) in Utah, which learned lessons from the Chicano movement. These groups attempted to transform local politics for Latino empowerment. I describe several contemporary organizations that challenged unequal social conditions to reduce gang violence. I explore how these nonprofit organizations have worked to address the social conditions in the barrio. Working with these activist groups and different state agencies influenced my perception of how to decrease gang membership and violence.

Chapter 8 offers an analysis to make sense of these themes of inequality and resistance under a theoretical model of racial oppression that combines various actions used to control the perceived threat posed by marginalized group members. I borrow from structural and conflict theories and integrate them with the study of internal colonialism and critical race theory. These control efforts were used against people with the least amount of social power and legitimatized as beneficial for everyone. Urban Chicano neighborhoods are presumed to offer few legitimate opportunities, and this trend has been reinforced historically to maintain inequality. The war on gangs, in conjunction with the war on drugs and the war on terror, targets those with the least social power who are labeled the most dangerous. I discuss how these have coalesced to form an effective war on race and ethnicity and explore how gangs can be transformed by social movements designed to eradicate racism for the ultimate purpose of destabilizing the colonial experience in an unlegitimated fight against the powers of the state.

CHAPTER ONE

Researching Gangs as an Insider

I am sleeping, but the doorbell of my townhome keeps ringing. Ding dong. Ding dong . . . Nonstop. "Damn, what do these fools want?" My doorbell keeps ringing. In a half daze I get up to see who is at my front door. I crack open the door and see two middle-aged men standing on the porch holding a picture of a little girl. They report she is missing and ask if I have seen her. I say, "Nah, I haven't seen her," when suddenly my front door is pushed open. The two men produce a gun as I am quickly pushed backwards down the steps. They identify themselves as police as they place me in plastic handcuffs. When I am lying face down on the carpet they ask who else is in my place. I say my girlfriend and baby daughter.

I'm 19 years old and belong to one of the most powerful gangs in the city. I feel untouchable, but not from the police who have the power to do whatever they want. I've been trying to stay away from gang-banging and instead have begun focusing my energy toward making money by selling marijuana. The plainclothes officer brings my girlfriend downstairs and places her on the ground next to me, also in plastic handcuffs. They say they have a search warrant and want to know where I keep my drugs. I say, "I don't have any drugs." "We will tear the place up, you fuckin' wetback! Tell us where you keep your drugs and money!" I tell the officers, I don't have any drugs and that I ain't saying anything. After a while they are throwing things around, so I dismissively say that I have money upstairs in a safe. One officer gets on the phone and asks what's taking so long for backup. They report that SWAT will be arriving shortly and that I'm headed to prison. They threaten me and my girlfriend with other criminal justice consequences, such as forfeiture and removal of our baby daughter from our home. I think to myself, this encounter with law enforcement is going too far. They must have a lot of evidence against me to raid my home. I tell my girlfriend that I'm probably headed to prison. She is crying.

My girlfriend and I both realize that decreasing my level of gang activity couldn't prevent me from going to the pinta. I tell her not to worry because I shouldn't do more than three years. I feel sad that I will leave behind my baby daughter, who is upstairs crying. Only about three weeks prior my closest brother was charged with first-degree murder. I realize that I will be joining him in prison. The two men say they are going outside to brief their backup about the situation. My baby is still crying. After a while no one shows and things begin to become suspicious. My girlfriend and I get up off the carpet and go upstairs to help our daughter. She has a blanket thrown over her head. As we remove the blanket, she is very red, her face covered in sweat, and she's crying at the top of her lungs. We both walk outside and there are no police cars, SWAT, or undercover officers. We have just been jacked: a home invasion robbery. Damn, how could this happen to me? How could I be caught off guard? I thought I was untouchable, and now I want payback for violating the gang rule of involving family. I want to kill these two putos. Now I have to find out who pulled off an attack that I had not imagined possible.

The event described above was one of the deciding moments in my life. No matter how badly I wanted revenge or how badly I wanted to maintain my lifestyle, in the long run my options were limited: prison or death. I wanted a better future for my daughter and girlfriend.

Contrary to stereotypes, I was not born a gang member. My parents weren't involved in gangs. My dad worked at one of the biggest open copper mines in the world, Kennecott Copper. He woke up early and came home late five days a week for thirty-four years. My mom raised eight children and made sure we attended school and church. My father's ancestors lived in New Mexico for hundreds of years, long before this area of the country was considered a part of the United States. Being a Durán symbolized the principles of family, respect, religion, and strength, all of which were maintained with certain behaviors. When my dad was a young boy his family moved to Utah for work. They lived in Dinkeyville, a very poor part of Bingham, which was close to the open copper mine. Bingham's diverse residents included Chinese, Filipinos, Greeks, Italians, Japanese, Native Americans, Puerto Ricans, and individuals from southern Colorado and New Mexico. My mom, on the other hand, was born and raised in East Salt Lake City, the daughter of an up-and-coming Catholic family of second-generation Czech and Scottish immigrants. She lived in an affluent part of town and attended Catholic schools. When my parents married and moved to Bingham, they combined two separate cultures under a common theme of Catholicism.

When Bingham Copper Mine began to push local residents out of the town in 1955 to expand operations, most, including my family, moved to Midvale, which was twenty miles away. The closer community of Copperton didn't allow non-Mormons or individuals of Mexican descent. Midvale, especially the older sections of town, had one of the highest concentrations of Latinos in the state. In elementary school during the 1980s, my life was relatively care-free. I attended a semidiverse Catholic school. I didn't know anything about gangs at this point in my life. My older brothers were active in sports, partying, and starting to get in trouble with the law.

When I was approaching junior high school my parents decided to move to Huntsville, Utah, which is a quiet, rural, all-white Mormon community an hour north of Salt Lake City and twenty minutes from Ogden. The town includes a popular Catholic monastery along with a beautiful scenic lake and mountains, all of which attracted my parents. They wanted to retire in a place that was more peaceful. From day one I felt different in this new location and wanted to move back to Midvale. My happy, class-clown days were beginning to change as I became more withdrawn and rebellious in junior high. I sought an escape from rural living and the popular cliques of white students when I transferred to the more diverse high school in Ogden. It was in Ogden that I found my home and identity within the subculture of gangs.

This chapter provides an overview of ethnography and how I began my research in both Denver and Ogden. My goal was to capture the social world in which I grew up with thick description (Geertz 1973) by developing a methodological approach that had the potential to be less colonial and more reflexive (Blauner and Wellman 1973; Hertz 1997; Ladner 1973). I gathered my data using a multimethodological approach of historical analysis, nonparticipant and participant observation, semistructured interviews, and urban mapping for which the information was recorded through field notes, photography and film, tape recording, and transcribing. The method that emphasizes these techniques is ethnography.

Ethnography

There is no single, universal methodology to study socially disempowered people or groups that remain secretive. I chose ethnography precisely because it offers the best ability to push past the multiple fronts
presented by gang members, media, and the police. I felt that telephone
calls and surveys provided little ability to validate what people say and
do, and I wanted to understand gangs from the inside as a researcher.
Ethnographic methods allowed me the opportunity to comprehend the
life of gang-involved individuals and their families on an intimate basis, within their own social environment—an environment maintained
through lived experience and impression management portrayals (Goffman 1959, 1963). Atkinson et al. (2001:4) reported that "observation
and participation remain the characteristic features of the ethnographic
approach." This methodology contrasts with the "armchair philosophy"
of quantitative studies (Deegan 2001).

    In 2000 I began receiving guidance from Patti Adler, an established
and respected ethnographer (Adler 1993; Adler and Adler 1987, 1991;
Wax 1971), and started my training in ethnographic research. I started
my dissertation "opportunistically" (Reimer 1977) with access to Ogden
gangs, but my mentor recommended that I establish a local research
setting. I began initiating contacts in Denver and was particularly influenced by several urban ethnographies (Anderson 1999; Bourgois 1995;
Moore 1978; Vigil 1988; Whyte 1943). These researchers were situated
differently in sharing the same characteristics as the people they were
studying, but they all worked to attain trust. They were intensely committed to studying impoverished neighborhoods and the people who
lived there, and their ethnographic research challenged widely held
stereotypes.

    Ethnography enabled me to conduct a multiyear study that drew on
my general cultural understanding (Douglas 1976) and specific subcul-
tural participation in gangs as a firsthand research tool. Therefore my
subjective experiences and relation to my research have been critical to
understanding how I gained access to researching gang members in two
cities. My knowledge about gangs began with my own experiences, but
gathering information systematically from a variety of sources helped to
inform my overall understanding of the gang phenomenon and determined the findings presented in subsequent empirical chapters.

Starting Where You Are

Lofland and Lofland (1995:13) stated that "much of the best work in sociology and other social sciences—within the fieldwork tradition as well as within other research traditions—is probably grounded in the remote and/or current biographies of its creators." While attending high school, I began to associate with Ogden's oldest Mexican American gang. The lifestyle felt welcoming, and I was in awe of the *cholo* subculture. These gangsters had a Catholic upbringing and were like one big family. They were respected, and when I hung out with these young men it felt like the whole city finally recognized me. Other friends were not involved in gangs and we hung out on the weekends. But many of these friends were increasingly getting initiated into a growing gang from the other side of town with a history of gang activity of its own. I began negotiating a thin line between rival gangs, and for a short period of time this was beneficial because it prevented me from being physically attacked when I came across different groups.

Walking the line between two gangs did not last long, and I eventually accepted the threat to become a member. Afterwards there was tremendous pressure to follow the rules of the gang or suffer its internal punishments. Growing up in a family that valued toughness provided a good transition into this social group, but the mental preparedness of fighting complete strangers was awkward. When I was younger my older brothers taught me that doing things that other people were afraid to do showed heart and earned respect. In practice a locote[1] lifestyle brought instant status. I began to devote my entire life to upholding the gang image, but accomplishing the group's ideals was not easy. In my late teens I wanted to move toward large-scale drug trafficking. Pressuring friends to join the gang became normal, but I never truly hated our rivals. As a gang member I hung out and responded to the challenges presented by a wide variety of people, including peers, police, teachers, and regular citizens. In my view success came from the streets. Going to school or work was for people who were suckers, afraid to take risks.

My involvement in the gang was daily for two years, but it began to decrease as many of my fellow gang members were sent to prison and a lot of internal problems arose. I was 18 years old and there were so many things occurring in my life that I began to question this lifestyle. I had a baby daughter, and my girlfriend constantly pressured me to quit hanging out with my friends and getting in trouble. The responsibility of fatherhood made me feel as if I had someone to live for, and I wanted to make sure she grew up okay. Molony et al. (2009) found fatherhood as a potential key turning point in young gang members' lives. Yet breaking away from hanging out every night was difficult, so I continued to remain marginally connected to the activities of my friends. During this time my closest brother was charged with a serious felony. Four of my five brothers have served time in prison, and I was probably next in line. I didn't want to go to prison. I decided to move back to my parents' house with my newly formed family after experiencing the home invasion robbery that tested my ability to resist street reciprocity.

I began to read books that raised my consciousness by focusing on cultural empowerment and Latino and black history. The most notable book was *Malcolm X* (Haley 1964), which describes how Malcolm X transformed himself in prison with critical consciousness to become a leader. The movie *Higher Learning* demonstrated the subtle and overt forms of racism and the importance of gaining knowledge. Learning about culture and history in the form of historical revisionism felt empowering and made me question everything. As I became socially conscious my mixed background of cultures, geography, and gangs pushed me to observe larger issues of structural inequality.

By the time I was 19, my activity in the gang had decreased with growing information that my gang had police informants and even undercover officers acting as members, which led to many internal disputes about who could be trusted. The gang was splintering into different pieces. When I began to fade away (too busy with school, work, and my own family to hang out), several leaders within the gang threatened to jump me out, but I refused to accept this open threat of a beat-down. Whether this will one day occur is unknown. Gang membership is a socially constructed identity, and there is nothing that establishes when people join or leave. There are people from the neighborhood who would argue that I am still a member of the gang. There are police officers who argue the same. Nevertheless, most people do not get jumped out of the gang, and I know of only a few instances in which people went through this exit process. Most people fade away from the gang scene. I moved past my previous gang membership by joining Chicano cultural groups and participating in community empowerment through education. Neighborhoods and gangs ceased to be my rivals, and I began working toward uniting the oppressed.

Collins (2000:257) reported that the cutting distinction between academic knowledge and wisdom is experience. She argues, "Knowledge without wisdom is adequate for the powerful, but wisdom is essential to the survival of the subordinate." My experience as a gang member provided me with a knowledge of gangs largely kept secret from nonmembers. When I was a gang member my closest crew and I hung out only with people we could trust. Occasionally a friend brought someone around whom we didn't know, and we tested that person until we felt okay with his or her presence. Our friend's integrity was also at stake in terms of who they attempted to bring into the gang network.

My growing critical awareness developed into a curiosity about why there were different opportunities in neighborhoods separated by class, ethnicity, and race. In my neighborhood (barrio), a lot of friends were joining gangs, getting shot, going to prison, and working low-end jobs or having no employment. On the other side of town, the white suburbs, where many of my elementary school friends lived, young people were preparing for college to become doctors, lawyers, and teachers. They were partying and using alcohol and drugs but rarely came into contact with the police. The difference in these outcomes helped encourage the importance of changing my future path in life.

Obtaining a full-time manufacturing job at age 19 allowed me an opportunity to begin making legitimate money. As I moved farther away from the drama in Ogden, my perspective began to slowly change. I registered for business school with a desire to open my own lowrider shop and obtained an associate's degree. Getting a professional job or having the money to open my own business were not realistic at this point in my life, and so I decided to continue learning and pursuing the opportunities available with a bachelor's degree. I took an Introduction to Sociology course, and my life was changed forever. I didn't want to be a statistic. I had turned 20 and school provided me the ticket to begin this intellectual journey. Chicano student organizations and lowrider car clubs became my new forms of identity.

I began studying Ogden gangs in 1995 for several courses I took as an undergraduate. My early interviews included Gang Unit community liaison members, friends who were involved in gangs or ex–gang members or associates, and young leaders in the Latino community who chose to stay away from the gang life. These conversations were documented with detailed notes. In addition, I began accumulating official statistics from the Gang Unit in Ogden describing the nature of gang-related activity and membership. I even learned how my personal notes from 1992 could be a source of insight.

Determining Insider and Outsider Status

Two primary forms of discussion are needed to articulate the issue of insider and outsider status: those of race, history, class, and segregation (standpoint) and those of membership in particular groups (methodology). Both of these analytical nuances affected my decision to choose ethnography as the methodology to enhance my insight into gangs.

First, issues of structural inequality have created divisions within society. Issues of race, class, gender, age, and religion can position human beings in vastly different circumstances for describing and analyzing social conditions. These varied life chances can affect the interpretation of experiences. Most individuals in academia have focused on one point of view, often characterized as being elitist or an ivory tower (Acuña 1998; Ladner 1973). Scholars from underrepresented groups have often argued for an opportunity to have their voices heard and told by themselves instead of by traditional dominant groups in society (i.e., middle- to upper-class whites). Critical race theorists (CRTs) argue that people of color are often viewed as outsiders, and their ability to make claims is restricted because white and middle- to upper-class residents are primarily presumed to have "access to the social and cultural truth." Collins (2000) argues that scholars, publishers, and other experts have come to decide what is considered knowledge to reflect their interests. This enterprise is largely controlled by elite white men. She argues that the people whose status should allow the ability to propose new knowledge claims about a certain topic become opposed by outsiders, who then condemn insiders for lack of credible research. For these reasons, many authors have attempted to create their own framework to understand society.

CRT offers the voice-of-color thesis as one of its four central tenets. These authors argue that members of minority groups bring competence to speak about race and racism because of different histories and experiences with oppression. The other central tenets include (1) the institutionalization of racism as normal; (2) white-over-color ascendancy offering both psychic and material benefits; and (3) the socially constructed nature of race and ethnicity despite no biological difference between human beings. Together these four tenets have influenced the number of scholars of color who have questioned dominant white frameworks (Bell 1992; Delgado 1995; Delgado and Stefancic 2001; Gómez 2007; Segura 2003).

Merton (1972), one of the most highly respected sociologists, argued against the polarization of "insiders and outsiders." He considered such monopolistic access to knowledge as ethnocentric and elitist. As an Ivy League educator and a white man, Merton critiqued the argument made by black studies advocates for a space of recognition, because on its face such an argument was logically invalid. Merton provided a critique of how human beings are often located within not one status but rather a status set. Thus it is impossible to be a complete insider or outsider; we are more likely a mixture. For example, one is not simply a man but also young or old, rich or poor, of different religions, and so on. Merton argues for the unification of insiders and outsiders to expand knowledge. By providing such an argument, he assumes academia is a level playing field on which anyone conducting research has an equal opportunity to influence knowledge building.

Merton fails to capture the full argument brought forth in Ladner's *Death of White Sociology* (1973). The same theme that Merton argued against—one perspective—characterized academia at the time and still does. Moreover, polarizations within standpoints among a race are also described among scholars of color. Malcolm X described a difference between "house Negroes" and "field Negroes" (Haley 1964). Gómez (2007) and Montgomery (2002) describe a similar separation between Mexicans (Spanish and mestizo) and Native Americans (genízaros, pueblo Indians, and nomadic Indians). Fanon (1963), Freire (1970), and Memmi (1965) describe how the colonial condition affects consciousness and the inability to alter subjection. Thus historical experiences and socially stratified positions in society can greatly complicate simple membership claims based on ascribed characteristics. These small-scale forms of inclusion do not alter the larger proportion of the population, who continue to be held under inequality. Bell (1985) argued that the incorporation of token minority leaders can create a feeling that everything is fair and equal without having to alter the structural landscape. Although racial and ethnic groups are not monolithic, their voices deserve to be included as not only the "researched" but also as the "researchers." Gang researchers by an overwhelming majority are white academics who study racial and ethnic groups different from themselves. Such monopolistic access deserves critique.

The second issue for exploring insider and outsider status centers on the topic of membership roles used to gather data. Adler and Adler (1987) describe the "complete membership role" as entailing researchers having the greatest amount of commitment and the most similar backgrounds and experiences to the people they are studying. These researchers do not experience the shock of studying groups of people and settings different from their own. They argue, "We believe that the native experience does not destroy but, rather, enhances the data gathering process. Data gathering does not occur *only* through the detached observational role, but through the subjectively immersed role as well" (84). Adler and Adler describe how multiple forms of membership roles within ethnography can enlighten the social science community about the worlds in which we live.

Individuals with membership roles in certain groups or stigmas can also use the knowledge for social transformation. Brown (1991:166) labeled individuals who capitalize on their former deviance by utilizing their knowledge to become professional counselors as "professional ex-s." Brown found that professional ex-s were convinced "that they possessed the necessary qualities for making substantial difference in the lives of individuals still suffering from addiction." Changing from a layperson to a professional required the credentials attained in formal schooling, but inside knowledge was crucial for understanding. Similar to Brown, I too wanted to use my previous deviant status to create a bridge between the streets and academia to bring greater awareness about gangs and develop solutions.[2] Breaking away from false consciousness and no longer identifying with the oppressor is argued as the first step toward deconstructing colonial and unequal structural arrangements (Fanon 1963; Freire 1970; Marx 1869; Memmi 1965).

Quantitative research treats race as a dummy variable and dismissively argues that issues of race for the researcher and the participant will not bias the study. The researcher is presumed to be "objective," "neutral," and free from value bias. According to Kirk and Miller (1986), this "positivist" or hypothetico-deductive model argues that there is an external world, but only *one* correct view of it. Ethnography, on the other hand, understands how race, culture, language, class, and physical characteristics affect the ability of the researcher to gather data and its own subjective influence on the researcher. These researchers reject the possibility of value freedom even as an ideal because scientific work is commonly political (Jorgensen 1989).

The academic unification of insiders and outsiders as argued by Merton (1972) is not realistic in the social world of gangs. In this context insiders are gang members and to some degree affiliates. Outsiders are everyone else, and in particular middle- to upper-class whites. This book will highlight attempts to unify gang insiders (former and current gang-involved individuals); yet creating acceptance by those in mainstream white society is much more difficult. My life experiences and gathering of research data involved forms of both insider and outsider statuses. In terms of gangs, I was an insider. Although I did not grow up in the neighborhood my entire life or claim a gang at the age of 8 as the stereotypes suggest, I was in the network. My ride, drug sales, and daily outings placed me at the heart of gang activity in Ogden. Moving away from this lifestyle created issues of whether I was still a member, but this identity was kept secret as I joined a field of employment considered in opposition to gangs: criminal justice. In time I learned that both roles were a lot more similar than depicted.

Criminal Justice Insider

At the age of 18 I began to maintain a clean criminal record, with not one misdemeanor. This was not easy to accomplish because I was regularly stopped and harassed by the police. My noncriminal status, along with my associate's degree, permitted me access to a job with Child and Family Services for the State of Utah. I worked with young kids from troubled families for three to six hours a week. I played sports with these youth and took one or two of the young kids to the university. I wanted to show them another social world. These kids were little versions of me. I felt obligated to guide them in visualizing an alternative future.

The work experience I obtained from Child and Family Services helped me secure employment as a deputy juvenile probation officer for Davis County, a primarily white, middle-class community, during my junior year in college. I was 21 years old and had become a member of law enforcement with an official state badge, access to state-owned vehicles, and a newly forming identity of moving past my previous deviant status. My registration was paid to attend a state gang conference in Salt Lake City that included law enforcement and correctional gang experts from around the country, who described gangs as criminally organized and very dangerous. I worked in law enforcement for a year, checking on those ordered by youth court to be on probation while developing the work experience for my next position.

During my senior year at Weber State University I was working full-time in a youth correction facility that housed boys and girls between the ages of 12 and 18. The facility where I worked had youth who were held in detention, observation, and assessment (sixty- to ninety-day detention) and within secure housing (usually a year or more of detention). I worked in the observation and assessment unit and developed good rapport with the youth by encouraging a nondelinquent lifestyle. It was here where I began to perfect my skills in verbal de-escalation. My work in youth corrections was short-lived as I received the opportunity to attend the University of Colorado for doctoral studies. My dreams of gaining more knowledge to develop solutions for my neighborhood were set in motion.

In 2004, while in graduate school, I once again worked for the government, supervising and mentoring delinquent youth. I was hired by Colorado's youth detention facility that housed their "most violent and dangerous offenders." The youth housed at this secure facility were all male and between the ages of 15 and 21. The building where I worked held about fifty-five youth, whereas the entire facility housed around four hundred individuals. My strategy of verbal de-escalation to mediate conflicts contradicted the preferences of many of the staff, who preferred to use physical restraint methods.

Entering Denver Gangs

To help ease my initial transition from Utah to Colorado, my cousin Ramón allowed me to stay with his family, where I first began to learn about Denver gangs. While I no longer felt like a gang member, I still frequented clubs with individuals portraying a gang image. Afterwards fights occasionally occurred. Two months into my stay I had my first confrontation with a gang member. After a late night of drinking, my cousin Ramón brought an individual from East Los Angeles over to his house. Ramón thought the two of us would be friends. I was asleep at the time but awoke to hear them arguing. The man from East Los Angeles thought my cousin wanted him to beat me up. Ramón became angry at the suggestion, and things quickly went downhill. Somehow I became the designated driver to drop off the guy at his apartment complex. Ramón and the man continued to argue, and when we arrived at the apartment a fight between them quickly ensued. I soon separated them, and my cousin and I left in the vehicle while the man shouted the name of his gang. This incident made me question why I wanted to get back into the gang social world to do additional research on this topic. There were definitely some gang members I despised, and alcohol didn't bring out the best in some of these characters. School, work, family, and a new social environment began to provide a buffer between this lifestyle, and now my mentor was encouraging me to get back involved to conduct research.

To gather research data on gangs in Denver, where I was never a gang member, I became involved with a variety of groups focused on gang prevention, high school reform, police observation, and community empowerment. A significant part of my research in Denver was carried out with a community group, Area Support for All People (ASAP). Current and former gang members started this group in 1991 with the goal of decreasing violence. A group of five to twenty gang members from around the city who were between the ages of 13 and 18 met once a week for three hours with the adult mentors. I attended group meetings for more than two years, from December 2000 to September 2003. The director of ASAP, D-loc, became a key partner in developing my networks and providing the initial information on Denver gangs. I consider him to be one of the most knowledgeable individuals on the city's gangs. The gang group brought many different gang members together to settle their differences nonviolently.

Attending ASAP was similar to self-therapy. For the first time I was experiencing a group that directly questioned my previous lifestyle. Consciously, I had struggled with my gang identity as the division between past membership and criminal justice created feelings of confusion. To my surprise, no one in the group believed that I had left the gang life behind. The ASAP youth thought that I was either selling drugs or involved in some other form of criminality. The volunteer and ex–gang member staff assumed it was possible that I was working on my master's degree, but they didn't grasp what a Ph.D. degree entailed. I said I was researching gangs, but everyone thought I was a gangster and possibly ordered by the court to attend. This image was conducive to gaining access to a lot of Denver youngsters who were active in gang banging. For those released from prison or pursuing a role in the distribution of drugs, such blatant promotion of the gang decreased as public displays of membership

were no longer an asset. It was frustrating to me to see these youth acting like I had eight years before. At that time, no one could reach me.

Besides ASAP, I became involved in three other groups working to
challenge the conditions in the barrio that overlapped with gang issues.
The first group I volunteered with from 2002 to 2006 is called People
Observing Police (POP). My key partners in this group included Pam
and Randolph. POP's goal was to ensure police accountability, and its
members observed all areas of the community, especially areas where
people felt harassed or were regularly stopped by the police. I sometimes
went out with this group during the day, but mostly at night to document
police stops with a camcorder and notepad. After the stop had ended, if
possible, we talked with police officers and the person(s) of interest. If
there were problems that developed with certain officers or stops, I simply documented the behavior and made it available to be used in court
at a later date.[3] I observed over two hundred police stops during four
years in Denver and Ogden. This information was used to compare and
contrast Latino claims with those of police officers and the media. These
data served as my own direct, personal, firsthand observation of police
practices and gang behaviors, which supplemented and served to cross-
check (Douglas 1976) accounts provided by individuals in the community. The data collection method involved monitoring all sections of the
city with a scanner and personal observation, thus removing the criticism
that selective and aggressive policing may have also been occurring in
white neighborhoods but my methodology failed to study them. Most
police officers acted in a professional manner, yet the amount of police
harassment I found while working with POP gave me another view of
Denver policing that people living in segregated white suburbs often find
hard to fathom.

The second group I became active with in 2003 included several community activists and community workers who provided me with additional knowledge and connections with gangs and police that led to
the creation of an organization called the Gang Group. The purpose
of the Gang Group was to focus specifically on gang-police-community
relations. This group took community knowledge and experiences to
city council members, protest activities, community forums, and media
sources. Members wanted to counter the stereotypes about the black
and Latino community. The key partners I developed from this group included Doc, Militance, and O.G. Fifty. They lived and breathed bringing

reform to Denver. Several news articles featured members of the group, including myself. This helped me to learn about and visit other programs operating in the city. Decker and Van Winkle's (1996) study in St. Louis also benefited from the media attention received from their ethnographic fieldworker.

The third group I became involved with in 2004 was a youth and parent group attempting to institute reform at an inner-city high school and to stop the schoolhouse-to-jailhouse track. I was greatly impressed by these active Latina/o youth. They remain key role models for how youth from horrible inner-city schools can actively pursue empowerment for themselves and their educational institutions. Many of these youth are now attending or have graduated from major universities.

Going Back to Ogden

Beginning in 2001 I returned to Ogden during my summer breaks and began my ethnographic research there. I met with old friends and stayed involved in the urban scene two or three times a week; the rest of the time I spent with my kids and family, who were glad to have me home. Bridging the gap from ex–gang member to researcher was more complicated in Utah because I was known in this community as a gang member. Thus challenging preconceptions became my first hurdle. I wanted to interview people not just from my own gang, but also from rival gangs.

As a researcher I reentered this social world with some time distance. I had begun breaking away from gangs in the mid-1990s, and many people had forgotten that I had become an enemy. In fact many of them thought I had been a member of their own gang, and this helped me to build rapport. I was welcomed as someone doing a school project with a desire to contribute to the community. I was able to mend many past rivalries. In the beginning I hung out regularly with people from four different gangs, which were the largest and most well-known groups. No one who saw me could identify me as someone working on his doctorate. I was back in my element. Ogden was my 'hood. My key partners in Ogden were Anne, Cyclone, Lucita, and Tone. In 2004, with the help of friends, I started my own POP group in Ogden to counter and document discriminatory policing occurring within the city. I have continued to stay in the Ogden area for about two months every year since then, where the local suppression efforts have kept me collecting more data.

Participant Observation

Atkinson et al. (2001:4) defined ethnographic traditions as being "grounded in a commitment to the firsthand experience and exploration of a particular social or cultural setting on the basis of (though not exclusively by) participant observation." The impressions gang members worked to create provided much insight for my research because there was frequently a discrepancy between what people reported and how people lived. My observations were key in validating self-reports. Bernard (1988:149–52) listed five reasons for insisting upon participant observation: it facilitates data gathering, reduces people's reactivity, helps researchers form questions in the language of the people studied, provides intuitive understanding of meanings in that culture, and enables general understanding of how something works. My direct observation of gangs involved living in Denver and Ogden and interacting with present and past gang members/associates. It involved going to clubs, events, meetings, house parties, conferences, and protests where gang members/associates were present. I maintained an overt status as an ex–gang member from the University of Colorado who was conducting research on gangs.

I developed informal networks (Werner and Schoepfle 1987; Whyte 1943) to begin and continue my associations with gang members, ex–gang members, and associates in both sites to create a membership role that balanced having inside access, based on past gang membership, yet no longer identifying as a present gang member.

To help with my data gathering, I maintained six key partners in Denver and at least four in Ogden, and a larger number informally. While ethnographers have traditionally used the term "key informant" to describe their closest research allies, these words have come to assume a negative connotation in the field, particularly in criminological settings. Both postmodernists (Denzin 1970, 1989) and feminists (Stacey 1988) have urged ethnographic researchers to narrow the distance between the people they study and themselves by adopting more collaborative working relationships. This offers the advantage of both empowering and giving voice to the people being researched.

I use the term "key partners," then, to signify both the collaborative and empowering relationship I forged with my closest helpers in the field and to indicate their participation at my side in a shared enterprise of exploration. Working closely with several people in both cities contributed greatly to my research, and without the help of these people I could not have gained such a large collection of data. These key partners included me in social worlds to which I would not have otherwise had access: ex-convicts, Denver gangs, Crusade for Justice, POP, and women gang members and associates. I documented the information that I learned with field notes (Bernard 1988; Lofland and Lofland 1995).

Some of my most interesting insights came from researching communities and groups different from my own. I studied the spatial dimensions of these cities with the use of census tract data and maps (Cromley 1999). I selected the five most concentrated black, Latino, and white neighborhoods in Denver, and the proportionately highest Latino and white neighborhoods in Ogden, to conduct comparative field research on the impact of race and ethnicity. In total there were fifteen neighborhoods in Denver and ten in Ogden.[4] During my walks through these areas I brought my still camera, tape recorder, notepad, and map. Afterwards I returned home, transcribed my tapes, and incorporated the pictures taken.[5] I compared gang-labeled neighborhoods with nongang neighborhoods. I did my best to dress the way I assumed people in the area did. I took written notes about things of interest and covertly spoke into the tape recorder to describe neighborhood features.

Semistructured Interviews and Field Notes of Conversations

In the fall of 2001 I began conducting semistructured interviews. My goal was to capture members' and associates' perspectives on gang culture. I followed a guide of ten specific themes to discuss, including demographic identity, people's life histories with gangs, their experience with the criminal justice system, neighborhood, family, police, and school, as well as their history of employment, their experience of race relations and their dreams for the future. I asked general, open-ended questions and allowed the interviews to develop along the interviewees' expertise. I treated my interviewees as fellow experts and did not judge their responses. Everyone I interviewed knew that I was knowledgeable about gangs, and this helped to develop rapport by including information that only people inside the gangs knew. I actively probed to learn more about their perspective.

I made little use of snowball sampling (Biernacki and Waldorf 1981) and instead followed what I call "judgment sampling." For this, I individually selected each person for an interview based on that individual's inside knowledge relating to gangs. I used my extensive knowledge of people in the communities acquired through my participant observation (Bernard 1988; Pelto and Pelto 1979), my inside knowledge of gangs, and the aid of my key partners to exclude certain nonaffiliated individuals from my sample. Utilizing this extensive knowledge base helped me determine which people in the community were known phonies (not who they claimed to be) and which could be trusted to give me reliable information and insight. Although I was not opposed to developing networks or snowballing to gather more interviews, I was embedded in these communities and wanted to increase rapport before inviting someone to be an interviewee. All the participants in this study had also been observed in the field for a period of time prior to their interviews.

My analysis of the data included transcribing 32 in-depth interviews that merged with my field notes on 145 individuals gathered during five years of participant observation. Early in my research the issue of tape recordings and consent forms became problematic. Moving from a formal research role to someone interested in learning more about the local gangs was more conducive to developing rapport but definitely limited the number of quotes that could later be helpful when capturing voices accurately. In some ways, I believe that prolonged hanging out with people made the transition to acquiring a formal interview more awkward and less compelling. In Ogden I talked with 93 individuals: 45 members or past members, 35 associates, 9 from the neighborhood, three Gang Unit officials, and a prosecutor at the district attorney's office. The members belonged to eleven different gangs. In Denver I talked to 52 people: 33 members or past members, 13 from the neighborhood, 3 Gang Unit officials, 2 associates, and a Gang Unit prosecutor at the district attorney's office. The members belonged to thirteen different gangs. My conversations were primarily with males (78.6 percent) rather than females (21.4 percent), which reflected gang membership patterns in both cities. My respondents were primarily Latino (70 percent), black (10 percent), or white (9.6 percent) but included 5 Asians, a Native American, a Tongan, and individuals of mixed black and Latino or black and white backgrounds. The average age of gang-involved individuals was 24—slightly older in Ogden (26.1) than in Denver (19.3).

I categorized quotes and field notes into themes relating to my initial questions about the gang experience (Lofland and Lofland 1995). I color coded themes into key areas (e.g., interesting topics, gang involvement by women, people's feelings, how I was seen by people in the gang scene, gangs and drugs, structural opportunities) for numerical comparison. Compiling and sorting the enormous amount of data I compiled from 1992 to 2011 helped immensely to make sense of it. I interviewed my ten key partners multiple times and paid them $25 each for their time and contribution to the research. The interviews were conducted in English, with some minor use of Spanish. Most of my respondents had been in the United States for two to six generations and thus spoke English as their first language. The interviews lasted between one and two hours.

Researching the Criminal Justice Response to Gangs

During my research in the two states, I interviewed seven gang officers. Six of these interviews were conducted inside police facilities and one was conducted over the telephone. I regularly requested police department data relating to gangs during the years 1995–2006 in Ogden and 2001–06 in Denver. When I interviewed or interacted with members of law enforcement I maintained the demeanor of an objective professional researcher. I wanted to learn as much as possible about how law enforcement acted toward gang members to help understand, validate, or refute Latino claims of gang profiling. To help establish rapport with the police, I mentioned that I too had worked in law enforcement and youth corrections (Durán 2011). I understood that members of these agencies were much more comfortable talking about gangs than about how they themselves operated.

I felt that going on ride-alongs with the police in these two cities might make me complicit with the police culture of secrecy, which several researchers on gangs had failed to explore (Katz and Webb 2006; Klein 2004; Sanders 1994). Hagedorn (1990) offered an excellent critique of "courthouse criminology" and its inability to accurately measure gangs or their level of activity because of the methodological social distance that is created between the researcher and the researched by surveys or by relying on the viewpoint of public officials. With such an approach, gangs become defined as a law enforcement problem. Hagedorn also criticized "surrogate sociology" for the snapshot sampling bias created when interviewees are obtained through the recommendations of public officials, relying on individuals who are incapacitated, on probation or parole, or selected by community centers. Hagedorn encouraged researchers to study gangs and gang members in their own settings.

Archival Analysis

I gathered an extensive number of newspaper clippings and primary documents to develop a history of gang activity in both sites. Earl et al. (2004:76) reported that newspaper data "facilitate longitudinal research, and make quantitative research on social movements more viable." Although newspapers and official statistics suffer from description and selection bias, they offered my only link to how gangs were being publicly described at that time. In Denver this research was supported by the Denver Public Library, which had indexed the two major newspapers by subject. I located all articles pertaining to crime and delinquency, gangs, Latinos, and the police. The library also housed a collection of tape recordings of interviews conducted during the reign of the Ku Klux Klan. The University of Colorado archives held several valuable collections on the early history of Denver.

In Ogden I was able to access newspaper microfilms from the local library. In addition, my own newspaper clippings on crime, gangs, Latinos, and police collected after 1992 gave me insights into early history of gang suppression. Documenting the early experience of Latinos was significantly aided by the oral transcripts available at the University of Utah's special collections library, which stored interviews conducted from 1970 to 1975 and 1984 to 1988. I included forty-two of these interview transcripts to gain an overview of Latino experiences in Utah from the 1920s to the mid-1980s.

The training I received in the ethnographic methodology allowed me to conduct research opportunistically. Entry to Denver gangs was made possible by my ex–gang member status, and my access to gangs in Denver came from a variety of sources: gang members, ex–gang members, associates, individuals actively involved in providing alternatives, and those working to suppress gangs. My research in Denver began in 2001 and lasted until 2006. In Ogden I returned home to build on my previous research studies and notes in an ethnographic project that spanned from 1992 until 2011. I merged the interviews of gang members, associates, and individuals within the neighborhood to contrast them with law enforcement and youth correction claims. Issues of difference were explored in both cities through archival data collection as well as by walking in the five neighborhoods with the highest concentrations of each racial and ethnic group. Interviews and field notes from 145 individuals are used to present the story of gang life in two cities told in this book.

CHAPTER TWO

The War on Gangs in the Post–Civil Rights Era

I'm driving through the 'hood of Ogden one evening and notice two undercover police vehicles stopped with their lights flashing. A friend and I park and walk over to the scene with my video camera. I've been recording police stops for two years as part of a local community group pushing for police accountability called POP. As I get closer to where the two white plainclothes officers are standing, I notice they are talking with three young Latino males in an apartment complex parking lot. Such a profile of officers and suspects equals the Gang Unit. As I begin recording the scene, a red undercover police car pulls up behind me and begins observing our actions. The three Latino youth look young standing in front of the larger adults. Police lights spin in the darkness while spotlights shine on the scene. Shortly after my arrival, several sheriff's vehicles pull up and the officers exit and begin observing the area. There are now nine officers present. The two cops begin taking pictures of the youth, who appear to be only 13, 14, and 16. Toward the end of the stop, the three youth appear to be joking with the officers as they are patted down and questioned. After some time goes by they are released.

A middle-aged Latina comes out from the apartment complex frustrated and begins yelling at the officers to quit harassing her nephew. She says, "You should be chasing the real criminals, not my nephew. Quit harassing my family or I will press charges." The white gang officer responds, "We didn't pull over anyone, Ma'am, who is your family?" She responds, "The one over there. Don't be judging a book by its cover. He works. He has a license. He is in no gang." The gang officer responds, "We stopped the vehicle for a traffic violation. No one is harassing, Ma'am. He didn't even receive a traffic violation." The Latina responds,

"You told him that if he didn't cooperate you would take him to jail. Get the real fucking criminals." The gang officer quickly challenges the comment: "What was that, Ma'am? What did you say?" The aunt's male companion encourages her in Spanish to remain calm. The officer looks towards me and states, "Did you get that? [Video-record the woman swearing.] Probably not, you are just after the cops." I respond calmly, "I'm capturing everything." As the police officers leave the scene I give the woman a business card and contact information for POP. She repeats, "This ain't right," but she seems unsure of how to stop the police from doing whatever they want. Individuals that I interview tell me that filing a complaint is a waste of time because it goes nowhere or results in only enhanced police harassment. The pattern of Latino and black submissive compliance with a high number of police stops and questioning is continually repeated in Denver and Ogden. Individuals who are stopped hope for the chance to be released without an incident. Some individuals are not so lucky and are led away in handcuffs or are demeaned, brutalized, or occasionally killed.

The early 1980s in Denver and early 1990s in Ogden can be seen as a period of early formation of gang enforcement as an institutional framework for responding to actual and perceived gang activity. This was not the first time authority figures targeted gangs, as this book will outline, but it was the first time in which gang enforcement became federally funded and organized around a gang suppression model involving intelligence gathering, aggressive law enforcement, and prosecutorial interest. In the post–civil rights era, such a strategy to suppress gangs ensured that the level of cultural activism never again achieved the momentum that was attained in the 1960s and 1970s. Law enforcement took the lead as the authorities began identifying who gang members were and what they were perceived to be doing.

The concept of gangs began to legitimize and open the door to more aggressive forms of law enforcement. Violating an individual's civil rights became less of a concern as barrios and ghettos began to be equated with breeding grounds for gangs and criminality—the two terms were used interchangeably. Gangs were characterized as nonwhite and then were argued to be more criminal. Gang labeling is important for at least three reasons: (1) it is overly broad in definition but specific in terms of whom the label is applied to; (2) it allows for selective and aggressive

enforcement; and (3) it responds to groups formed from racial oppression with neutral-sounding code words that perpetuate a cycle of increased oppression.

In response to this image of a gang member as a new "urban preda-
tor," a large number of cities since the mid-1980s have created specialized
gang units to support a "war on gangs" that will eliminate this alleged
threat. Through a survey of 261 police departments, Klein (1995) found
that intelligence gathering, crime investigation, and suppression were the
most common police actions against gangs, and that many states had
instituted increased consequences for gang-related crimes. Spergel (1995)
agreed that a vigorous "lock-'em-up" approach remained the key action of police departments, particularly in large cities with acknowledged
gang problems. Police officers routinely recognize how such a war on
gangs is hindered by traditional constitutional protections but have developed support to create methods and tactics to sidestep disapproval; in
essence they have become legitimated. Diaz (2009) argued that the federal government became involved in gang suppression after the 1992 Los
Angeles riots. The Safe Streets Initiative allowed for joint federal, state,
and local agencies to participate in combating gangs. The Department of
Justice continued this pursuit to bring down gangs by merging organized
crime statutes under federal racketeering laws (Racketeer Influenced and
Corrupt Organizations Act, or RICO) that required making street gangs,
which primarily lacked a leader hierarchy and military structure, fit their
needs.[1] These ongoing efforts have institutionalized the war on gangs
by targeting immigrants and social groups that are deemed a threat to
national security.

Understanding the impact of the criminal justice system on the lives
of gang members and the communities they live in was a significant part
of my research because it was constantly mentioned and observed as a
problem. The substantial impact of criminalization on barrio communities is all the more amazing when one realizes that many gang researchers have failed to explore what role the executive branch of government
plays in altering life chances. This chapter seeks to correct this omission
in the scholarly literature by highlighting law enforcement's role in the
definition of the situation by labeling gang behavior as primarily involving people of color. The chapter introduces the argument of contemporary racialized oppression, defined as the actions and motivations of the
state to utilize the stratification of racial and ethnic group hierarchies in

the United States to exercise power in a cruel and unjust manner for the purpose of maintaining colonialism.

Legitimated Profiling

In both Denver and Ogden, police officers were primarily deployed in high-crime districts (Sherman et al. 1989). These were more often neighborhoods with a higher concentration of Latinos and blacks (50–90 percent) and economic poverty (20–70 percent) (United States Census). The police departments' diversity paled in comparison to these neighborhoods. Approximately 20 percent of Denver police officers and 5 percent of Ogden police officers were Latino. Since most street crime did not occur in plain sight, police officers had to determine which people were engaging in criminal activity.

The police focused on making stops based on the legal justification of reasonable suspicion and probable cause. Probable cause includes a belief, based on objective facts, that supports the suspicion that a person is committing or about to commit a crime (Hall 1996). A lead prosecutor in northern Utah described reasonable suspicion as "facts and circumstances that would lead a reasonable officer to believe that there is a particular problem or indication of criminal activity" (2003 interview). Together, reasonable suspicion and probable cause legitimated a wide-ranging assortment of stops.

However, this led to a confrontational relationship between police and many residents in Denver's and Ogden's barrios because residents often believed that police officers were using gang and criminal stereotypes to predicate stops. Most of my respondents reported that they had been stopped for a variety of reasons that were not criminally predicated; in other words, they were profiled. Latino youth reported that common reasons the police gave for the stop included, "It looked like I was wearing 'gang' clothing" (i.e., clothing from sports teams and hip hop clothing), "I was assumed to be out too late," "People matched my description," "There were reports of shots fired," "We had more than three people in the car," or "We looked suspicious." Other community members were stopped because of minor traffic violations that could be detected only with strict scrutiny. If there were no traffic violations, police officers had the option of using vehicle safety ordinances, such as lacking a front license plate, violating noise ordinances, having overly tinted windows (Utah), hanging rosaries or objects from the rear-view mirror (Colorado), standing or driving around in a known gang area, or driving a customized (i.e., lowrider) vehicle. In sum, police officers had a full range of reasons to initiate and later justify a "criminal" stop when speaking with barrio residents.

The wide array of justifications created confusion on the part of Latino and black youth. D-loc, a 25-year-old ex-gang member from Denver, described a meeting between community members and police officers. He attempted to learn more about the legal term "reasonable suspicion":

> We were really trying to have some meaningful conversation with 'em and say, "why you pull us over, because there are four of us in a car?" [Police response:] "Agh, reasonable suspicion." "What if we were just walking down a street?" "Agh, reasonable suspicion." "Well how come you stop our little brothers and sisters on the street, they ain't doing nothing." "Agh, reasonable suspicion." It could be anything. We started getting upset because every answer they gave us was reasonable suspicion. So I said, "What's reasonable suspicion?" They said, "There could have been a crime in your community and the description they gave might fit the description of someone walking down the street. There was a robbery that happened in a house and the suspect was described as a possible Hispanic male between 5'6" and 5'9", ugh, between 120 lbs and 170 lbs." "Shit, that's almost every male in my community between those ages and that description. That's half of the population in my neighborhood. So that gives you any reason to stop any one of us and be a bunch of assholes to anybody walking down the street because you feel like it?"

D-loc stated that he started attending police presentations about gangs to critique their phony criteria of gang identifiers. To the police, everything in terms of urban style was considered to be affiliated with gangs, from how your shoes are tied, to hats and how they are worn, to how you sit, to every imaginable symbol or article of clothing. D-loc argued that most of the time this has nothing to do with gangs but is just the style of youth fitting in with their peers.

POP observations supported Latino and black claims of harassment. During their five years of watching the police in Denver, Randolph and Pam, two middle-aged white police-observers reported the countless

times they witnessed Gang Unit officers searching suspected gang members' vehicles for drugs and weapons. Pam reported that officers would
stop young men for unclear reasons and take them all out of the vehicle.
Randolph said the officers would then ask everyone in the car for identification, check them for outstanding warrants, search their pockets, and
then send them on their way. He explained:

> So that happens over and over again, and it's the same general age
> group, ethnic group, gender group that it happens to time and time
> again, and no one is arrested. Like detention and searches are sup-
> posed to be based on a reasonable suspicion that a crime has been or
> is about to be committed, so what is the crime here? It seems that being
> a Chicano youth for the Denver Gang Unit is reasonable suspicion of
> criminal activity. . . . So a lot of times, what we see is the Gang Unit
> rides around using bogus traffic violations as an excuse to stop any car
> that has more than one young man of color. It can either be black or
> Chicano, or even Asian sometimes. A little-known fact is that whites
> get in gangs too, but they never get stopped.

Pam and Randolph thought that maybe if Latino youth began dressing
in suits they wouldn't be stopped by the police for meeting a profile, but
they wondered how unusual that would be to stop the harassment. They
both argued that the police net was long and broad in its application to
youth of color.

Traffic violations were highly discretionary and also very difficult to
prove or disprove. Several researchers have attempted to determine the
role and significance of this practice as racial profiling and how it is used
to further an investigation into the identity of occupants and search for
possible contraband (Bass 2001; Browning et al. 1994; Cole 1999; Fagan
and Davies 2000; Meehan and Ponder 2002). In November 2000 Denver
initiated a task force to assess racial profiling in the city by requiring officers to fill out contact cards. The study found that from June 1, 2001,
to May 31, 2003, the number of stops experienced by each racial and
ethnic group was similar to their numbers in the city population, but that
Latinos and blacks were searched at two to four times the rate of whites
(Thomas 2002; Thomas and Hansen 2004).

Based on POP observations, the city of Ogden utilized racially profiling far more than Denver, possibly owing to the lack of organized community resistance. Chicle, a 26-year-old ex–gang associate from Ogden,

said, "They would make up reasons for maybe going too fast or going too slow, or maybe you were swerving. I've been pulled over fifteen to twenty times and I haven't gotten a ticket." Although happy to not receive a ticket, Chicle believed a legitimate stop by the police entailed a consequence, whereas a fictitious reason included being released. Cola, a 27-year-old ex–gang member from Ogden, recalled, "They stopped me for everything. They even stopped me a couple times to tell me they liked my car. I'm not sure what that had to do with anything. At the time I thought it was nothing, but now that I think back, I realize they would take down all of our names. We were just glad that we weren't in trouble for anything." Cola recalled purchasing low-profile tires for one of his vehicles that resulted in a higher than average number of stops, but such selective enforcement appeared odd when large trucks driven by white cowboys did not result in similar treatment.

The observed and described police discretion produced an elusive standard for establishing reasonable suspicion and probable cause because it was highly influenced by extralegal factors (e.g., age, class, gender, neighborhood, and race). Anderson (1990) found that police officers become "willing parties" to "color-coding" that entails making race, age, class, and gender presuppositions as to who commits crime and who will be perceived as dangerous. While researching as a member of POP, I found Gang Unit stops were particularly influenced by age, gender, race, and local gang stereotypes in 100 percent of the forty-seven observed police stops. In Ogden it was observed that when dispatch reported Hispanic males involved in an incident, the Gang Unit was more likely to accept the call to investigate. The rationale for many of these stops and subsequent detentions appeared far-reaching. Compliance with picture taking and information resulted in release from custody. The rationale of gang officers would leave researchers believing that most people stopped were gang members. However, gang members in both cities were a small percentage of barrio youth. The average number of youth who join gangs continues to be very low. Even in Los Angeles, the gang capital of the world, it is estimated that only 4 to 14 percent of youth join gangs (Vigil 2002). According to the data I accumulated over five years, there were definitely a greater number of associates than actual members of the gang—probably a 20-to-80 ratio.

Barrio youth faced greater difficulty entering different parts of the city because law enforcement often associated this behavior with causing problems with rival gangs. Randolph, the POP member from Denver, described a situation in which a car was stopped:

> And the officer will say, "I recognized the people in the back seat of that car as being from East Denver and I wanted to know why they were in West Denver." Now that's not a reasonable suspicion of a crime. People in the United States are supposed to have freedom of movement. . . . Obviously the reason they were there was because they were cruising during Cinco de Mayo. . . . It's a famous event for a lot of youth and so they will go cruise Federal [Boulevard] because it's a big thing. So it's a ridiculous reason to say someone is from another jurisdiction and that's why I stopped them.

Pam and Randolph described how, along with several additional groups from the community, they became involved in observing police stops during Cinco de Mayo. They reported that the number of tickets or citations decreased from 2,500 in 1996 to 15 in 1998. The police observers provided a presence to document that many of the citations given were not illegal and the reasons for the stops were also fabricated.

According to the Gallup Poll as cited in the *Sourcebook of Criminal Justice Statistics*, Latinos (63 percent) report a greater belief that racial profiling is widespread in motorist stops on roads and highways than whites (50 percent). Latino youth in the barrio believed they were stopped simply because of their profile, and most had witnessed experiences where their white friends were treated more leniently. A large number of researchers have reported police harassment within Latino communities (Acuña 2000; Bayley and Mendelsohn 1968; Durán forthcoming a; Escobar 1999; Mazón 1984; Mirandé 1987; Moore 1991; Morales 1972; Rosenbaum 1981; Vigil 1988). Bayley and Mendelsohn (1968:109) reported: "The police seem to play a role in the life of minority people out of all proportion to the role they play in the lives of the Dominant majority [whites]."

A third demographic factor community members believed they were stopped for was their gender. Men or teenage boys were perceived as more highly targeted than women or teenage girls. Thus the women interviewed described fewer negative interactions with the police than the men, but they believed that the police would try to use them to gather information. The young women who attended ASAP thought the men were stopped and harassed more by the police. Randolph, the POP member in Denver, commented on this pattern: "If it's a car full of girls, they are far less likely, we saw, to be stopped. So, like, for every car full of girls they stopped, they stopped ten cars full of guys and we know that multiple passengers were much more likely to be targeted." If ascribed characteristics were not enough for police to profile individuals as gang members, many Latino youth matched the criteria by their clothes, haircuts, numbers, or tattoos (interviews with Denver and Ogden Gang Units and gang protocol). Most youth dressed in clothes that were fashionable with their peers. This created great confusion for the police, and even for gang members, when the majority of youth dressed in baggy clothes from urban hip-hop brands (e.g., Ben Davis, Dickies, Johnny Blaze, Karl Kani, Phat Farm, Roca Wear, Sean John) and clothing with numbers (e.g., Fubu 05, Joker 77, Sports Jerseys). Fine et al. (2003) reported that urban youth in general felt disrespected by police, and that adults in positions of authority often equated youths' urban clothing as a symbol of their criminal inclination. Lucita, a 25-year-old gang associate from Ogden, recalled seeing the police approach her Mexican American friends: "They get harassed, they get questioned, they get pulled over for any reason because they wear their pants a certain way, which is funny because you catch these white kids trying to do the same thing but they never get asked those questions. They never get asked 'Why you dress like that?' or 'Where are you going?' "

Latino youth who dressed similarly to others in their neighborhood increased their differential treatment by both authority figures and peers. Urban attire brought the possibility of negative treatment by authority figures but also approval from peers. Whites, on the other hand, were more likely to escape negative gang connotations being associated with their identity.

With gang officers making a high percentage of their stops based on extralegal factors related to age, gender, neighborhood, race, and gang stereotypes, community members were skeptical about police officers' stated primary objective as targeting crime. Rather, a large number of residents believed that police were there to enforce social control over the neighborhood and the people who lived there (Fagan and Davies 2000). Police officers often faced difficulty legitimizing their actions with the people they were policing. The profiling increased conflict, but individual officers lacked the structural power to alter where they were deployed and how they prevented crime. Their structural vulnerability led officers to dismiss claims of racial profiling. Nevertheless, the everyday motions of police work legitimated a focus on extralegal factors.

Interacting with Suspected Gang Members

The interactions between police and the Latino community members were very tense because of the vagueness of the encounters and their unknown outcomes. Several people who observed police interacting with suspected gang members noted that the police often attempted to incite provocations to justify a search or arrest. The U.S. Commission on Civil Rights (1970) found that Latinos viewed the police with tension and fear because of frequent arrests on insufficient grounds for "investigation" and "stop and frisks." Such findings mirror the nearly one hundred studies I reviewed regarding Latinos and the police over the past 186 years (Durán forthcoming a).

Intelligence gathering was a key component of police suppression tactics. Donner (1980) reported that surveillance conducted on people and groups was justified on preventive grounds as counteracting against violence. However, police intelligence gathering has allowed the labeling of entire racial and ethnic groups, especially men, as gang members (*Westword*, June 3, 2004b; *New York Times*, Dec. 11, 1993; *DP, Dec. 5, 1993*). Once people land on such lists, it becomes more likely that their future acts will be discovered, prosecuted, and dealt with punitively. Denver and Ogden gang lists do not require criminal activity for admission, and they remain on file for at least five years. Prosecutors often use these lists for sentencing enhancements and in the incorporation of a broad array of individuals for gang injunctions, which makes legal activity—such as associating with family and friends, drinking alcohol, and possession of a firearm—illegal even though the individuals may have never committed a crime.

In order for police officers to create these lists, Latino youth were repeatedly asked what gang they belonged to. According to the police department gang protocol, people who admitted gang membership satisfied the first and primary requirement for being placed on a gang list, yet most people denied membership. The police used different tactics to discover gang involvement, ranging from talking nonchalantly to coercion. Most respondents interviewed who were not involved with gangs believed that officers suspected them of lying in denying membership.

Officers searched for clues by asking individuals to pull up their shirts and looking for tattoos, or asking what high school they attended. Tone, a 28-year-old "convict" who chose to stay away from a gang lifestyle, said, "They [police] would throw a couple different gang names at me and ask me which one I belonged to and I would say none. But they would always look like they didn't believe me if you didn't tell them what they wanted to hear."

Anne, a 24-year-old gang associate from Ogden, said:

> I was pregnant and me and my friend were cruising on Washington and we were just sitting there parked and the cops came over and a couple other people were parked there and they were in a gang but they said we couldn't be loitering around there. And right away they were yelling at us what gang were we in. I said, "I'm not in a gang," and he said, "Don't lie," like yelling at me, "Don't lie." I was like, "I'm not in a gang." And then he asked, "Why you around all of these gang members if you're not in a gang?" I was pregnant and a girl hanging out with another girl and so it made me pretty mad. And frustrated too because I kept telling him but he wouldn't let it go. He kept saying, "You're in a gang! Tell me!"

Although Anne was associating with gang members, she was not a member. A large number of people in the barrio know someone in a gang, but this does not make someone a member. Individual gang membership created a stereotype that spread to everyone of this particular racial or ethnic background who lived in the barrio. Police officers could then use the gang label to legitimate all interactions with the Latino community. These labels were then maintained by the presumption of clear, precise policies and guidelines that countered all forms of legal challenges and complaints, yet no one outside of the Gang Unit had access to the police files to verify their accuracy. A Gang Unit detective reported that of the one hundred individuals entered into the gang database since his arrival, not one had been screened out by a sergeant or lieutenant for not meeting the gang criteria (*SE*, Sept. 15, 2010). Thus a police officer labeling someone a gang member was confirmation of the database's own internal accuracy.

Others whose family members were involved in gangs were often treated as members of the gang. Monique, a 22-year-old from Ogden who had two brothers involved in gangs, mentioned how the police automatically assumed she was a member and treated her poorly. Lucita, a 25-year-old associate of a traditional gang with two brothers who were previously involved in gangs, concurred with this negative treatment when she said:

> For a while there I was getting pulled over a lot. They assumed I was affiliated with so and so, they see you one time with this one person, therefore you have information that you are withholding from them or they think you know the whereabouts of an individual. Stuff like that. You get harassed and you get them on your back you can't get them off. They are on you constantly, and they will pull you over for anything. I think they put the word out, look for this vehicle with this person driving.

Lucita wished the police were friendlier with her and the Latino community. A higher level of trust and mutual support could live up to the ideal that the police were actually there to protect and serve.

Almost all respondents reported frequent disrespect from the police, and it took them little time to recall instances of verbal and body-language abuse. Although Mastrofski et al. (2002) reported that police disrespect was very rare—4 percent of all police stops—almost half these incidents were unprovoked. The police attempted to dominate these interactions with the power of the law, authority, and entrusted discretion. Mack-one, a 24-year-old ex–gang associate from Denver, said, "They treated me bad. They thought I was a gang member. They didn't do really do any physical harm to me but, ugh, verbally they definitely thought of me as a lower human being." Although acting civilly and cordially may not be a requirement for policing, these stops produced feelings of anger, distrust, and hopelessness, particularly when police could do whatever they wished and get away with it. Everyone interviewed could cite examples of being treated like dirt and then simply being told to go on their way once officers found no reason to take the stop further (the majority of the time). Police officers' "fishing expeditions" would not always pay off.

Anne, the 24-year-old gang associate from Ogden, said:

> They're dicks; they don't care, and they don't care if you're a girl. I had one of the gang cops search me, and I know that is against the law. Not search me but pat me down, like really pat me down! I know

they are not supposed to do that, and I told him, "You can't pat me down." I'm like, "You're supposed to have a female officer." He was all, "You don't tell me what to do." You know, just their little attitude, they'll put you down to your face. You're nothing, you're a piece of shit. They totally don't have any respect for anybody who is a gang member or who they think is a gang member. I don't know how they choose the gang task force, but they don't seem to understand anything about gangs. All they focus on is getting them off the street and into jail. It's awful.

Anne didn't think the officers serving on the Gang Unit were very educated. She thought that diversity training could help them become more open-minded and stop viewing every Latino or black person as a gang member.

Mirandé (1987:153) argued that "perhaps the most persistent overriding concern expressed by Chicanos is that the police treat them with less respect and courtesy, and with less regard for their rights." Mastrofski et al. (2002) reported that minorities experienced disrespect at twice the rate of whites. Smiley, a 23-year-old ex–gang associate, said, "They treat you like you are lower than everybody you know, like you are a bad person, like you are always committing felonies or that you are involved in crime. They just treat you with no respect. They just treat you like you are scum or something, like you are a bad person." A perception developed in the community after the formation of the Gang Unit that the police were attempting to gather intelligence to bring individuals down and disrespect them during the process.

Gang-labeled Latinos—those who were on the gang list—were approached differently because they were seen and treated as constant criminals even when following the law. Police perceptions shaped gang membership as a "master status" (Hughes 1945) that combines ascribed and achieved statuses with the belief of lifelong gang involvement. Changing this image was very difficult for gang members, particularly those attempting to leave the gang lifestyle. Police primarily applied the gang label to Latinos and African Americans, and thus the only people who could be perceived as non–gang members were whites. Many police stops of gang members would begin with ordering Mexican Americans out of their vehicle and telling them to put their hands in the air or lie face down on the ground. The officers more frequently drew their guns and attempted to investigate assumed gang involvement and planned activities. Cyclone, a 25-year-old ex–gang member and ex–prison inmate, said:

> I got labeled as a known violent gang member and never been caught of a gang crime with anybody and it's odd because they label you as that and it's not a good label because it sticks with you for life. When I get pulled over it doesn't matter who I am with, they pull me out of the car and pat me down. Every time. I mean they run my name, the NCI report comes up that says I am a violent person, and they wait for three or four more cops to show up, and then they get me out of the car just to check me. While I am with my family, my kids, I am getting discriminated. They've embarrass me in huge way with the people I'm with. They will tell the people I'm with I'm a bad influence or I'm trouble.

Cyclone was adamant that the police have consistently tried to hurt him and did not provide personal protection to prevent his victimization by rival gangs.

Pam and Randolph concurred that police officers depicted gang members as dangerous when they described an observed police stop at a Denver carwash:

> [Pam:] So we pulled up and started filming and the [police] interaction ended shortly after that. Before they left, we went and got the officers' cards and we had our cameras and the Gang Unit officer said, "Oh we're leaving now and we suggest you do the same because these are very dangerous men and you will get hurt if you stay." [Randolph:] And once we are gone you are not safe. [Pam:] So then they pulled away and as soon as they left all of the guys just came running over to us and shaking our hands and saying, "Thank you thank you," they said, "[the police] would have towed our car, our ride if you hadn't been here." [Randolph:] They were going to arrest us but they let us go once you guys pulled up here. So rather than them attacking us, they ended up being our best friends.

Based on their observations, Pam and Randolph thought the police were actually more dangerous than gang members. They described the police as violent and the community's fear of the police as well founded because they have destroyed people's lives with absolute impunity. They believed the actions of law enforcement in Denver drove individuals to join gangs because youth of color were constantly treated as criminals.

Klein (2004:42–45) found that gang officer perceptions of gangs often did not match research findings. Klein found that most gang crime is minor; most gang activity is noncriminal; street gangs are social groups; street life becomes a part of gang culture; and the community context in which gangs arise is often ignored. The police, on the other hand, portrayed gangs as violent criminal enterprises, fundamentally different from other social groups and divorced from local community problems. Raul, an 18-year-old ex–gang member from Denver, said:

> They [police] mess with you all of the time. Like if you are a gang member they be stopping you all of the time. Checking to see if you have any weapons, some of these police officers are racist, they think we are all violent and do bad crimes, but I think we are different. One time they stopped us and they were taking off our shirts and checking if we had any gang tattoos. Writing things on their computer, about when they stopped you, what gang tattoos you have. They even took pictures of me one time, and I don't know why.

Raul was shocked by the treatment he received, but over time he began to see these incidents as normal encounters with law enforcement.

Gang intelligence gathering was blatantly discriminatory when Gang Unit officers stopped countless Latinos and left groups of whites alone. If there were whites involved in gangs, as the self-report studies (Esbensen and Osgood 1997) and my research confirmed, the majority continued to go unnoticed by law enforcement. Winfree et al. (2001) found that "Hispanics are no more likely to be gang members than Anglo youths." Conducting sweeps on groups of white youth and justifying them with gang reasoning had the potential to put Gang Unit funding and con-tinued operations in jeopardy. Police officers' repeated profiling based on stereotypical perceptions and coercive intelligence on Latinos and blacks justified increased funding, increased gang legislation, and aided the movement to relocate greater numbers of this population to the peni-tentiary. Pam and Randolph, observing the police in Denver, thought there were huge discrepancies in how blame was attributed to whites and youth of color. They mentioned how the Columbine shooting was a per-fect example because in that incident Marilyn Manson and society were blamed, whereas for minority youth the blame was laid on the parents or children of color being born violent. Cultural holidays reinforced their perceptions of racism, which led them to draw the following conclusion:

[Randolph:] The whole thing with crime and gang violence, and violence in the inner-city, is a red herring, you know? They are not addressing the problem. They are just trying to keep certain people down. If everybody in the Latino community has a criminal record before they are 20, there is no chance that they are going to get the job that rich white people have now because they are not going to be qualified. They are going to have a criminal record. [Pam:] Or even have a vote, if they get a felony. [Randolph:] Yeah it's a way of maintaining the status quo, that's the real purpose of the police. That's what I say.

Pam and Randolph remained critical of the police. They challenged numerous wrongful shootings of black and Latino men by the police and observed countless stops where profiling continued to alter race relations. Individuals interviewed lived these experiences on a regular basis and became locked in a cycle of future incarceration or criminal justice involvement.

Respondents interviewed claimed that both Denver's and Ogden's police departments often used excessive physical force. Although researchers for the Bureau of Justice Statistics (Greenfeld et al. 1999) reported that the use of force occurred in less than 1 percent of all encounters with citizens during the year of their survey, at least one-third of my respondents had experienced physical abuse one or more times. Eighty percent of this misconduct occurred during an arrest and in an isolated area during evening hours. People were more likely to be victimized by police in impoverished black and Latino neighborhoods. The level of abuse and misconduct in these cities was different from that noted in the infamous Rampart division case but currently remains underresearched and veiled in secrecy.[2]

Denver had a high rate of police shootings: from 1982 to 2011 there were 232 people shot and 105 people killed by the police department (data gathered from various newspaper reports, historical records, and the district attorney's office). The captain of the Denver Gang Unit assured me that many policies and protections were instituted to prevent misconduct within his city. Nevertheless, two Denver gang officers were charged for not logging at least eighty pieces of drug evidence into the police department's property bureau after making numerous arrests and issuing tickets for marijuana possession and paraphernalia (*RMN*, July 20, 2000). One of these officers was accused of harassing and brutalizing gang members within the Denver area, and this was the likely reason he was shot by a suspected gang member during a questionable traffic stop (Ritter 2003; interviews in 2004). The alleged gang member was also shot to death during this incident.

In another Denver case, an off-duty gang officer was driving home late at night after getting off work and became involved in a road-rage incident in which he fired six shots at a Salvadorian immigrant, who died at the scene (Ritter 1997). Forensic evidence contradicted the officer's testimony about whether the immigrant was holding a gun (*RMN*, Nov. 24, 2001). In yet another incident, an ex-military and highly decorated African American man filed a racial profiling complaint against the Gang Unit. He described how several gang officers stopped him without cause, crashed into his wife's car, and held him down at gunpoint while making lewd remarks toward his wife (*RMN*, Apr. 21, 2004). Nevertheless the Gang Unit claimed it had received few complaints (2004 interview). Rodney, an African American Latino resident who was a gang associate from Denver, told me:

> I wish every gang member would actually report the abuse that they would go through by the Denver Police Department. Then we would have a better picture of what the role is that unit plays. But the gang members don't feel like they have a right to report when they have been beat up. If they actually took the time to document this stuff we would actually see the Denver Police is putting in more work than anybody. They function as a gang. [They said they had low amounts of complaints that come from that unit?] They said they have a low amount of complaints; yeah they do, because the people they are attacking are scared to complain. A lot of times, I don't even want to say scared, they don't feel empowered to complain. They feel like they are a gang member so they just have to deal with what they got.

Rodney had been beaten by several police officers in the past and was unsuccessful in his attempts to get the officers fired for brutality. He thought his vocal protest of brutality only encouraged the police to go after him and his family with more determination.

The Ogden Gang Unit was the least prepared for dealing with harassment practices by its officers because white officers were rarely challenged or questioned about how they operated. Therefore the Ogden Gang Unit practiced a higher number of profile stops than the Denver Gang Unit. Jay, a 27-year-old ex–gang member in Ogden, said:

> I think that some of their methods and tactics are a little on the borderline of police brutality, or excessive force. One of my friends, who works at the police department, is in close contact with the Gang Unit. He told me that this one officer hates little gang members. He calls them on whether it be a fistfight, a weapons fight, whatever. He will physically challenge them, you know, you bring your stick and I'll bring mine. I guess they figure they got to do what they got to do.

Jay saw the need in the community for better policing. This drove him to continue pursuing the possibility of one day becoming a police officer himself.

Several community members challenged Ogden Gang Unit officers for their role in inciting a riot of about seventy-five African Americans at a hip-hop concert. The officers had received a call that alcohol was present, and when they attempted to enter the building security officials denied them entrance. As a result, several people were beaten with police batons and charged with felony rioting (*SE*, Oct. 23, 2003). After this case was turned over to the FBI for investigation, one of the key officers suspected of brutality began to target the individual who filed the complaint (*SE*, Feb. 22, 2004; Apr. 1, 2004).

Human Rights Watch (1998:2) argued that "race continues to play a central role in police brutality in the United States. Indeed, despite gains in many areas since the civil rights movement of the 1950s and 1960s, one area that has been stubbornly resistant to change has been the treatment afforded racial minorities by the police." Human Rights Watch's research involving fourteen cities reported that habitually brutal officers, usually a small percentage on the force, might receive repeated complaints but were usually protected by other officers and poor internal police investigations. Cyclone, the 25-year-old ex–gang member and ex–prison inmate, said:

> I've been beaten by cops before. I was running from the police and I was drunk. I wrecked a car and I got out and started to run and I noticed there were five different counties of cops. There were cops from every district surrounding me. I lay down on the ground and

the cop that jumped on me started punching me in back of the head. I went into County [Jail] and let them know that I was having serious migraines and I showed them the bumps on my head. They took a report and that's all that was ever said. They didn't do anything to the officer that whupped my ass. I got charged with resisting arrest and was tied to the bumper of a car. [How many times do you think he hit you in the back of the head?] Probably about four of five. [What were you doing?] I was in handcuffs on my stomach while his knee was in my back, and the other cops were watching. They know something happened. If I wasn't in cuffs when he was hitting me I would have defended myself. They have the reports on the bumps on my head, severe handcuff marks on my arms; I couldn't feel my left hand for nearly an hour after they took the cuffs off.

Cyclone thought the law was hypocritical in allowing officers to abuse the law and justify abuse by claiming fear for their safety. Cyclone didn't understand how he was a threat when in handcuffs.

Several interviewees believed that undocumented immigrants were treated worse by police. Mirandé (1987) suggested that immigrants were especially vulnerable because they lacked resources and familiarity with the justice system. Immigrants also reported fewer instances of abuse because they feared deportation. Nite Owl, an undocumented 17-year-old gang member, said:

One time I was walking, and they [police] told me stop, and I stopped, and they didn't tell me to turn around or anything they just came up and tackled me. They hit me two times with their stick and put the cuffs on my hands. Maybe they could say "I'm sorry we messed up" or something, but they didn't say nothing like that. They just [said,] "Sorry, it wasn't you." I said, "It wasn't me," and they said, "Shut up," so I didn't say anything.

Nite Owl viewed his situation as being in the wrong place at the wrong time, but there was nothing he could have done to prevent a severe beating.

Problematic urban conditions and minority presence have resulted in police violence being used proactively rather than simply in reaction to a criminal threat (Jacobs and O'Brien 1998; Terrill and Resig 2003). The Latino and black community recognized that a simple stop or interaction with the police had a variety of outcomes that were seen as legally permissible, but that law enforcement officers were not going to treat whites living in their racially segregated neighborhoods with the same type of aggression. Holmes (2000) reported that there are reliable data to conclude that southwestern Latinos are targets of police brutality based on his study of civil rights complaints filed with the U.S. Department of Justice. Furthermore, Kane (2002) reported that an increase in the percentage of the Latino population increased police misconduct.

Accommodating the Legitimacy of Gang Units

Rosenbaum (1981) argued that the preferred tactic to colonization for the majority of Mexicanos from 1846 to 1916 included spatial and social separation from the Anglo community. In Denver and Ogden the barrio was spatially separate from whites, but since gangs were perceived as synonymous with Latinos and African Americans, the number of police interactions increased. The post–civil rights Latino community primarily responded to police aggression by accommodating to police tactics, thus instituting an oppressive component to the barrio experience. Thus gang enforcement added a new level of surveillance and community oversight onto an already tense relationship with the barrio. According to interviews and POP observation, when Gang Unit officers interacted with community members, law enforcement officers expected deference; without this submissive demeanor, many became vocally and physically abusive. Faced with consequences that included criminal charges, jail, fines, and even death, most Latinos in the neighborhood told the cops what they wanted to hear. When citizens failed to demur, many Latinos reported seeing their friends thrown to the ground with guns pulled on them, even physically roughed up and arrested. Morales (1972) reported that "perhaps the most discouraging fact is that even if a Mexican American police brutality victim were to survive initial police and prosecutor obstacles in the path toward justice, it is highly improbable that a court would rule in his favor."

Ninety-percent of the individuals interviewed were fearful of filing a complaint, and only three people knew anyone who had done so. Human Rights Watch (1998:50) reported that in the fourteen cities it studied, "Filing a complaint is unnecessarily difficult and often intimidating." Pate and Fridell's (1993) research indicated that even when blacks filed complaints, they were less likely than whites' to be sustained. None of the three people who filed complaints ever had their charges substantiated. Anne reported her accommodation strategy:

> [Was there anything you could do to stop that from happening?] No, not really. I never really thought about it, I guess. I could stop hanging out with my friends or cruising around with my friends just so I wouldn't get pulled over. It wasn't always me driving though either. Maybe I would be with my friends in their car, and they would get pulled over. [Your friends ever, like, complain to the police department?] No. [Do you think that would help?] I doubt it. I don't think so. They don't care at all. If I said anything he would probably try and take me to jail. And if you go to someone higher they are going to laugh at you. People don't mess with the cops. Then you're just going to be targeted more. Nobody did nothing, or said nothing. They [police] would be mad. They would try and find something on you to get you in jail.

Thus it was not surprising when Bayley and Mendelsohn (1968:129) reported that "for all the suspicion shown by minority people toward the police and the unpleasant personal experiences they have had with them, very few have made formal complaints about police behavior." Cola, a 27-year-old ex–gang member from Ogden, said:

> The police have pulled so many guns on me. I don't know how many times I have had to lay face down on the ground with a gun to my head. All the while they end up letting me go because I didn't do anything. But feeling and seeing guns pointed at you, you damn well know they can do anything they want. The police have pulled their guns on me way more than gang members have, and each time I am told to go on my way, like nothing ever happened. It didn't matter the time of the day, or how many people were around. I don't know how you might feel about this, but constantly seeing my life in their hands made me reluctant to go outside.

Cola stated that there were sections of Ogden where simply driving down the street at night resulted in getting pulled. My observations with POP revealed a heightened enforcement in the barrio and even ticketing of vehicles for parking more than twelve inches away from the curb, resulting in additional forms of punishment.

During undergraduate school Ray, an 18-year-old African American student in Ogden, came over to my apartment after a stop and was crying. I was surprised; I had never seen my friend cry, and he was always getting stopped for no reason. The cumulative number of stops was overwhelming. He told me, "I am sick and tired of the police pulling me over for nothing." I asked what happened, and he said he was driving his white girlfriend's car and the police pulled him over and made him lie down on the ground because they thought he had stolen the vehicle. Once the police found out the vehicle was not stolen, they simply told him to stay out of trouble. Nevertheless, the shame and humiliation he felt in front of everyone did not go away.

Anne, the 24-year-old gang associate from Ogden, said:

> One time we were just standing outside my friend's house and this gang Detective pulls up and he went off. I think he said something like, "What are all of you assholes doing out here?" "Nothing, we were just talking." Right away he started telling everybody, "Don't you have a warrant? I think you do. I'm going to check right now. If you do, you are going down." Cops were called for backup and wouldn't let anybody leave. Then somebody asked, "What did we do? We were just standing here talking." He responded, "I don't need a reason to pull you guys over and ask what you are doing. You are trouble makers." He wouldn't let anybody leave or go in the house. Even the girl's mom tried to come out and he told her she better get back in the house.

Based on personal experience, no one was allowed to challenge the actions of a police officer. Doing so brought consequences. Thus participating in POP in Ogden always carried a feeling of doing something different because it was definitely not the norm to observe police actions. In Denver a compromise between the police department and POP had been reached after several court cases and the ACLU determined that people had the right to observe the police. The police learned to accept individuals with cameras and notepads observing their behavior, and it became departmental policy to give business cards stating the officer's name and badge number when requested.

The small percentage of officers convicted of criminal wrongdoing or even charged with such behavior leads community residents to believe that officers are above the law and cannot be reproached. D-loc, the ex-gang member in his mid-twenties, said, "The police speak with attitude, they automatically assume they're above all. I don't care if you're a gang member or just a regular citizen on the street, they talk like their power goes to their head and they lose it. When it is a gang member they are three times harder on a kid because they are gang involved."

In Denver this reached the point of absurdity as questionable and outright wrong beatings and police shootings were upheld as legally justifiable. If the officers were in the wrong they were only temporarily suspended or had their consequences minimized by comparative discipline. In both cities Latino and black community members who questioned differential policing and the behavior of officers were seen as ignorant or criminal. Donner (1980) reported that negative images created about groups, often without evidence, became self-perpetuating, and questioning the validity of law enforcement practices merely confirmed the groups' subversive nature.

The self-defense response against agents of the state in the form of violence became legal justification to kill or brutally assault the Latino and black community. Hemmens and Levin's (2000) research described early common law that allowed people unjustifiably stopped by the police the power to resist arrest. They noted that over the past forty years this right has been effectively eliminated. At the same time more aggressive tactics and enforcement erode and undermine the legitimacy of these stops. If such resistance were ever attempted by members of the Latino or black community, it would surely result in felony charges for resisting arrest and assault on an officer or would justify officers' excessive use of force.

Self-Protection and Police Underprotection

Latino gang and community members believed that the police, as agents of the state, often neglected to enforce crimes that were committed against them. They felt that with limited compassion, time, and resources, the police selectively chose those victims they considered worthy of protecting. The majority of Latinos interviewed, and especially those who were gang members or ex-cons, described how when they were beaten up, robbed, stabbed, or victimized, the police only investigated the person who initially made the complaint. Therefore these respondents felt underprotected (Weitzer 1999). Anderson (1999) found that the majority of inner-city African Americans believed the police did not care about their safety and that when a crime was committed against them showed little concern. Neglectful policing encouraged gang members to settle problems themselves. Anderson (1999:34) spoke about a code on the streets that "emerges where the influence of police ends and personal responsibility for one's safety is felt to begin, resulting in a kind of 'people's law,' based on 'street justice.' " Cyclone, the 25-year-old ex-inmate and prison gang member, said:

> Cops drive by every day at least maybe every two to three hours just to see what's going on. Make sure there ain't no gang activity. And it's weird that they miss it when shit is happening. When you are getting hurt they miss that, but they use it against you. Your house gets robbed; they want to take you to jail because you got jumped when you were asleep. They know exactly who the hell did it and what happened, and they look at it like they never did, and being a cop they have to notify it no matter what and they didn't. You want to believe they are there and they ain't. Also how they look at gang members. Shit, they are like, who are they, you tell them about a problem you got; they are not ready to go kill for you anymore. It makes you wonder, what the fuck.

Cyclone understood that he was not perceived as a model citizen, but he was truly amazed that he could be attacked and the police didn't care or respond by investigating his victimization.

Kennedy (1997:29) reported that "deliberately withholding protection against criminality (or conduct that should be deemed criminal) is one of the most destructive forms of oppression that has been visited upon African Americans." Therefore when "street-committed" individuals were robbed or assaulted and the police did not respond the same way as they did to other crime victims, it fueled the pressure to retaliate against the people who were getting away with the crime. Street-committed members become pressured by norms of neighborhood respect and honor to avenge their victimization. This pressure was felt most keenly immediately after a crime had happened, tearing away at the victims' decision making.

Klein (2004) reported that Gang Unit officers had little sympathy for gang member victims, and that involvement in a gang condoned whatever victimization they would suffer. The police seemed to thrive off situations of gang members fighting each other, creating an opening for them to go in for the arrest that would set up a long prison sentence for one individual while the other one could be shot, stabbed, or wounded. My respondents believed that through this practice the police could accomplish "justice" and retribution. Ex–gang member D-loc said:

> Some people that got killed because these cops went and talked to these gang members, and after they talked to them they went and talked to these other gang members and repeated what other gang members just told them. And then they cause conflict between each other, and no one is like, I heard it from the cops, they are just going, oh those fools are talking shit, oh those fools are the ones who did this or that, we're going to get them pussies. And they wind up shooting each other and the cops just kick back and pick up the bodies and their hands are clean when they're the ones who started the whole beef and the fighting and the murder.

Police officers, on the other hand, were often hindered in their investigations because street-committed individuals and those who feared retaliation were unwilling to talk to them. The Latino community worried whether the information they provided to the police might implicate themselves as a snitch or lead to themselves being criminally investigated for doing something wrong.

Gang enforcement by Gang Units and patrol officers involved several theoretical patterns. First, the increase in the number of young, poor, and urban Latinos was seen as a threat for gang membership. Second, structurally vulnerable areas became targeted with concentrated aggressive gang enforcement that supported gang assumptions and fueled the moral panic by labeling non–gang members as gang members (ecological contamination). Third, aggressive policing of marginalized and oppressed communities did not eliminate crime but rather led to greater divisions between barrio residents and law enforcement.

In my observations and research I did not find that Gang Unit officers or law enforcement officials were incorrect in all criminal stops, but rather the majority of gang enforcement stops were predicated on noncriminal activity and included more non–gang members than gang members. The barrio residents were not antipolice; they *were* against profiling and demeaning treatment. The end result of aggressive differential policing was greater division between the barrio and law enforcement.

The actual practice of gang enforcement included racialized profiles, fabricated intelligence, and suppression of marginalized communities.

The social control placed on the young, urban black and Latino community by the police, and in particular by the Gang Units, seriously challenged individuals' abilities to move through life without a criminal record and thus be able to rise through poverty-stricken urban neighborhoods. Such practices built on a long history of racialized oppression. Although this chapter primarily focused on the police, they were not alone in participating in the war on gangs. Other officials and agencies that vigorously pursued gangs included correctional facilities, parole officers, prosecutors, and the new, multijurisdiction federal law enforcement initiatives designed to arrest and incarcerate larger numbers of gang members.

CHAPTER THREE

Racialized Oppression and the Emergence of Gangs

*Denver's population of half a million residents feels superlarge compared
to Ogden, a city of 75,000 residents. Maybe it's the skyline of tall buildings or the greater density, but I feel like I'm in uncharted territory, far
from my 'hood and the homies who watched my back. I'm sitting shot-
gun one afternoon as D-loc drives me through the Westwood projects.
Eighty-three percent of residents living in this neighborhood are Latino,
making it one of the neighborhoods with the highest concentration of
nonwhites in the city. In the next ten years, this neighborhood will be
the site of broken-windows policing, which is focused on zero tolerance
for misdemeanor activity. In New York City, this style of policing was
criticized for racial profiling and increasing the number of arrests for
minor offenses. The federal government will also supply funding as part
of the Office of Juvenile Justice and Delinquency Prevention's Comprehensive Gang Model in the name of Gang Reduction Initiative in Denver (GRID). Westwood is similar to other neighborhoods in Denver in
that it has experienced an increase in Latino immigrants moving into
neighborhoods where Mexican Americans have lived for more than half
a century.*

*As an ex–gang member from the Crenshaw Mafia Bloods, D-loc
wears the color red, which contrasts with the color blue that I wear. The
simple fact of having two individuals hanging out who were socialized
into hating a certain color demonstrates progress. We are both 25 and
Chicano, but he has a level of political and cultural consciousness that
I've never observed before in my lifetime. For the last three years, D-loc
has been working with other ex–gang members to reduce the level of
violence in Denver through a group known as ASAP. Such an approach
is unheard of in Utah, where the criminal justice system seems to be*

the only response to gangs. I've been shadowing D-loc for over-a-year and find him very outgoing and likeable. Individuals in the community give him a lot of respect. He is not afraid to challenge authority figures, whether they are police officers, school officials, or individuals who are white. He brings with him a presence of authority, demanding respect.

D-loc is telling me about the drama of gangs in Denver: the shootings, the murders, the police brutality, and the Chicano activism that transformed the city. Many of the gangs and gang members he mentions coincide with my year of observations attending ASAP. The local gangs are becoming more familiar to me: Bloods (Crazy Chicano Bloods, Crenshaw Mafia Gangsters—CMG, and Westside—CMG), Crips (33 Gangster, Compton Crip Riders, Raymond Avenue, and Rolling 30s), Sureños (Florencia 13, Lennox, Playboy, South Central, Varrio Grande Vista, along with nonneighborhood-based Sureños), North Side (Criminals, 41st Diablos, Hotboys, North Side Mafia, and Untouchables), and other gangs including Bella Vista, Chi 30, Gallant Knights Insane (GKI), Inca Boys, Kings of Denver, Oldies 13, Quinta Loma, Criminal Wreckin Society, Westside, Tiny Rascals, Viet Pride, and Asian Pride.

Mexican Americans, Mexicans, blacks, and Asians are considered by law enforcement as the dominant racial and ethnic groups that make up the gangs in Denver. The youngsters attending ASAP are livin' the gangster life in terms of style of dress, language used, and promotion of their particular gang identity. As I have been attending the group and listening to the conversations, I have begun to wonder how these marginalized racial and ethnic groups became the city's gang population. Stepping back in time provided a context to understand the origination of Denver gangs, in particular the experiences of Latinos—the largest number of reported gang members in Denver (73 percent of all new gang members in 2003 according to the Denver Police Gang Bureau statistics).

This chapter provides the historical context of how gangs emerged in Denver. Karl Marx (1994:188) reported, "Men make their own history, but they do not make it as they please; they do not make it under self-selected circumstances, but under circumstances existing already, given and transmitted from the past. The tradition of all dead generations weighs like a nightmare on the brains of the living." Making the link between contemporary issues required understanding how and why gangs first emerged into an informal institution that fit a niche provided by no other formal organizations. In outlining this history, I argue how gangs developed from racial oppression and their level of activity decrease when social movements challenge these inequalities and increase during times of gang suppression.

Denver emerged as a community in 1858 as part of the Kansas Territory. It was seen as inhospitable because of the presence of Native Americans and its wilderness setting, but the discovery of gold quickly changed the geographical and social landscape (Dorsett and McCarthy 1986; Leonard and Noel 1990). Gold and the railroad brought Anglos from the East, and by 1880 the city population was estimated to be 35,629. A police force was created in 1874 to help manage drunkenness, gambling, prostitution, and theft but was largely deemed ineffective owing to lack of political and public support. Native Americans and blacks did not benefit from any form of justice in the area and their murders often went without punishment. Dorsett and McCarthy reported that "the promise of American life in frontier Denver was largely the preserve of white men" (53). Themes of racial inequality were clearly present in local politics and day-to-day operations (Arps 1998; Delgado and Stefancic 1999).

According to Walsh (1995), the first mention of gangs in Denver occurred in the 1889 *Denver Times*, but group conflicts among whites did not cause much concern for residents. Whites were not seen as a problem, and various Italian, Polish, or Russian immigrants did not receive special focus as they did in Boston and Chicago (Thrasher 1927; Whyte 1943). According to Colomy and Kretzmann (1995), Judge Ben B. Lindsey, known as the "Father of Juvenile Court," served as judge from 1901 to 1927 and followed a philosophy of uplifting good children from misdirected energy. Lindsey's version of social justice was challenged by the Ku Klux Klan, a racist organization that rose to prominence and began pursuing the removal of the famous juvenile court judge from office in 1923, and it eventually accomplished its goal (Rodgers 1976). In the beginning this organization did not bring the city outrage but rather tremendous growth in the number of individuals who desired membership. The general ideology after World War I was in favor of Protestants and against blacks, Catholics, foreigners, and Jews.

The Ku Klux Klan emerged as a political powerhouse, wielding community pressure for law and order and resisting demographic and cultural changes. As Robert Alan Goldberg (1981:12) reported, "The Denver klavern was the largest and most influential member of the Colorado Klan federation." The Klan reached the height of its influence in the winter of 1924–25. In 1924 it had grown to an estimated seventeen thousand members in Denver, and a total of fifty thousand members in the state of Colorado (Davis 1963; Goldberg 1981). It controlled every aspect of city and state government: attorneys, city appointments, the governor, the House of Representatives, judges, police, senators, and school boards (Davis 1963; Goldberg 1975, 1981; Ku Klux Klan Tapes 1962). The Klan's symbol was the American flag, providing an association with patriotism and a whites-only form of law and order. Klan members constituted the majority in the Republican Party and operated in a secret society with handshakes, symbols, and covert words to maintain a community stronghold (Davis 1963).[1] A backlash arose against the Denver Klan when national attention increased largely because of public attention to bigotry from chapters in the South. This opposition coincided with internal disputes among the Klan leadership, an opposing Republican faction, and an outcry from two groups despised by the Klan: Catholics and Jews.

Mexican Americans continued to live in Denver and the state of Colorado despite encountering Anglo hostility. Individuals of mixed Native American and Spanish descent had lived in southern Colorado since the land was controlled by Mexico and Spain; however, in most parts of the state they continued to encounter second-class treatment. Employment opportunities in the sugar beet fields surrounding Denver brought many Latinos from rural communities in New Mexico and southern Colorado. In 1930 an estimated 7,000 residents of Mexican descent lived in Denver, an increase from 1,390 in 1920 (Dorsett and McCarthy 1986). As early as 1936 the Latino population was considered too large, Governor Edwin Johnson declared martial law to have over 100,000 Mexicans escorted out of the state by the National Guard (Dorsett and McCarthy 1986). The National Guard was placed along Colorado's southern border to make sure Mexicans did not reenter. Such forced removal was eventually declared unconstitutional (Meier and Ribera 1996; *Rocky Mountain News* [*RMN*] 1936). Thus political leaders had to develop new forms of maintaining social separation, and in Denver this largely resulted in the creation of barrios.

In the late 1930s the black and Latino neighborhoods eventually became a context for producing disparity as both groups remained segregated from white society (Mauck 2001). The *Rocky Mountain News* (Oct. 23, 1936) reported that in 1936 crime was relatively low in Denver, with the majority of arrests being for drunkenness. In 1938 the Youth Survey Committee (YSC) of the Adult Education Council of Denver conducted a study on "The Youth Problem in Denver." The YSC looked at issues facing youths 16 to 21 years of age. It reported that the area along the Platte River contained the highest rates of delinquency (at least 33 percent) and unemployment (at least 29 percent). According to the U.S. Census, the majority of the city's people of Mexican descent lived in this area (United States Census 1940). Black neighborhoods had the city's second-highest rates of delinquency and unemployment. White neighborhoods were reported to have less delinquency (11 percent or less) and lower unemployment (10 percent or less). Delinquency patterns became only more pronounced when individuals reached adulthood. Colorado's prison in Cañon City reflected the overrepresentation of black and Latino adults. According to Hans von Hentig's Colorado Crime Survey (1940), the rate of whites incarcerated per 100,000 was 233.0, Mexicans 497.4, and Negros 735.9. Thus Mexicans were more than twice as likely, and blacks more than three times as likely, as whites to be incarcerated. The white opposition to minority residents and Latino attempts to confront this unequal society eventually collided during the 1940s.

1940s and the Origination of Latino Gangs

The growth of the Latino population was intertwined with city neglect, racism, and urban decay, creating ripe conditions for gang development. The Mexican population increased to 4 percent of the population as a whole in 1940 (12,345), nearly double the percentage in the 1930s (Carmichael 1941). The population growth remained concentrated along the Platte River within four primary neighborhoods (census tracts 11, 12, 16, and 22). The Mexican barrio housing lacked central heating, refrigeration, and indoor plumbing. F. L. Carmichael (1941) reported that nine of every ten Spanish American families lived in substandard housing, compared with 23.9 percent of all Denver residents. The 1940s began with many Anglo officials and administrators remaining from the Klan years. World War II, much like World War I, had increased U.S. patriotism as well as hostility toward perceived foreigners.

The fear of Mexican American gangs in Denver escalated on December 19, 1942, when the Rocky Mountain News ("Hoodlums Watched by Police") reported "flashily dressed youths" participating in property crimes. The captain of the police department stated that the majority of these youth had "no malicious intent" but were believed to belong to a

group called the "zoot-suit commandos." A few days later a police sergeant reported to the media that a 16-year-old girl had been held captive
by four boys while another youth dragged a 17-year-old girl down an alley, where she was repeatedly attacked (*RMN*, Dec. 21, 1942). Authorities attributed the assault to "wartime pressure on youthful morals."

In June 1943, the Zoot Suit Riots occurred in East Los Angeles, California. The *Rocky Mountain News* (June 8, 1943) reported five nights
of rioting in Los Angeles between well-organized gangs and military sailors. The hysteria that swept Southern California resulted in Mexican
Americans getting attacked and arrested while white sailors were left
untouched (Bogardus 1943; Escobar 1999; McWilliams 1948; Obregón
Pagán 2003). Many people, including Eleanor Roosevelt, considered
the terror waged by servicemen against the Latino community as con-
stituting a race riot. Newspaper headlines in Denver fueled community
anxiety as the Denver Police Department had received increasing reports
of California zoot suiters relocating to the city (*RMN*, June 19, 1943).
The police emphasized that *local* zoot suiters had not received community complaints, but outsiders would be watched carefully because "the
zoot suit apparently has become a sort of insignia for the hoodlum and
that element will not be tolerated here." Zoot suiters were uncommon
except in the Five Points district, an area with a high concentration of
blacks and Latinos. Their criminal activities were limited to drunkenness
and vagrancy. On August 31, 1943, Denver had its first media headline
that zoot suiters from California were in the area. The *Rocky Mountain
News* reported, "The shadow of violent death moved forward yesterday
to darken further a series of abductions, slugging and terrorization of
Denver women by a hoodlum gang of zoot-suitists who styled themselves
The Order of the Wolf." The Order of the Wolf hailed from Los Angeles,
and its members traveled in a car that had hit a 19-year-old Denver resident, who later died. The Order of the Wolf had also allegedly abducted
three women.

In the spring of 1944, one year after the Los Angeles Zoot Suit Riots,
reports of people wearing zoot suits in Denver continued, as did efforts
to counter this perceived threat. On May 5 thirty people wearing zoot
suits were arrested for fighting and charged with loitering. Three Lowry
Air Force Base soldiers reported that they were attacked by a "group of
nine zoot-clad youths." A *Rocky Mountain News* reporter became curi-
ous about zoot suiters and drove to 18th and Curtis, where he saw forty
of them hanging out at 1:00 A.M. taunting cars (*RMN*, May 8, 1944).

The following day, city officials requested more police patrols along the areas bounded by 14th, 20th, Curtis, and Larimer streets (*RMN*, May 9, 1944). These streets bordered the growing Latino neighborhoods adjacent to the downtown district. City officials wanted dance and age curfews enforced, along with charges for loitering, following an assault on two women by a group of thirty youths that included several girls (*RMN*, May 13, 1944). The Denver City Council reported that zoot-suit hoodlumism in downtown Denver had recently subsided because of vigorous police action but added that legislation could prevent future violence (*RMN*, May 10, 1944). City Council members agreed that targeting hoodlum behavior required changing the age of those subject to the city's 10:00 P.M. curfew law from 14 to 17. They formed a committee composed of residents and members of city organizations who were notified any time zoot suiters were picked up for loitering, so they could meet with the parents to discuss how to correct the youths' behavior, or pursue the possibility of charging the parents for failing to supervise their children.

The *Rocky Mountain News* (May 9, 1944) exacerbated the panic with such headlines as "A Terrible Denver Tragedy": "GANGS OF YOUTHS, 16 to 18 years old, wandering the downtown streets, beating up women, assaulting soldiers, dragging spectators from movie houses, kicking them and pulling their hair! . . . It is the pathetic picture of certain unhappy members of minority groups venting their fury in a blind, confused way on innocent persons." The reporter argued that the city's punishments needed to be harsher and more strictly enforced. In response to the gang reports, the May 11, 1944, issue of the *Rocky Mountain News* described the police and city officials waging a "war on gangs." The war included fines and ninety-day jail sentences for people charged with vagrancy, in an attempt to curb "outbreaks of hoodlumism on Denver streets." Within several days fifty "gang members" had been arrested for vagrancy, which means "wandering" or walking around a city. Walsh's (1995) research on Denver's early gangs included interviews with numerous people who described the use and abuse of the vagrancy law. One woman described being put in jail for seven days simply for being in the park. According to Walsh, the Denver Police Department's "Annual Report" indicated that 31 percent of those arrested for vagrancy between 1945 and 1954 were Latino.

Fourteen arrests were made on May 14, 1944. The demographics of those arrested were somewhat surprising: six were young women. They wore the zoot-suit counterpart: blue jean overalls and jumpers decorated with embroidered names and designs (*RMN*, May 14, 1944). The increased legislation and police patrols coincided with a four-day seminar on Spanish Americans held by Regis College in October 1944. More than forty delegates from six states discussed issues such as the role of prejudice, inadequate education, and employment discrimination (*RMN*, Oct. 8, 1944; Oct. 18, 1944). Several letters to the editor questioned the double standard of unequal treatment, but racial disturbances persisted.

On March 11, 1945, at least eight people in military uniform were among sixty-five youths picked up by police for invading a community center and beating up "Spanish-speaking" youths. The names of the Anglo youths were taken, and they were released without charges. Mexican American citizens were outraged that the Klan-backed mayor, Benjamin Stapleton, and the Denver Police Department were not providing protection for them. People of Mexican descent were upset that their children were dealt with more harshly than whites. Walsh (1995:124) reported, "The police department was not a protective unit in these communities as much as it was a force of repression and surveillance." Walsh's interviewees described beatings by police and an overwhelming show of force when Latinos were apprehended. District Attorney James T. Burke corroborated Latinos' negative experience with the police. He accused Mayor Stapleton and the chief of police of "doing nothing to weed misfits out of the police department" (*RMN*, Aug. 12, 1946). Burke argued, "The policemen committed crimes [ranging] from murder to petty larceny," and neither official did anything about that behavior. A grand jury investigated charges of police brutality and indicted three officers: one had stolen linen, another had beaten two Latinos with a billy club, and the third had obtained money under false pretenses (*RMN* 1946). James Fresques, a City Council member, presented evidence that Latinos were treated badly by police (*DP*, Sept. 8, 1946). The majority of the police force was white, with only one Latino and two black officers. The police department refused to change its aggressive practices against Latinos, and no person or law could make it change. A district judge upheld the police chief's refusal to answer questions about the death of a Spanish-surnamed man, along with other cases of police brutality (*RMN*, Jan. 11, 1947).

In 1947 James Quigg Newton succeeded Stapleton as mayor. Newton honored a pledge to establish a task force on human relations in an attempt to end discrimination and to reach out to the minority community

(Delgado and Stefancic 1999). The eleven-member Denver Commission on Human Relations (DCHR) reported "a linked spiral: job discrimination means that minorities earn less; their lower income drives them to poor housing areas; prejudice keeps them there; the neighborhoods become full to overflowing; facilities break down; the inhabitants try to escape but run 'into a wall of prejudice" (Delgado and Stefancic 1999:38). The DCHR found the cost of prejudice staggering and described it as an "expensive luxury." The DCHR developed the first documentation of racism in Denver.

Although governmental and public interest problems in Denver began to increase, gang feuds reported in the *Rocky Mountain News* grew in severity from 1946 to 1948. Gang activities resulted in wars between East Side and West Side neighborhoods (*RMN*, April 8, 1946). The use of guns increased, and more Latinos were being shot or arrested for carrying weapons. Juvenile Court judge Gilliam thought the rise in the use of weapons was influenced by the movie "*City Across the River*," which was based on the book *Amboy Dukes* and dealt with juvenile gangs in New York (*RMN*, Oct. 23, 1949). Several of the people interviewed by Walsh (1995) corroborated this theory by describing how they had learned to make zip guns from watching the movie.

Sam Lusky, a writer for the *Rocky Mountain News*, described his version of gang members in a report titled "Rich and Poor Kids Alike Want to Be 'Tough Guys' " (*RMN*, Oct. 24, 1949). He viewed the rising popularity of this lifestyle with disdain:

> They're suckers. Fall guys for somebody else. Or just Chumps. Deep down they know it. But they shove it farther and farther back into their consciousness, and block it out with more swaggering and strong-arming. They think they look hard to the cops [but] these juveniles look silly. . . . These gangs recognize only one law—force. They beef about discrimination and unfairness. Sure there's discrimination. It's rotten and unfortunate. But, even where it doesn't exist these gangs pretend it does.

Lusky reported that the police preferred to use their billy clubs to help gang members understand, and these officers resented the "current straight-down-the-middle attitude of the Piloce [*sic*] Department and the city administration." Near the end of 1949 Lusky found sympathy for his aggressive stance when a Denver judge issued a three-point ultimatum: work, go to school, or go to jail (*RMN*, Oct. 26, 1949). The youths before him had been charged with vagrancy and some with illegal possession of firearms. The judge saw no reason for these youths "being idle, staying up all night, and sleeping all day." Perceived gang members received very oppositional press coverage that pushed for Mexicans to be punished until an unachievable goal of conformity was achieved.

Contrary to the view of newspaper editors, writers, and the general white public, Walsh (1995:1) vividly captured the Latino worldview of the time with his interview of Jack Chavez, who reported his experience in this complex and troubling social environment:

> You walked with pride. People had walks. We called them Pachuco walks. It was a strut. It was a real strut. It was designed to put fear in the enemy, whoever the enemy happened to be. The enemy could be the guy two or three blocks over; or if you went downtown on sixteenth street, not knowing what the white element happened to be. That created fear. So you strutted down the street scared to death. You didn't know what the Anglo element happened to be. So it was a matter of strutting down the street saying, "Hey, I can conquer the world."

Latinos were growing up in the midst of white racism, external opposition from law enforcement, and increasing legislation to control their perceived misbehavior. In addition to the external opposition, Latino youth faced a rising threat from rival gang members. Gangs took on the image of becoming more organized by using gang names, whereas before they had been primarily a clique of boys known by their leader (interview with Ernesto Vigil, 2004). According to the documents reviewed, the names of male gangs in 1949 included the Aces, Dukes, Heads, Lefties, and Lincoln Park Brothers. There were three girl gangs: Jeans, Proxies, and Sisters.

1950s and the Acknowledgment of a Problem

Latino youth faced many challenges. They organized to confront discrimination and urban decay, but these groups were beginning to pose a threat to Latinos' overall safety in Denver. The Latino population increased to between 40,000 and 45,000, or 10 percent of the city's population (National Committee Against Discrimination in Housing 1951). The 1950s included a gang fight, in which two youths were stabbed and a member of the Aces gang ended up in critical condition. The *Rocky Mountain News* reported that residents in the lower East Side neighborhood said youthful gangs were on the prowl (*RMN*, Jan. 23, 1950). Ernesto Vigil, Denver's Chicano historian, described the early 1950s as filled with high racial and ethnic tension in which white gangs dominated:

> My neighborhood became the first significant one that had people of Mexican descent, and there were fights and rivalries. Some of it was gang rivalries, but a lot of it was neighborhood and ethnic violence. Our neighborhood was becoming increasingly Chicano, and Globeville, being heavily white ethnics and usually southern Europeans, first- and second-generation, was working class. In retrospect, I didn't see it at that time, they [the residents] were really concerned into proving their own Americanism. . . . They used to call Globeville the United Nations neighborhood because you had all kinds of first- and second-generation immigrant families, and I think their status was threatened in their eyes by competing Mexican laborers, and one of the first things they did, immigrant communities in acculturating, it became as racist as the U.S. is, and so Mexicans were good people to look down upon, and it would help them to feel superior and reinforce their own ideas about their status, but Mexicans were typically victimized. I remember families that would try and move in[to] the neighborhood, the Globeville neighborhood, and people would throw Molotov [cocktails] on their front porch. . . . So my recollection of the gang Los Santos was primarily about their fights with the young men from Globeville. . . . Part of that was an ethnic fad for the youth in the community. I also think in terms of the racial conflicts that existed, part of it was self-protection. In particular, I remember in elementary school when we would want to go swim it was dangerous to go to the Globeville neighborhood, and they had a much bigger and better swimming pool. . . . The only time that we would go was when there would be a big number of us because if we went individually there was a good chance that you would get beaten up. . . . [W]hat those guys on Globeville would do is they would contaminate the pool. They would throw in gasoline, oil, because they didn't want Mexicans to use it, so they would throw that type of stuff in the pool and it would shut it down for everybody, but that was a way of sending a hint that we weren't wanted so I think it should be stated as a supposition; clearly I never asked these older

guys, I was too little, but I got the strong impression that one strong motive for them to join the gang was protection against the white gangs that existed, and they were very aggressive, very violent, and very racist.

Vigil recalled the harshness of growing up during these times. The media and community officials blamed Latinos for their circumstances.

Judge Gilliam in the Juvenile Court took proactive steps to decrease gang feuds. He became an honorary member of the Heads gang in an attempt to help these forty to fifty members "reform" (*RMN*, Mar. 12, 1950; *DP*, Mar. 11, 1950). The *Denver Post* labeled the Heads "one of Denver's most notorious hoodlum gangs." However, the youths told Gilliam that they would become good citizens. More than half of these members had been expelled from school, and their crimes had ranged from assault to car stripping. The gang members started to work on keeping each other out of trouble. Gilliam loaned three of them money to buy bicycles so they could get to work (*RMN*, Mar. 12, 1950). Although Judge Gilliam gave the Heads a way out of the gang life and a path into the conventional middle-class Anglo worldview, fellow youths in the barrio responded with ridicule. Heads gang members were taunted by various gangs as being "sissy" and "junior policemen" for their attempt to reform. This led the Heads to second-guess Judge Gilliam's plan. Thirty-five Heads gang members were arrested for fighting or preparing to fight. Judge Gilliam urged the Heads to stay the course for change (*RMN*, Mar. 30, 1950).

Gilliam conceded to the media that he had strong feelings that adult communists were "masterminding the epidemic of juvenile gang warfare sweeping the country" (*RMN*, May 9, 1950). The consensus across the nation, according to Judge Gilliam, was that adults were guiding these new gangs, helping them to last longer and causing more trouble for the police. Gilliam worried that most of the youth appearing in his courtroom lacked parental supervision (Gilliam 1950). This concern about outside influence initiated a trend that was repeated consistently through law enforcement's response to gang activity: linking them with the major fears of the time. Despite Gilliam's reported benevolent feelings toward wayward youth, the general community's orientation toward punishment was difficult to resist.

In May 1950 police and the news media portrayed girl gang members as "more vicious than the boys" because they continued to fight until someone was severely injured. Young women gang members were reportedly "waging a war among themselves." The female gangs went by the names of Heads (auxiliary to the male Heads gang), KC's, Legs, and Sisters (*RMN*, May 4, 1950). On December 10, 1950, the *Denver Post* published a special section entitled "Girl Gangs: A Civic Problem. They flaunt authority and fight among themselves for the sake of excitement." The reporter wrote, "Emily was an attractive, dark-haired girl with one very ungirlish talent: She could punch like a pugilist." The reporter interviewed a female Denver probation officer who said, "When boys get to fighting they quit when somebody gets the worst of it. Not the girls, though. They fight like animals. They're fearless. They just seem to like to fight." Juvenile authorities reported that the young women carried knives, and they were surprised that none of the fights had ended with a fatality. The girls reportedly came from homes with delinquent parents or from broken families, and often from blighted living conditions. They were described as lonely girls seeking companionship because they lacked fathers or father figures. A psychiatrist reported that "girl gangs" often engaged in sexual promiscuity to show that they were not afraid. According to the Juvenile Hall data, 1950 had the second-highest percentage (35.2) of girl court cases and hearings in a decade, slightly less than 1944 (35.3) (Juvenile Hall 1960). However, in 1944 delinquency among young women was mentioned only briefly.

By the summer of 1952 the *Denver Post* once again reported that "City Police Open Drive Against Teen-Age Gangs" and that the police had reimposed a "get tough attitude" (*DP*, June 3, 1952). Several unprovoked community muggings occurred in which the perpetrators were identified as Latin American "pack-running hoodlums." One man was stabbed in Lincoln Park, another on his way to church, and another in front of a liquor store. Police were planning on stopping gangs to look for concealed weapons. During the early 1950s switchblade knives were being used and confiscated with increasing frequency (*DP*, Nov. 12, 1950).

By February 1953 organized gangs reportedly had decreased (*RMN*, Feb. 22, 1953). Civic organizations, juvenile court, and the police department were praised for breaking up most of the gangs. Judge Gilliam reported that the Dukes, Heads, and other gangs had pretty much died down. No information is available from outside sources or primary documents to verify the reasons why gangs were decreasing. Ernesto Vigil, the Chicano historian, believed a change occurred in the 1950s when

the parks and recreation department began to open its doors to neighborhood gangs and got them to turn into sports clubs. Captain Nevin
of the Denver Police Department was quoted as saying, "The last big
gang outbreaks were in late summer of 1951. At that time gang warfare
broke out in the downtown and East Side areas, resulting in stabbings,
beatings and shootings. That period probably was the worst Denver had
seen in many years." The news media hinted that gangs had become
more territorial in the 1950s. On the West Side, an East Side gang of
boys and girls invaded a dance and stabbed a 20-year-old in the stomach. The brawl reportedly involved "40 howling boys and girls" (RMN,
Mar. 29, 1953). There had been several attacks on people parking along
lover's lane near Sullivan Dam, which resulted in at least six people
being beaten or threatened for being in the wrong neighborhood. The
Hoods gang reportedly claimed that it attacked motorists just for kicks,
and that it had been going on terror raids for the past year. Members
armed themselves with short rubber hoses and carried six-inch knives.
None of the girls were bothered, just their male companions (RMN,
May 31, 1953).

In 1954 the *Rocky Mountain News* published a seven part series of
articles concerning Denver's "Spanish-American Problem" (Jan. 31–
Feb. 6, 1954). This was the first set of news articles attempting to conduct in-depth research on the status of Latinos. Years later, Martin Luther King, Jr. (1967) criticized the language of the so-called Negro problem. He argued that the true issue was the white problem, as the disease
of racism affected U.S. society. Not until the white majority began to feel
empathy toward the ache and anguish of blacks would the problems of
the ghettos be solved. The writer of the *Rocky Mountain News* article
argued that Spanish American people faced problems kept silent because
statistics were not kept by race or ethnic group. He found them "Underpaid, Ill Fed, Badly Housed: Can We Blame the Poor After Half-Century
of This?" (RMN, Feb. 2, 1954). He quoted Archbishop Lucey: "HOW
much exuberance, vitality and enthusiasm could any people show who
had been underpaid, undernourished, and badly housed for half a century?" Lucey described the Mexican American as the "poorest of the
poor." The 1950 median family income in Denver for Spanish Americans
was the lowest of any racial or ethnic group. Perkins wrote that Spanish
Americans were poor because of low levels of education, language difficulties, cultural backgrounds, large families, and bitter experiences of

employers since they were considered unskilled labor. He found almost half the city's employers practicing overt discrimination against Spanish Americans and other minorities.

Denver property deeds included "restrictive covenants" against Spanish Americans that banned the sale of property to such individuals regardless of their level of income, culture, education, or manners. A sampling of Denver public opinion suggested that the majority of people (whites) did not want Spanish Americans as their neighbors under any circumstances. Only 30 percent reported that Spanish Americans should be able to live anywhere in the city, while 61 percent claimed they should not. According to the 1950 census, fewer than half (nineteen) of the forty-nine Denver census tracts contained more than 250 white persons with Spanish surnames. The majority of people of Mexican descent lived in four census tracts: 8, 12, 16, and 22.[2] Three of the four neighborhoods contained the highest percentage of Latinos found during the 1940 census. Perkins found no running water, baths, electricity, heat, or toilets. The households included more people than average in each room. According to the *Rocky Mountain News* and the United States Census tract data, Latinos occupied the city's worst homes. Six out of 10 of Denver's Spanish Americans lived in homes that were unfit for use (*RMN*, Feb. 5, 1954).

The final section of the series focused on solutions to this "Denver Problem," and thus a more collective responsibility was starting to be acknowledged (*RMN* Feb. 6, 1954). Perkins concluded, "Poverty impoverishes. Morally, spiritually, mentally, socially, physically." He emphasized that Denver needed to come to grips with its Spanish American problem. He argued, "Left alone the problem will not go away and stop bothering us." Perkins offered seventeen areas for improvement that emphasized changed treatment, increased data collection, and support for Spanish leadership. A year later, commemorating the seven-part series, the *Rocky Mountain News* again looked at the situation of Denver's Spanish Americans and found indications of progress (*RMN*, Jan. 27, 1955). Specifically, the principals of two schools reported increasing retention rates, "not startling but encouraging." The dropout rate among Spanish Americans had been as high as 90 percent in the past.

The increased focus on the social conditions that led to gangs brought additional attempts to achieve gang reformation. In 1954 Judge Gilliam came up with another new idea to target gang behavior and juvenile delinquency. He formed his own gang, the Friday Nighters, to combat the high delinquency year of 1953. The group began with twenty-four eager members. The gang members who attended the group discussed problems and attended a movie (*RMN*, Feb. 20, 1954). The objectives included therapeutic meetings, building relationships between probation officer and probationer, changing group loyalty to the community, learning to "humanize" officers enforcing the law, learning to release aggression in socially appropriate ways such as sports, receiving recognition for socially appropriate success, and helping the general public learn more about the role of the court system (Poremba 1955). Poremba found the program successful because it helped youth on probation to see the human side of the law.

Although local initiatives were gaining momentum, gang activity in Denver was discussed at the national level. A special Senate committee in Washington, D.C., on juvenile delinquency included a probe of Denver's teenage gangs. Three gangs were cited by the committee: Aces, Heads, and Hoods. The probe warned that the nation was losing its fight against juvenile delinquency, and the committee declared an all-out war on juvenile crime in order to decrease the rising tide (*RMN*, Mar. 16, 1954). The newspaper did not discuss what actions the committee was planning to use in its all-out war, but did mention that it involved using whatever efforts and resources necessary.

In 1957 police allegedly stopped the first full-scale gang battle in Denver since 1945; fourteen youth were placed in jail. The battle began when the Demons arranged a fight with another gang in the sunken gardens near West High School. They were reportedly armed with baseball bats, chains, iron clubs, wooden clubs, and zip guns (*RMN* 1957). The continuance of gang activity coincided with additional research. A master's degree candidate named Ronald C. Johnson at Denver University studied fifty Denver boys at the State Industrial School and concluded, "White delinquents are found worst-adjusted" than blacks and Spanish Americans. The thesis claimed that many Spanish American boys centered their life on their gangs, "which were formed in part to oppose the discrimination of the Anglo-American." It added that Spanish American boys fought back against discrimination, but blacks appeared to have surrendered (*RMN* 1957). This may have been the first analysis in Denver of this particular time in which gangs were depicted as a form of resistance to unequal treatment.

In October 1957 the *Rocky Mountain News* continued to report that Spanish Americans were showing social gains (Oct. 9, 1957). However, racial prejudice and poverty had still combined to provide no more than minimal housing integration for Denverites of Spanish descent. The writer reported, "Crime rates for the group are still far out of proportion to its numbers." Spanish Americans were overrepresented in hospital admission rates (30 percent, with an estimated Latino population of 10 percent) and underrepresented in high school graduation rates (5.6 percent of all graduates). Mayor Nicholson's Commission on Human Relations reported, "The lot of Spanish Americans is being improved with slow progress" (*RMN*, Oct. 10, 1957).

The research on this slow progress was complemented by several city and county agencies working together to compile a report titled "Problems in Relation to Work with Spanish Speaking People in Denver" (Parks and Recreation Department, Mar. 10, 1958). The section on education was written by the Joint City School Project, which reported that "very, very few Spanish parents exhibit an active interest in the academic progress of their children. They do not communicate with teachers by commenting on report cards, visiting school, asking how they can assist the pupils at home or by criticizing the school program." Most Latino youth were not finishing high school. The report stated that "one fourth, or more, of the Spanish children have only one parent in the family." The police department section had the most critical presentation. Spanish American adults were criticized for establishing false alibis, deliberately antagonizing the police to claim brutality, hiding stolen property, selling drugs, sheltering family members and others from police, and being unwilling to give information to police. The Spanish American youth were criticized for disrespecting authority, running with gangs, and accepting advice from possibly subversive outside sources.

The police department compiled a list of adult and juvenile arrests, and these data highlighted that Latino adults and especially their children were overrepresented in arrests compared to their population. The worst two years were 1953 and 1956, when Latinos comprised 30 percent of all arrests. When Escobar (1999) analyzed the official statistics given by the Los Angeles Police Department in the 1940s, he found that "police did arrest more Mexicans, especially more Mexican American youths, than they had in the past, but these increases in arrests resulted more from changes in the law and changes in police practices than from changes in Mexican Americans' behavior." He also found that curfew laws led to a higher number of arrests, and these types of responses were practiced in Denver. The high number of Latinos being arrested by the

Denver Police Department brought with it an interest in who the police were and how they operated.

A special *Denver Post* news report on the Denver Police Department questioned, "How Good Is Denver's Police Force?" (April 5, 1959). The police department had 700 policeman and 120 civilian employees—about 1.33 police for each thousand of the city's 530,000 people. The *Denver Post* argued that the number of police officers needed to be increased in order to decrease crime rates. Overall the police department had apparently suffered from low morale owing to several problems, including issues of police brutality (*DP*, April 5, 1959). The paper's writer took it upon himself to look into these community claims of police brutality during the past four years and found they were often untrue or distorted. Never stating the method for determining complaint legitimacy, Weiss found that two-thirds (22 of 33) were false and that officers' actions were justified or unsubstantiated in these cases. The other eleven officers were no longer with the department, reportedly because they had been fired or forced to resign. Weiss assured *Denver Post* readers that "Since the brutality furor a few years ago, the men have had lectures, instruction, and new rules and procedures on the proper way to deal with citizens." The chief of police created a new unit to deal with complaints against the police department, which included eighteen cases involving charges of brutality; twenty involving drunkenness, swearing, rudeness, or disobedience; and nine involving charges of theft (*DP*, April 5, 1959). The police felt their efforts were not appreciated by citizens, nor were they treated with respect. The chief of police instituted six target areas to decrease crime: clear rules and procedures, reduced paperwork, an intelligence bureau to keep tabs on criminals and gangs, an internal affairs bureau, a police garage, and a new records section.

In 1959 newspapers continued to describe the attempt to "smash" youthful gangs after several purses were snatched on Colfax, Lincoln, and Park streets (*RMN*, Dec. 9, 1959). The *Denver Post* conducted an in-depth report examining why Spanish American children got in trouble (Nov. 29, 1959). The newspaper reported that while only about 10 percent of Spanish American children ever tangled with the law, they accounted for about half the delinquency cases in the city. This was a rate five times higher than their population. Black youth were claimed to have a higher delinquency rate than their share of population, but it was only a fifth as numerous as that of Spanish Americans. Blacks were found better off in terms of economic standing, industrial working, and urban living. The reporters claimed that the individuals with Spanish surnames seemed to share a feeling that they were strangers in Denver. Those with Spanish surnames described the Anglo world around them as hostile and unwelcoming. The reporters claimed that delinquency appeared to be based on discrimination, father abandonment, few skills, a lack of interest in sports and other conventional Anglo activities, poor knowledge of the English language, and poor school records. The youth were reported to look at troublemakers as heroes. The paper concluded, "Everyone has a stake in helping the newcomers to make hard adjustments that lies ahead of them." Denver was urged to deal with these issues before they reached a crisis stage. This recommendation mirrored several others that had been made twenty years prior. Delinquency, discrimination, gang involvement, and urban decay continued to overrepresent Latinos. Most city tactics increased social control, but the 1950s brought interest in studying the underlying issues behind these problems and initiating small-scale reforms. The problem remained, however, that city leaders were not willing to take aggressive measures to bring improved treatment for minority communities.

1960–70: Developing Chicano Resistance and the Decline of Gangs

The 1960s gang reports started with the same flair as those in previous decades. Young women were reportedly forming gangs at a shocking rate (*RMN*, Mar. 15, 1960). Dr. Norbert Shere reported, "They're organizing not only for shoplifting and sex offenses, but also vicious assaults and extremely malicious mischief. . . . Many of the girls involved come from respectable families, and the girls themselves have white skins and high IQs—but dirty necks, and low morals." He told a story about five high school girls entertaining twenty boys in an abandoned building and argued that boy gangs had disappeared, but girl gangs were increasing. Dr. Shere blamed parents for neglecting their children. Mayor Batterton publicly called for gangs to receive sterner punishment (public whippings or manual labor). Congress was once again updated on teenage hoodlumism in Denver, with the Hoods being the primary focus (*RMN*, April 26, 1960). Judge Gilliam again attempted to decrease gang involvement by creating a work gang. The people assigned to the work gang were dressed in army surplus green and were required to pick up trash, pull weeds, and rake lawns along the highway (*RMN*, April 27, 1960).

The enhancement of anti-Latino propaganda and legislation in Denver after the 1940s created efforts on behalf of the community to challenge unequal treatment. Branches of the American GI Forum (1948) started in Denver to help initiate reform along with a local organization named Los Voluntarios in 1963 (Vigil 1999). These groups were active and beginning to establish new ground, but they struggled to get the Mexican American community involved. In 1966 this began to change, as urban Chicanos in Denver organized under the leadership of Corky Gonzalez to create a group called the Crusade for Justice. Gonzalez, along with many others, began to realize that attaining change by working in the system created minimal impact. According to most indicators, the statistics accumulated in the1960s indicated that "Spanish Americans" in Denver were still worse off than blacks (*DP* 1960; Census 1960). The Crusade for Justice worked under the philosophy of self-determination and cultural pride. The organization responded to two primary issues: police brutality and the hostile educational system. It became involved in protests (police, schools, Vietnam) and opposing anti-Latino public figures, laws, and policies, creating networks with black, Latino, and Native American leaders around the nation. By the end of the 1960s, the Crusade for Justice created bridges with youths by organizing dances and offering support for the creation of Black and Brown Berets (a national Chicana/o youth group).

During the 1960s the police department began to receive greater scrutiny from several research studies (Bayley and Mendelsohn 1968) and civil rights complaints. By 1969 most youth had put aside their gang involvement to join these activist youth groups (Vigil 1999). This created for the first time a counter social movement to gangs by allowing youth to fight discrimination while offering status and approval from peers. Black and Chicano efforts to counter racism from the police, schools, and media led to significant transformations in the community. Police officers were regularly challenged for wrongful shootings and brutality. The community called for a civilian-led police review board and for the removal of officers engaged in misconduct.

Coinciding with increased forms of Chicano resistance were enhanced efforts by the Federal Bureau of Investigation (FBI) to undermine political activism of which numerous counterintelligence programs (COINTELPRO) are the best-known examples. The FBI, in collaboration with local police departments, implemented these strategies, and by the late 1970s the Crusade for Justice "ceased to be a powerful organization" as internal and external pressures exerted a toll and produced an eventual vacuum that only encouraged the reemergence of gangs (Vigil 1999:364). The actions of the executive branch of the government in resisting Chicano empowerment for altering second-class treatment are critical for understanding the response to gangs that occurred afterwards. In the post–civil rights era, gangs as a social movement to fight racialized oppression became transformed into a federally funded tool to legitimize criminalization of Latino and black youth.

The 1980s and the Reemergence of Gangs: Crips and Bloods

The demise of the Crusade for Justice and the remaining local problems led to the revival of gangs. During the early 1980s gangs reemerged as the police received new sources for funding and support to combat gangs. The Denver Police Department's Juvenile Delinquency Prevention Unit received $300,000 from a federal Law Enforcement Assistance Administration fund in 1980 to begin monitoring perceived gang members (Vigil 1996). Gangs became identified under several names: Varrio Unida Chicano (VUC), 38th Street Specials, 44th Street Conquistadores, South Side Steels, and Warlords. Rodney, a middle-aged African American Latino who is an ex–gang associate, described the evolution of gangs:

> I have been in Denver since 1978. When I first came to Denver there weren't really any gangs. I moved to the La Baca park area, which is a predominantly Chicano neighborhood, and the stuff going on was all about Chicano power and there was a unity thing going on. I would say about 1980 to 1982 somehow that started changing. That's why I was talking to you about COINTELPRO. It fit right in and those individuals are central players that came into creating the 44th Street Conquistadors and started the gang epidemic in Denver. It really started on the Latino side of town. Didn't even get over here yet [Northeast Denver, a neighborhood with a higher concentration of black people].

Toward the end of 1982 and during the entire year of 1983, gang activity and violence escalated in the Latino community. Kenneth Alva became Denver's first gang killing victim in the 1980s on December 28, 1982 (*RMN*, Dec. 30, 1982). He was 16 years old and, according to police, a member of the 44th Street Conquistadores. West Denver gangs were suspects in nine additional shootings that took place within a month. Four boys died in 1983 (*DP*, Dec. 12, 1983). Two youth suspiciously committed suicide at gang houses. A gang member described how the gang provided status to neighborhood residents. Police and officials responded by forbidding the use of an alley behind North High School, creating a law that allowed for mandatory jail or public service for youth caught with lethal weapons, sweeping neighborhoods with police to find curfew violations, shaking down suspected youth gang members (*DP*, Nov. 10, 1982; April 25, 1983; June 20, 1983; *RMN*, June 18, 1983).

Denver gang officers began receiving funding and training from Los Angeles, but they lacked community outrage in the intraracial feuds between Latinos. After 1986 public perception was altered, as black youth began identifying themselves as belonging to well-known California gangs. Rollin' 30 Crips were reportedly involved in three slayings and becoming increasingly active in the black community (*RMN*, June 7, 1986), where several other gangs operated but received much less attention: Brick City, Greeks, Members Only, Nasty 5s, Player 5s, and Untouchables (*Westword*, 2007). Crips activity soon brought the rival gang, Bloods (*RMN*, Mar. 27, 1994), an outgrowth of a group that had been mentioned as early as 1983 and was known as the BOYZ (*DP*, Dec. 1983). In 1987 the Colorado General Assembly authorized the Colorado Bureau of Investigations to collect and track information on gang members and their associates. The politics of gang enforcement was forming. In 1988 police estimated that 480 metro-area youth were involved with the Crips and Bloods, many of them reportedly from Los Angeles (*DP*, Sept. 4, 1988). Gang shootings occurred between these two gangs (*DP*, May 12, 1988; Dec. 9, 1988; *RMN*, July 15, 1988). Innocent people in the community were being attacked and shot, and several individuals were killed for wearing blue or red clothing (*DP*, Nov. 6, 1988; *RMN*, Nov. 5, 1988; Nov. 10, 1988).[3] Crack dealing emerged during the same time, only heightening the concentrated effort, even though Sgt. Dave Dawkins of the Gang Unit stated that the majority of dealers were not involved in gangs.

Denver responded in various ways to combat gang activity. Ministers from various churches rode with police to soothe tensions after 17-year-old Rashid Riley was killed by an undercover police officer when he raised a firearm at a plainclothes Latino officer (*DP*, Dec. 17, 1988; *RMN*, July 15, 1988a; July 15, 1988b; Denver District Attorney Report). The Gang Task Force was expanded to forty officers who began observing an estimated six to seven hundred gang members (*DP*, Nov. 10, 1988). Police patrols increased at night and in certain neighborhoods. Denver mayor Federico Peña proclaimed, "We won't put up with it," and he called for seventy-three officers (twenty-four motorcycle officers, forty-five SWAT and K-9 officers, and four Mall Unit officers) to be stationed in Northeast Denver (*DP*, Nov. 5, 1988). The Colorado Black Roundtable feared Denver had become a "police state" and suggested that additional police were not the answer. Its members criticized the media for worsening the situation by publicizing the exploits of gang members (*DP*, Nov. 10, 1988).

The opposition to gangs continued in 1989 as the police sought $1.5 million for a gang crackdown. They planned to create a new, thirty-member Gang Unit that focused specifically on gang members, thus easing some of the pressure on the Gang Task Force (*DP*, Jan. 7, 1989). The police operated with a zero tolerance toward the estimated eight hundred gang members in the city (*RMN*, Feb. 23, 1989). Alternatives to gangs were created by other members of the community. A city councilman initiated a program called Operation Gang Busters, which had dual purposes. It offered rewards for arrests of gang members to individuals using a special tip line and presented educational rap videos to help youth resist gang membership (*RMN*, Nov. 18, 1989). A minister developed a program called Open Door Youth Gang Alternatives that incorporated professional athletes to show youths a better road (*RMN*, Dec. 2, 1989). A parent group, Youth Train, formed to provide an adult presence at youth events (*RMN*, Nov. 19, 1989). The various levels of responses and attention ensured that gangs were once again a central issue in Denver.

1990–2010: Institutionalizing Gang Suppression

The 1990s saw a tremendous increase in the number of newspaper articles devoted toward gang and gang violence in Denver. Colomy and Greiner (2000) found that the number of news stories on violent crime increased from 73 in 1992 to 196 in 1993, which included the so-called Summer of Violence. These stories were more likely to be on the front page and include pictures than in previous years. Seven high-profile incidents initiated the reporting: four black and Latino children victims and four "exemplary adults" who were white, middle class, college educated, and lived in perceived "good" or "nice" sections of the city. The authors found the fear of innocent victims, unprecedented violence, encroaching violence, and random violence combining to conjure a belief in a new type of young lawbreaker. Colomy and Greiner analyzed the monthly crime report data for 1992, 1993, and 1994 and found the actual number of youth crimes in 1993 did not explain what happened during that year in terms of reporting and the push for new legislation. Instead, they argue, "The visibility of youth violence in Denver and Colorado was largely contingent on the claims making efforts of the news media" (688).

The media, however, was very perceptive and incorporated new data attained from the Center for the Study of Prevention of Violence at the University of Colorado to help support their argument. The Denver Youth Survey was developed from a probability sample of high-risk neighborhoods that resulted in a five-year (1987–91) study of 1,527 boys and girls (Browning and Huizinga 1999; Huizinga et al. 1998). These researchers found that over a five-year period, 85–87 percent of the youth between the ages of 7 and 19 were victims of violence or theft. However, they found that only 5–6 percent of the youth were involved in gangs, and 20–25 percent of them were female. Most gang members were involved for only a year, but during their involvement in a gang they accounted for the majority of serious violence and property offenses. Instead of focusing on the small number of youth who join gangs and their short duration of involvement, the media reported that slayings by teenagers nearly tripled from 1988 to 1991, and that gang–related homicides in Colorado had increased from 1984. Professor Del Elliot of the University of Colorado attributed this rise to an increase in single-parent households, drug dealing, and access to handguns (*RMN*, Nov. 18, 1993).

The result of the Summer of Violence media reporting and the inclusion of Denver Youth Survey findings led to several major initiatives to respond to gangs and youth violence in Denver: bans on cruising on certain streets, raising the age to buy spray paint to 18, establishing stricter curfew laws, lowering the age for certification as an adult court, creating stricter youth gun laws, forming a youth boot camp, increasing the number of youth incarceration beds, starting a gang witness protection program, having landlords at apartment complexes deny housing to gang members and felons, getting schools to enact clothing bans and a policy to suspend students who got in trouble off campus, and expelling students charged with a violent crimes. The most significant change in terms of gang suppression was the creation of three specialized units: multijurisdictional and federal (the Metro Gang Task Force), local (the Gang Bureau), and prosecutorial (the District Attorney Gang Unit).

Denver became the federal government's "test city" for bringing federal and local officials together to counter youth violence. The Metro Gang Task Force was responsible for a higher order of investigation and involved both multijurisdictional police units and federal agencies. Although this agency began formally in the 1980s, it was not until the late 1990s that its tactics received increased support by way of the Safe Streets Violent Crimes Initiative (SSVCI) that the FBI announced on January 9, 1992. This allowed the FBI to deal with gang- and drug-related violence by giving support to local agencies. Prosecution and gang enforcement were aided by the RICO Act and the Colorado Organized Crime Act (COCA). From 1999 until 2009, the Department of Justice along with local law enforcement pursued indictments against more than 260 individuals and more than a dozen street gangs.

The Denver Gang Bureau, also known as the Gang Unit, began in 1993 and employed between thirty-seven and fifty-four personnel (depending on the year and funding). A Gang Unit officer described its inception: "Well initially, prior to becoming the gang unit, it was called the Urban Street Crime Unit in 1987 and they focused on Urban Crime, that type of thing. [In] 1993, the Summer of Violence, they changed the function of the unit and made it a bureau and it became the Gang Bureau in 1993 as the result of several shootings and several homicides that summer."

The Gang Unit existed separately from other police patrols to focus on investigating gang crimes, enforcing laws, gathering gang information, and providing awareness of gangs. The officers admitted into the Gang Unit were selected for their initiative and a good overall record. Once in the unit, these officers tended to stay and were often promoted after several years. The Gang Unit maintained specific policies and procedures (2004 Gang Unit interview).

In 1990 the Denver district attorney's office created its own Gang Unit, which included prosecutors trained in gang legislation, vertical prosecution, and removal of gang members from the streets. Vertical prosecution allowed prosecutors to intercept potential gang cases from their initial filing and follow these cases all the way to their completion. They handled gang-motivated and gang-related cases, and they used the Gang Bureau–created gang lists to determine their caseload. The DA

Gang Unit averaged 400–450 gang cases a year. The goal was to incarcerate criminally involved gang members until they were no longer
in their prime gang-banging years of 13 to 27 (interview with Gang
Unit DA).

The primary consequence of gang enforcement, legislation, and prosecution was incarceration. In 1985 the passage of the Mielke-Arnold
Bill doubled the maximum sentence for all felons, which resulted in a
substantial increase in Colorado's prison population. In 1980 the rate of
incarceration was less than 100 per 100,000, but by 2008 it had grown
to almost 506 per 100,000 (Colorado Criminal Justice Reform Commission [CCJRC]). The funding grew from $57 million during fiscal year
1985–86 to $825 million in 2008. Colorado now has twenty-three state
prisons and contracts with six private prisons. In 2008 Latinos (30 percent of the inmate population) and blacks (20 percent) were two to four
times overrepresented in prison compared to their populations, while
whites were nearly two times underrepresented (CCJRC).

Although I moved away from Denver in 2006, I continued to visit
during the summers of 2007 and 2008 to study Denver police shootings.
On January 1, 2007, Darrant Williams, an NFL football player with
the Denver Broncos, was murdered after leaving a downtown club. The
individuals convicted of the shooting were listed members of the Tre Tre
Crips, a subset of the Rollin 30s. After this shooting increased acts of
vengeance were initiated to reduce gang activity, with the Department of
Justice and Metro Gang Task Force launching a three-phased initiative to
bring down the gangs. Local leaders in gang prevention joined with the
other agencies in responding to gang violence with the $2 million dollar
federal grant titled the Gang Reduction Initiative of Denver. Fears of immigrants continued after Denver police officer Donald Young was shot
and killed while working off-duty at a baptismal party in 2005. A Mexican national and alleged Sureño was sentenced to eighty years in prison
for the crime. Tom Tancredo, an anti-immigrant politician, used this case
along with others to continue spreading a nativist agenda in Denver.

Based on a review of Denver's early history using various forms of primary documents and interviews, it is clear that the city was racially hostile
in both behavior and ideology for Latinos and blacks. The data indicate
that the 1943 Zoot Suit Riots in Los Angeles increased the Denver community's focus on individuals of Mexican descent who wore zoot suits
and were portrayed as gang members. At the time Latinos constituted

only 4 percent of the population. There are no data to indicate that these individuals were in fact identifying as gang members until the late 1940s when groups of youth of Mexican descent began giving themselves names, often devised from neighborhood friends or movies. People of Mexican descent thought Denver was unwelcoming because they were forced into the worst housing and jobs. Although white membership in the Ku Klux Klan was drastically reduced after the mid-1920s, the ideology of the Klan continued with racially discriminatory policies and social treatment of minority groups. Latino tensions with the police go back to the 1940s when Latinos were beaten, harassed, underprotected, and left unsupported with complaints of brutality. If law enforcement agents' behavior was perceived as illegal, the law was changed to make it legal by imposing a curfew or by punishing cruising, loitering, and vagrancy. Membership in a gang later became the illegal activity for which federal prosecutors could pursue COCA and RICO indictments.

In the past sixty-eight years, Denver has launched several initiatives to combat gang activity, involving City Council members, district attorneys, judges, mayors, and police officers. The various wars on gangs that began in 1944 had risen and fallen until the early 1980s, when federal funding seemed to offer a continuous supply of energy for maintaining a gang-control enterprise. From the beginning gang-involved individuals were overwhelmingly labeled as Latinos, followed by blacks and then Asians. The news media headlines that coincided with these antigang efforts reflected accusatory and sensationalized accounts that depicted Latinos as animals "howling" or "pack running." The reemergence of gangs was enhanced by feuding between the Crips and Bloods, which provided justification for antigang efforts to become institutionalized with agencies designed to investigate, arrest, and prosecute gang-involved individuals.

More empathetic initiatives have also been present in Denver to improve relationships between the white majority and racial and ethnic groups. These efforts include the seminar held at Regis College in 1944, the investigation into racism by the Denver Commission on Human Relations in 1947, and the increasing number of studies outlining inequality, beginning with the *Rocky Mountain News* report in 1954 focusing on the "Spanish American Problem." The actions of Judge Gilliam in becoming an honorary member of the Heads in 1950, creating a gang called the Friday Nighters in 1954, and establishing a work gang in 1959 definitely departed from the mainstream response of the time (Gilliam 1950; Poremba 1955). The parks and recreation department also departed from traditional practices during the 1950s when it opened its doors to gang-involved youth and encouraged them to pursue sports clubs.

The grassroots community response to inequality took on a form of activism in Denver. Pachucos/as became symbols of resistance. Latino/a gangs originated in the face of racial hostility, police neglect, police abuse, and victimization. Over time and with governmental pressure, Latinos were no longer able to maintain gangs primarily for ethnic support. Thus Chicano organizations were developed to fight for equality but fell to governmental pressures under COINTELPRO. In the gap of organized resistance, the gang-control enterprise grew stronger after the mid-1980s, with several community-based groups originating that attempted to reduce gang violence and offer better futures for gang-involved youth.

CHAPTER FOUR

Demonizing Gangs Through Religious
Righteousness and Suppressed Activism

*Researching gangs in Ogden is my primary reason for attending gradu-
ate school, and during the summers from 2001 to 2011 I continue the
data-gathering process. When I first arrive back home during the summer 2001 I am still seen as a gang member, but since it has been a
period of time many of my previous rivalries during the mid-1990s are
pushed aside. Former members and previous rivals remember me as a
friend, which builds on the rapport I developed in high school and while
participating in a lowrider car club. My persistent emphasis on Chicano
empowerment helps to reduce the idea that I am maintaining a gang
lifestyle. Many in the community are aware that I have been attending
college for a long time. My primary interest is in giving voice to all of
the drama that goes on in the city. I'm working to uncover the history of
gangs in Ogden, which leads to an exploration of religion and its role in
shaping race and ethnic relations. Most of my friends are non-Mormon
and becoming marginalized because their ethnicity is repressed and they
are being seen as unrighteous.[1]*

*It is amazing how everyone changes after high school. Everything that
was once seen as cool (self-protection, multiple girlfriends, party lifestyle, risk taking) has begun to take a toll. Several of my close friends are
more involved in serious drug use and drinking alcohol all day long. My
homies released from prison have been forever altered in the way they
see the world. Their new form of social capital provides enhanced street
credentials but decreased opportunities to move beyond this lifestyle.
The number of children has increased, as has the number of failed relationships. The gang identity that provided so much excitement during
high school has been transformed into simply a part of life. The gang as
a group of resistance offered few other trajectories for our lives beyond*

incarceration and a continuous struggle with a system that hoped for our demise.

During my second year of ethnographic work in Ogden, I go visit my homie Cola, one of my best friends during high school. His family tells me Cola was kicked out of the house for stealing things. He is hooked on methamphetamines. I try to visit him at a motel, but a heavily tatted vato tells me Cola is not here, so we don't hang out much that summer. My homie Cyclone, who is also all tatted up along his arms and neck from when he served time in prison, is ready to hang out. He is glad I am back in town. We lived together before I moved to Colorado. We go to the strip-club and hang out with one his friends from prison. A couple other vatos with bald heads and wearing the color blue join us. Cyclone tells me that his street gang ties have faded away and it is his prison con- nections with a gang that have become stronger. Everyone thinks it is cool how I live in Denver. They want to continue pursuing their GEDs or see what options exist at the university in auto mechanics. My chang- ing networks of Denver activists, graduate students, and professors have started to allow me a new way to look at Ogden. I still look gangster, but my friends believe I have become soft, which really bothers me. True, my reckless abandonment is no longer present and I have begun to care about my future, but I try to hold on to my street identity. I block out my competing identities as we cruise the streets with marijuana smoke escaping from the back window because I feel really good to be back in the town that made me: Ogden.

The drama of the streets continually fluctuates. Most days are quiet, whereas other days confrontations arise unexpectedly. For example, I'm driving home and a young man throws up his arms to me as a challenge. I think to myself, "I don't know this person. Damn, people like to trip out here." Later in the day, on June 18, 2002, I learn that a 12-year-old boy named Jesse Martinez has been shot and killed after two rival gangs began firing at each other. One of the bullets traveled across the street and hit the young boy while he was sitting in the park with his mother. I knew both of the gangs and some of the participants. I prepared for a new version of a gang crackdown like those that have represented the police and mayor's response since the Gang Unit was created in 1992. This new version targets parolees. In a surprising turn of events, Jesse's father speaks out that he was a former gang member who worked hard to keep his son away from the wrong crowd. As a born-again Christian, the father expresses love toward the individuals arrested. Devastated by

his son's loss and the struggle of his own life, religion became his sal-
vation. This incident and many others continue to remind me that this
research project is bigger than me in terms of importance. How could I
prevent another young Jesse from becoming a victim of the madness in
the streets?

A month later I attend the Ogden Street Festival: an event where the
downtown boulevard is closed to traffic and little booths of activities and
shops are created for pedestrians to congregate. As I walk along with my
family, I run into several of my friends. I learn about the drama of who
has gone to prison or had kids, and about changing relationships. Matt
just got out after three years and now has a girlfriend and a child. He
tells me that he was given a one-to-fifteen prison sentence but is happy
to have served only three years. Later in the day they have a car show
where I recognize the family members of the boy who was shot. I feel
bad for the family who has lost a child. I go to hang out at my homie's
porch, sit back, and begin talking about how Ogden gangs began. Sev-
eral of the vatos on the porch are on parole, and they begin telling me
the history of Ogden gangs, which fills some of the pages that follow.
Other parts have been developed with the use of archival and newspaper
articles from the time.

In Utah the Mormon religion is the central framework for every institution and how individuals go about their day to day living (Yorgason
2003). Explaining gangs in the state of Utah requires the incorporation
of not only race but also religion. The history of how Utah became the
place for Mormons and their relationship with those considered nonwhite is the focus of this chapter, followed by a chronological overview
of Utah and the social construction of gangs in Ogden. The historical
countermovement against Mormonism in of Utah has led to changes in
politics but has continued to maintain white superiority, which has suppressed the voices of racial and ethnic minority groups (Cuch 2000; Iber
2000; Kelen and Stone 1996).

Origins of a Religious Zion and the Shaping of a Unique Identity

On April 6, 1830, the Church of Jesus Christ of Latter-day Saints was
established by Joseph Smith, a 24-year-old man from Vermont who had
begun having spiritually guided visions ten years prior while living in

New York (Bushman 2005; Walker, Turley, and Leonard 2008). During this same year Smith published the Book of Mormon, which is considered God's historical account of ancient inhabitants in America. The book and the religion's initial reception was negative, but a small following developed that resulted in the creation of several small communities in Ohio, Missouri, and Illinois. Difficulties in each state increased Smith's passion for establishing the religion and its communal philosophy. In every community where Smith and his followers lived they encountered difficulties with their neighbors. The religious practices of Mormons were seen as different and suspicious. Smith's emphasis on plural marriage later resulted in condemnation by a newspaper that was quickly destroyed by Mormon leaders. Smith's involvement in the destruction of the press only enhanced the increasing public tension. Smith was arrested and detained in Carthage Jail, Illinois, in 1844. While he was awaiting a court hearing, an angry mob went to the jail and killed Smith, his brother, and a friend. The individuals involved in the murder were never punished, leading to an overwhelming feeling of religious persecution. Both Missouri and Illinois only confirmed this discrimination when they pushed Mormons from their homes. Mormons began a journey to find a new location where they could safely practice their religious beliefs. The move from Illinois to Utah was described by Walker, Turley, and Leonard (2008) as the largest mass migration of a single group in the United States in the nineteenth century.

Under the leadership of Brigham Young, the new leader of the Mormon Church, the membership entered Mexico from July 21 to 24, 1847, in the area now known as Salt Lake City. The 148 individuals included men, women, and children. Among them were three slaves (Bringhurst and Smith 2004; McConkie 1979; Verdoia and Firmage 1996). The illegal entry into Mexico was seen as divine as Mormons also believed in manifest destiny and their own inherent right to the area (Solórzano 1998; Walker, Turley, and Leonard 2008).[2] During Spanish and Mexican control of these lands, few outsiders remained in the area. Native American tribes, however, were a significant presence as they had lived in the area as far back as 9000 to 7500 B.C. (McPherson 2000). Some scholars argue that the origination point for Aztlán (ancestral land of the Aztecs) was centered on Antelope Island, a 28,000-acre island within the Great Salt Lake (R. Rodriguez 2002; Solórzano 1998). The Native American tribes who lived in the area that became Utah included the Goshute, Navajo, Paiute, Shoshone, and Utes (Cuch 2000).

In 1849, a year after the United States took possession of the Southwest, the Mormon settlers drafted a constitution for the State of Deseret, which encompassed modern-day Utah along with parts of Arizona, California, Colorado, Idaho, Nevada, New Mexico, Oregon, and Wyoming (Verdoia and Firmage 1996). Despite such broad claims of empire, Young and the Mormons who settled in the area were actually squatters. According to MacKinnon (2008), Mormons possessed no public domain land holdings or titles. The high number of Mormons living in the area led to an uneasy compromise, which resulted in an agreement for the president of the Mormon Church to serve a dual appointment as governor of the state. A United States surveyor named Stansbury (1966) entered the Salt Lake area from 1849 to 1850 and documented the people and places within the area. Stansbury did not think any individual but Brigham Young could serve the role as the leader: "He was not only civil governor, but the president of the whole Church of Latter-Day Saints upon the earth, their prophet and their priest, receiving, as they all firmly believed, direct revelations of the Divine will, which, according to their creed, form the law of the church. He is, consequently, profoundly revered by all, and possesses unbounded influence and almost unlimited power" (86). Stansbury's expedition was possible only because of Young's support. Stansbury elaborated on Mormon fears of the U.S. government because of their negative encounters in Missouri and Illinois. Mormons anxiously waited whether the United States would try to remove them again; if so, they planned to resist with force.

From its beginning as a territory on September 9, 1850, the area that became the state of Utah faced many challenges. The first of these included the Mormon relationship with various Native American tribes and how the Mormon religion shaped race relations. In a book titled *A History of Utah's American Indians* (Cuch 2000), McPherson reported how Mormons' flight from adversity in other states led to their claim of Native American lands that furthered indigenous problems. The more than twenty thousand indigenous people living in the area had their ways of life greatly transformed by the increasing white presence. McPherson (2000:19) argued, "From a purely ideological point of view, the Mormons believed that the Indians were a remnant of a people who fell out of grace with God, were given a dark skin as a sign of their spiritual standing, and who now lived in an unfortunate condition awaiting restoration to an enlightened state."

The Mormon interactions with the indigenous populations began with the belief from the Book of Mormon that Native Americans were the Lamanites, who were cursed for their inequity and wickedness with darker skin (Bushman 1984; 2 Nephi 5:20–21; Solórzano 1998). Mormons saw their role to convert, save, and teach the Lamanites in order to prepare for Christ's second coming. The goal was to help Native Americans become "white and delightsome" instead of a "dark, and loathsome, and a filthy people." Young argued, "It is better to feed the Indians than to fight them," and he attempted to push their conversion into the only *true* religion. Non-Mormons were labeled as Gentiles and considered "progeny of Satan" (Wallace 1961) or "Satan's co-workers" (Madsen 1980). The primarily English, immigrant, and Mormon settlers lacked the cultural capital to create such an ideal of collaboration, and early encounters often led to murderous attacks on Native Americans, imprisonment, and blaming the indigenous for crimes perpetuated by Mormons (MacKinnon 2008). The population of Native Americans in Utah gradually decreased as they were relocated to reservations, used as indentured servants, or eliminated (Cuch 2000; Jones 2000).

Native Americans struggled to coexist in this new religious Zion. Blacks, on the other hand, were cursed for a different reason. According to scholars, some have used the LDS doctrine, consisting of four books (the Bible, the Book of Mormon, Doctrine and Covenants, and the Pearl of Great Price), to claim that blacks were unable to serve as priests since leaders associated Cain's seed with being cursed with blackness (Allred 2004), but Mormon historians seem unclear about how such a legacy developed and lasted until 1978 (Bringhurst 2004). Mormons began their new Zion by maintaining slavery and legalizing the practice in 1852 (Coleman 1996). According to Jones (2000), Mormons had an uneasy relationship with slavery, and they seemed to operate on a double standard: okay for us but not for others. Jones used the Trial of Don Pedro León Luján to highlight these contradictions. An Old Spanish Trail existed in Utah that provided a historical trade route between different Native American groups, Mexicans, and fur traders. The trade in Indian slaves became important along this trail. Goshute and Paiute children were often captured and sold to residents in New Mexico, where an underground form of indentured servitude existed (Defa 2000; Gómez 2007; Jones 2000). Officials in Utah wanted to stop this trade because it reduced their perceived ability to control activity within the state (Jones 2000). Pedro Lujan was found guilty of violating the Trade and Intercourse Act of 1834, and he attempted to appeal the decision based on irregularities in the trial, including confiscation of horses and pack mules; a prejudicial jury; and the claim of a new licensed trade. The indigenous children were prevented from being sold in New Mexico and were instead held in slavery by Mormon families. Jones (2000:93) argued that this trial, along with altering trade, brought many changes: "Utah institutionalized the purchase and indenturing of Indian children, open Mexican trade was effectively eliminated, and short-term Indian hostilities escalated, leading, in part, to a brief but bloody Indian war with the chief Indian traders." The overall impact was that land and everything that occurred in the territory was controlled by Mormons.

The second issue became known as the "Mormon problem" and resulted in conflict between church leaders and the U.S government. From Utah's inception as a territory, the issue of Mormons and Brigham Young's "autocratic theocracy" created concern (MacKinnon 2008). The Mormon practice of plural marriage and the conformist behavior of residents toward the Mormon leader created outside public condemnation. President James Buchanan pushed for removing Brigham Young as territorial governor, which resulted in the Utah War in 1857. Young prepared once again for battle and organized the Nauvoo Legion militia to fight the U.S. government. The events that transpired have been well covered in the book *At Sword's Point: A Documentary History of the Utah War to 1858*, by William MacKinnon. After the government and Brigham Young reached a compromise, many changes soon followed: Young was removed as governor; Mormon polygamists were arrested, prosecuted, and incarcerated under the Morrill Anti-Bigamy Act in 1862; and Mormon properties were confiscated in amendments that followed under the Edmunds and Edmunds-Tucker Act in 1877 (Larson 1971; Verdoia and Firmage 1996). Some Mormons who wished to continue the practice of polygamy moved to Mexico and established several colonies (Romney 2005).

As Mormons were encouraged to settle in locations outside the Salt Lake Valley, Ogden became home to an interesting mix of Mormons and non-Mormon influences. Mountain men and trappers established themselves in Ogden by 1825. The creation of Fort Buenaventura in 1845, the oldest permanent settlement in Utah, by Miles Goodyear preceded the arrival of Mormons. Goodyear sold his property, and by 1850 the population of Ogden was 1,141 residents. Early fears about Native Americans led to the creation of a fortress wall, which ranged from nine to twelve feet high (Roberts and Sadler 1985). The Ogden Police Department was created in 1860 and consisted of two officers who patrolled the streets (Sadler and Roberts 2000). In 1869 Promontory, a community outside of Ogden, became the connection point for the Union Pacific and Central Pacific Railroads, linking the East and West Coasts. Competition developed between the town of Corinne (considered the largest Gentile capital in Utah) and Ogden for which community would serve as the railroad transfer station to connect passengers (Madsen 1980). Brigham Young made sure the location chosen was Ogden by creating a north-south track through Ogden from Salt Lake City. The location of transfers between these railroads became Ogden, which developed a thriving economy (Roberts and Sadler 1985) and became known as the Junction City. Ogden competed with Salt Lake City, the state's capital, for national production and export and by 1890 had grown to 12,889 residents.

Efforts to change Utah's image were successful as it became the forty-fifth state of the Union in 1896. After the federal legislation against polygamy, the death of Brigham Young, and the ongoing federal pressure for Utahans to conform, non-Mormons and other religious groups began to take form and compete for political power. Yorgason (2003) described the cultural changes occurring in Utah from 1880 to 1920, during which time the conservative Mormon ideology shifted from communal economics and distrust of federal government to independent capitalism and superpatriotism. The Mormon pressure and struggle to fit in with non-Mormons led to their identification with white racial superiority and a belief that Native Americans, Mexicans, and Chinese were backward and required Mormon support to improve their level of civilization. Despite feelings of racial superiority, groups such as the Ku Klux Klan showed a presence during the 1920s but did not gain a stronghold presence (Peterson and Parson 2001). May (1987) and Madsen (1980) argued that part of the reason that the Ku Klux Klan did not rise to the same level of prominence in Utah as in other states was that the Klan and the Masons denied membership to Mormons.

The demographic, cultural, and non-Mormon influences were probably most acute in the Junction City, where the railroad continued to bring in residents from around the world. Ogden became the center of Catholicism in northern Utah with the establishment of St. Joseph's parish in 1875 (Mooney and Fitzgerald 2008). At the time most of Ogden's resident ancestors were from the British Isles or northern Europe, but the railroad brought Chinese (106 residents in 1890), Italians, and blacks, as well as a minimal number of individuals of Mexican descent (Sadler and Roberts 2000). In 1900 the federal census counted 40 people of Mexican birth in the entire state of Utah, and this number increased to 166 in 1910 (Iber 2000). Blacks, Chinese, and Japanese experienced segregation and discrimination, with several acts of racial violence that continued to demonstrate inequality (Roberts and Sadler 1985).[3] The interviews captured in Kelen and Stone's book titled *Missing Stories: An Oral History of Ethnic Minority Groups in Utah* (2000) describes numerous encounters of prejudice and discrimination during the 1900s. The authors argued that the majority group was unaware of such unequal treatment and thought such behavior only occurred in the South. Despite such majority group ignorance or denial of differential treatment, blacks and Latinos were often affected by segregation in dance halls, housing, movie theaters, restaurants, street cars, and swimming pools. Moreover, racial and ethnic minority groups encountered numerous instances of racially derogatory language and hostile treatment.

The central downtown district in Ogden known as 25th Street or "Two Bit Street" was often the center for diversity: behavioral, ethnic, racial, and religious. After the creation of the railroad, this area included a high number of bars, brothels, clubs, and opium dens where local residents engaged in illegal behavior, such as gambling, prostitution, and vice. For these reasons the area earned a reputation as "the most dangerous street in the world" (Iber 2000:58).[4] The downtown district was notorious for these activities from 1875 to 1950 (Roberts and Sadler 1985). Various crimes continued in this area after the creation of the railroad and continued until after World War II, leading to a reputation for Ogden as a "little Chicago." Illegal activities also resulted in challenges to informal practices of segregation. Nathan Wright, 67, described how 25th Street during World War II was full of black servicemen who brought a presence to challenge segregation (Kelen and Stone 1996). The Porters and Waiters Club provided a place for blacks to stay and enjoy entertainment under the leadership of Anna Bell Weakly from the 1940s until 1960.

The Emergence of a Latino Presence Along Utah's Wasatch Front

The Wasatch Front is 120 miles long and an average of 5 miles wide, stretching from Santaquin in the south to Brigham in the north. Both

Ogden and Salt Lake City are along the Wasatch Front, which is home to about 80 percent of Utah's population. Iber's (2000) research found that the number of people of Mexican descent increased in the area during World War I, with most people working in commercial agriculture, mining, and transportation. A large portion of job opportunities in Ogden after the 1920s came from the federal government, with a Defense Depot, Hill Air Force Base, and the Internal Revenue Service, but jobs rarely utilized Latino labor. As of 1930 an estimated four thousand Latinos lived in Utah, with more than half residing in Salt Lake or Weber County.

The narratives of individuals who immigrated to Utah's Wasatch Front describe the pursuit of a better life for their families and themselves (Hispanic Oral Histories [HOH] 1984–87; Spanish-Speaking Peoples in Utah Oral Histories [SSPUH] 1970–75). The Mexican Revolution between 1910 and 1920 pushed many individuals to pursue life in safer locations. Crossing the border during this time required paying a 10-cent toll—much different from the hypervigilant forms of border enforcement that began in 1978 and escalated with Operation Hold the Line in 1993 and Operation Gatekeeper in 1994 (Dunn 1996, 2009). Many individuals reported living in other states before coming to Utah. They moved from impoverished conditions in southern Colorado and northern New Mexico. Utah offered more stable employment, and an increasing number of industries required labor. The jobs pursued included agricultural work with beets and lettuce, cleaning occupations, working on railroad gangs, and mining. Many women worked in the canneries but were prevented from doing so until after World War I. Although there was work, families often continued to live in poverty, as $10 a day provided only the barest of necessities. Mexican families struggled to provide clothing, food, and heat for their apartments and homes. Living conditions were poor, but they were often better than in the places where Latinos had left, which kept many families in Utah.

Bingham, Utah, was a community with an interesting mix of immigration, work, and diversity. Kennecott Copper transformed the mountain into the largest open copper mine in the world, with the highest production. Bingham contained sections such as Dinkeyville, Copperfield, Frog Town, Highland Boy, and Tier Heights. All the Mexican labor started and primarily stayed employed in the powder jobs. Preparing and blasting the mountain were dangerous, so when individuals had opportunities to move into shoveling, truck driving, or line work they readily assumed those occupations, but rarely did Latinos become foremen. The continual strikes over the years pushed many employees to join unions. Since everyone in Bingham knew each other by where they lived and worked, the town did not experience the level of overt prejudice as in other places in Utah. When Bingham residents went outside their community, they were perceived as outcasts, but it was their street toughness that made them confident. Norbert Martinez (HOH 1985, box 3, folder 7), age 46, described fights as a normal part of growing up, whereas in the Salt Lake Valley the young men were considered "sissies." He described this tough demeanor: "We had a mean macho image. [We] were the miners, were the—big mean people—you know, the mean guys. The guys [from Salt Lake] just hated our guts. They were like 'There's them Bingham Boys!' " Jesse Lopez (SSPUH July 9, 1973, box 4, item 108), age 49, corroborated the toughness of Bingham and the prejudice outside the town. Lopez was the first police officer in Bingham and possibly the first Latino police officer in Utah. He described the roughness of Bingham in 1963: break-ins, drunk drivers, fist fights, gambling, knifings, and speeders, but no holdups because you couldn't get out of town. Despite his military service, Lopez was often refused service at restaurants in Salt Lake City. His overall treatment outside Bingham was negative: "Everywhere I went, even as I grew older, it was Mexican greaser this, spic, pepper gut, they say things, but I would tell them my ancestors were around this territory even before you came from Europe, you or your parents or your grandparents, and we were here just like the Indians. We are Indians: Mexican Indians." Lopez was born in Bingham but was proud of his parents, who came from Zacatecas, Mexico, in the 1920s in search of a better life. He found the prejudice in Utah strange as he had honorably served in the navy whereas most Mormons did not join the military.

Religion shaped many of the opportunities within the state. The majority of Latinos remained Catholic despite constant pressure and encouragement from Mormon missionaries for them to join the Church of Jesus Christ of Latter-Day Saints. Failure to join often led to different forms of exclusion. Hispanic converts to Mormonism were given more support. Most Latinos remained Catholic, whereas some joined other denominations, including the Church of God. The Catholic Church became a major institution providing various forms of emotional and social support, including access to education, food, and improved living quarters. The Church created a West Side Family Cooperative that offered better deals on food. It developed the Escalante Park housing units that offered cheaper rent for older homes. It operated a boxing ring, judo mat, and early learning program at the Guadalupe Center, in addition to Boy Scouts and Girl Scouts. Latino Catholics were devoted to church and prayer. The dogma of a strict and conservative belief system kept the culture tied to reverence and hope for a better afterlife since many things were perceived as unchangeable on earth.

Education was a central challenge. The school curriculum emphasized the positive view of European history and negative portrayal of Mexican history. Catholic schools often provided the only forms of education to non-Mormons but operated classrooms separated by gender; in the 1920s the charge was $5 a month to attend. Children were discouraged from speaking Spanish in school. Many Latino interviewees reported an interest in education but were definitely not encouraged in school; some were even pushed out. The unwelcoming atmosphere made it difficult to persevere in educational accomplishments. A noteworthy interview was given by Mike Melendez (SSPUH June 15, 1972, box 1, item 19), age 25, who described growing up in Bingham, where his father made $3,000 a year as a powder man. His mother, Edith Melendez, was very active in improving Latino rights in Utah by working for various organizations. Mike recalled how poor his family was when he was growing up, and how they even used Hercules Powder boxes as chairs for their kitchen table. He worked from the age of 6. He relished living in Bingham, where everyone knew one another, but experienced challenges when he moved to Midvale and was the only Mexican. He was called a Sambo and the n-word at school. Teachers told Mike that he talked too much. Mike's mother was born in northern New Mexico and his father was from Puerto Rico. Many Puerto Ricans moved to Bingham between 1941 and 1943. Mike gave an inspirational interview as he described wanting to be successful in school and working to change the image of Mexicans. He had 13 A's and 1 B; he also played baseball and maintained a 3.7 GPA. He hitched rides to high school when his family moved to Midvale. He was committed to helping human beings, but he realized later in life, after joining the military and graduating from the university, that change began with his daughter. He received his M.D. degree from the University of Utah in 1976 and proceeded to help people for the next thirty-five years.

Most of the interviewees reported a variety of experiences with discrimination. The experience of blacks in Utah was definitely racist, and very few black people desired to live in the state. They were not let into restaurants, and the popular amusement park, Lagoon, didn't allow them into the swimming pool, dance hall, or fun house. They were not allowed at Hotel Utah or Hotel Newhouse. The famous musician Nat King Cole couldn't even get a room in the 1960s. Native Americans were not sold liquor. Theaters in Salt Lake City often didn't allow Mexicans in the 1940s. Some of the youth of Mexican descent wore zoot suits that often brought negative interaction with businesses and the police. In Ogden Mexicans and blacks were required to sit in the back of the movie theater. Restaurants along the Wasatch Front often denied service to both groups during the 1950s and 1960s. Ellen Cordova (SSPUH 1973, box 1, item 7), born in 1904, remembered that whites "looked down on them [Mexicans] just like they were nothing really." Her husband, whom she married in 1924, was of Mexican descent, and she thought that Salt Lake City was very biased.

A significant part of maintaining social separation involved segregated neighborhoods. In Ogden blacks and Latinos were segregated in the central and western parts of the city, which contained older and poorer housing. Richard Navarro (SSPUH July 5, 1973, box 4, item 127), age 33, described how his family was segregated into the west side, which was 80 percent Mexican with a smattering of Italians and Japanese, as well as one black family. He was called Mexican greaser at school and after fifth grade began fighting when he heard these comments. There were no parks where he lived. When he and his friends went to other parks they often received comments such as "here come those God damn Mexicans." He found Ogden highly racialized, with the schools being a central part of the problem. By the time Navarro was in eleventh grade, he had had enough and dropped out of school to join the U.S. Marine Corps. He was happy to get away from the racism in Ogden. When he returned he noticed divisions between Spanish Americans and Mexicans that made it difficult for various self-help organizations to prosper. Richard thought blacks received greater support from the Community Action Programs at the Marshall White Center; whites didn't go to this recreation center because they associated it with only blacks and Latinos.

A public meeting was held in 1967 in Salt Lake City questioning why the Latino community in Utah did not organize itself like the black civil rights movement. Such questions later led to the development of a group named the Spanish-Speaking Organization for Community Integrity and Opportunity (SOCIO), which pursued various forms of justice by working to reform the system (Iber 2002; HOH and SSPUH Special Collection files). The organization developed into nine chapters around the state and was active in a variety of initiatives, which led one of its leaders, Vincent Mayer (SSPUH, Nov. 8, 1970, box 2, item 47), age 63, to argue that "many of our Chicanos here who sometimes feel that we are moving at a slower pace than other states and articulate this often go to other states and find that actually we have achieved more here in Utah they have there." He described how SOCIO was involved in getting school districts and the University of Utah to meet its demands. Some, however, characterized the approach as being too middle class when more activist organizations such as the Brown Berets developed several years later.

Ruben Jimenz (HOH 1985, box 3, folder 3), age 54, who graduated from the University of Utah in 1954, reported, "It's never been, I think, accepted that there has been a problem in Utah; somehow, it appears to me that people in Utah feel that we're different in Utah. And that we don't suffer some of these evils that exist in other parts of the country, but I think that people mislead themselves." He joined SOCIO to pursue justice. Many interviews described the division between individuals identifying as Spanish and Mexican. Father Merrill (SSPUH, Dec. 31, 1971, box 1, items 12–13) reported that challenges of the Chicano movement in Utah included uniting the group under a specific leader and a specific direction. He provided an overview of the challenges of discrimination in Utah and the belief by some that none existed, despite continuous examples of unequal treatment. Solomon Chacon (SSPUH, June 3, 1972, box 1, item 17) described white ignorance as the central challenge and noted that the culture in Utah was not prepared for the diversity of other racial and ethnic groups.

In the early 1970s the city of Ogden began to include an increasing number of Latinos and blacks struggling for self-protection. The minority population remained segregated primarily in central Ogden and West Ogden. The Latino population grew to 8–14 percent of the population, with blacks at 3 percent (National Change Database CD 1970–2000; U.S. Commission on Civil Rights 1977). The student body at the schools reflected this demographic change, but the teaching faculty and administration remained more than 96 percent white. In August 1970 the Office for Civil Rights (OCR) of the Department of Health, Education, and Welfare (HEW) encouraged the superintendent of Ogden schools to develop a desegregation plan of "racially identifiable schools." One elementary school in West Ogden was closed and the students were transferred to other schools. Teachers were required to attend multicultural

training, and by 1975 the initiative was reported to be working successfully but required continual monitoring, evaluation, and review. Despite
such optimism, Ogden's white residents increasingly struggled to deal
with racial and ethnic diversity.

1970–80: Ogden's Gang Development

Longtime Ogden residents claimed that the gang Ogden Trece was established during the early 1970s. In 2010 the Weber County Attorney's
Office argued a similar point of origination. Raul told me that Ogden
Trece began as Central City Locos but the original name was CCV, or
Central City Vatos and a split occurred between 1985 and 1987, which
resulted in the formation of Ogden Trece. Raul had been part of 27th
Street and one of its originators, but the majority of members were incarcerated. He attended Ogden High School in the late 1980s. Based on
interviews and ethnographic data about this period, inner-city residents
who were primarily Mexican American began forming gangs in two
neighborhoods: Central City and West Ogden. A large railroad station
and the river separated the neighborhoods. According to Detective Montanez (Salt Lake Area Gang Project 2000:54), "Before 1978 no documented Hispanic gangs existed in Salt Lake City." Thus gangs in Ogden
may predate those in Salt Lake City as the earliest labeled and socially
stigmatized gangs in Utah.

From 1980 to 1989 there were only minimal mentions of gang activity in Ogden.[5] The media and police did not appear particularly interested in the topic. On October 1, 1981, the *Deseret News* (*DN*) shared
the following headline: "L.A.-STYLE GANGS PLAGUE OGDEN NOW, PO-
LICE SAY" in a B section, page 3 article. It was reported that Mexican
American street gangs were a major source of crime and violence but
had only formed two months before. A police detective found an increasing number of confrontations between whites and Mexican Americans
along Washington Boulevard, and authorities believed that a homicide
was soon to follow. The Ogden Police Department reported that the
first gang activity that captured law enforcement attention developed
in June 1987 when it received notification from the Los Angeles Police
Department that Crip gang members were migrating to the Salt Lake
City/Ogden area for the purpose of selling crack cocaine and stolen firearms (Ogden/Weber Metro Gang Unit 1998:15). During the next eigh-

teen months, Utah law enforcement officers engaged in several criminal investigations involving California Crip and Blood gang members. The *Deseret News* also reported in a June 1987 article that law enforcement officers in Los Angeles had contacted the Ogden police, and by April 1988 there was a confirmed purchase of crack by a self-proclaimed Crip gang member from California. By August a Weber State college basketball player reportedly associated with Southern California gangs was charged with distributing crack in Ogden (*DN*, April 23, 1989).

A couple of incidents were reportedly gang related in 1989. In January Danilo Pascual was convicted of second-degree murder for a shooting that had occurred in 1988 and sentenced to five years to life in prison. The Weber County attorney argued that the confrontation was between two rival gangs. In March a San Bernardino, California, Crip was arrested, and investigators revealed he was responsible for a local cocaine distribution network and was also a major supplier to Milwaukee, Wisconsin (Ogden/Weber Metro Gang Unit 1998:15). *Deseret News* reported that several search warrants were executed in February and March 1989 involving crack and members of the Crips (*DN*, April 23, 1989). Desmond Seals was reportedly responsible for dealing crack in Ogden, but was killed in San Bernardino on April 1, 1989. Crip gang members were starting to be closely monitored, but the newspapers noted that Hispanic gangs in Ogden were already well established (*DN*, April 23, 1989). Officials feared that black gang members were spreading from Los Angeles for the purpose of distributing crack. Similar to Denver during the 1980s, it was black and not Latino gang members who were the focus of law enforcement and the news media. After the 1990s this trend began to change, with growing paranoia about Latino gangs.

In Salt Lake City gangs were reportedly more numerous and active during the 1980s than in Ogden. According to Rich Montanez (Salt Lake Area Gang Project 1999, 2000), the first gang was listed as the Precious Few Gang, which started on the east side of Salt Lake City in 1978–79. Latino, Tongan, and Asian gangs began to increase, along with prison and white gangs. Straight Edge was the white gang that was deemed the biggest threat. Montanez argued that conflicts with California transplants and the movie *Boulevard Nights* solidified gang culture and made the lifestyle popular.

Both cities' Gang Units and community members attributed much of the blame for California gang influences in the local area to the Job Corps, which was located in Clearfield, about thirteen miles from Ogden and thirty miles from Salt Lake (*DN*, April 13, 1990; Ogden/Weber Metro Gang Unit 1997–1999; Salt Lake Area Gang Project 1996–2001). Despite such claims by law enforcement, no systematic study was conducted to verify them. During my involvement in gangs and my research, there were occasional fights with individuals known to be in the Job Corps, but these individuals never set up locally in Ogden or the surrounding area to compete with gangs there.

1990–2011 and the Creation of a Gang Panic

When the Salt Lake Area Gang Project emerged through a federal grant in 1990, becoming the first gang suppression unit in the state, which had a labeled gang population of two hundred members, one of the first priorities became hosting annual gang conferences. The organizers brought gang "experts" from Chicago, Los Angeles, and other big cities to inform the local public, especially law enforcement, about gang activity. They described how gangs were spreading and becoming more lethal and organized (Salt Lake Gang Conference, 1990–2012; Stallworth 1995). A Chicago gang expert warned that "The next step for Utah's youth gangs could be into organized crime, particularly the illicit drug trade" (*Standard Examiner* [*SE*], n.d., in personal gang clippings file). Not to be outdone by Salt Lake City, Ogden quickly followed in securing a federal Byrne Grant in July 1992 to create the Ogden/Weber Metro Gang Unit, and by 1998 it too began holding annual conferences (Northern Utah Gang Conference, 1998–2011). The image of gangs presented at these conferences was similar to that of a virus—cunning, deadly, and spreading. Law enforcement strategized about various proactive and perseverant responses, supporting an ideology that they needed to be tougher and more prepared to meet this threat directly. Some sessions were for law enforcement only, whereas others included the general public, who registered and paid a fee to attend.

After the establishment of Gang Units, both Salt Lake and Ogden enhanced their level of attention devoted to the issue of gangs. The Los Angeles riot in 1992, which protested police brutality and a criminal justice system that did not hold law enforcement accountable for wrongdoing, increased the discussion of gangs and whether members were moving to the local area. The FBI became infatuated with the topic of gangs after this uprising (Diaz 2009; Hayden 2004). A Utah public safety commissioner reported at a gang conference in Salt Lake City that "youth gangs exported from Los Angeles to Utah and other states cannot be stopped by police and harsher penalties alone" (*SE*, May 1, 1992). Despite the recommendation to try alternative strategies, the initiatives for institutionalizing gang enforcement constituted the only strategy that received federal funding. The Byrne Grant that created the Ogden/Weber Metro Gang Unit provided $100,000 to $200,000 a year in additional income (State of Utah 1999, 2000). A Gang Unit community coordinator reported the following:

> We work primarily with state and federal types of funds and that's what funds the specific gang unit. . . . They pay for equipment, and they pay for whether it's a separate building or within. They [Gang Unit officers] are regularly citizen employees, but for equipment, overtime, and specific types of things it's funding by these programs. It's a year to year kind of thing, there is no guarantee that it will be here next year, even though it has been going since '92 there is no guarantee. . . . [I]t's a federal grant . . . called the Byrne grant. It's federal and each year units or departments have to apply for these funds. Right now, Salt Lake, Ogden, and St. George receive funding, and I think most other agencies also apply for this grant.

It is unclear based on newspaper reports, primary documents, and interviews whether any other approach to respond to gangs was attempted. Law enforcement became the central institution to socially construct and respond to gang activity. As most authority figures, elected officials, and members of law enforcement continue to be white and Mormon, the ever-present but unspoken influence of religion guides most forms of decision making that tends to support their personal feelings of superiority.

The reported purpose of the Gang Unit was to unify information and resources by utilizing two officers to monitor gang activity. Ogden Police Lt. Marcy Korgenski said, "Ogden gang-crime statistics are not available prior to 1992, but since then, gang crime in the city has risen significantly" (*SE*, 1999). A Gang Unit coordinator collaborated this report by stating that growing gang crime in 1992 led to the creation of the unit. However, the data provided by the Gang Unit covering the years 1992–2003 contradict this claim. In 1992, the first year gang crimes were recorded, there were only ten gang-related incidents, of which three were acts of graffiti, two were assaults, and the other five miscellaneous. In the years following, the Gang Unit recorded more gang-related incidents, the bulk of which (40 percent) involved graffiti and assaults (homicides were less than 1 percent of gang activity, and a significant portion involved miscellaneous incidents).

At the inception of the Gang Unit in 1992, there were 250 listed gang members and associates in Ogden, which was slightly larger than the number originally recorded in Salt Lake City. These numbers increased significantly as plainclothes police officers or officers dressed in black fatigues with bullet-proof vests began regularly stopping black and Latino youth and inquiring about gang membership. Such tactics selectively overrepresented those who were predefined as gang members. White Gang Unit officers patrolled inner-city neighborhoods and perceived certain clothing worn by youth of color as denoting gang membership. Gang Unit officers began telling youth uninvolved with gangs that they were gang members. The Ogden Gang Unit operated without any specific policies or procedures as of 2003 (interview with Gang Unit). Ogden had the second largest unit in Utah after Salt Lake City, with five officers augmented by sheriff's officers in the Weber County area.

I arrived in the city of Ogden as a teenager in 1992. My first contact with a gang officer occurred in high school when an unmarked vehicle stopped abruptly and a plainclothes white man stepped out of the vehicle and pointed a handgun at me and three friends: two Latino and one white. My white friend had exited my vehicle holding a BB gun. After the white Gang Unit officer confiscated the toy gun, he inquired whether my friends and I were forming a new gang called the *putos* (a derogatory term for male whores or prostitutes). He took down our information and gave us a warning. None of us was involved in a gang. After this event my contacts with the Gang Unit became more regular.

In 1993 there was one self-identified gang that was predominant at Ogden High School, called Ogden Trece. Its members were primarily Mexican American. Two other gangs were rivals to this gang: Moon Dogs and Hilltop. These two gangs were led by several gang members who claimed they were from California, and both were multiracial and ethnically diverse. These gangs did not have a strong presence in the school but were more significant in the community as their members were in their late teens or early twenties. In West Ogden the original group was West Side Players, which spawned several newer gangs, such as Ogden's Violent Gangsters (OVG) and West Side Pirus (WSP). West Ogden gangs were also rivals of Ogden Trece. Youth who lived in West

Ogden attended Ben Lomond High School, and those who lived in Central Ogden attended Ogden High. This high school separation followed many youth into their future in terms of gang and neighborhood allegiance.

During the spring of 1994 a Los Angeles–based gang named 18th street showed its presence in Ogden and became an intense rival of Ogden Trece. The Ogden/Weber Metro Gang Unit (1999) described 18th street as having over four hundred members in Ogden alone, of which most were considered illegal immigrants who had arrived from Los Angeles, Texas, or Mexico. 18th street grew into the second largest gang in Ogden. The various conflicts with Ogden Trece, Ogden's most historically based and institutionalized gang, resulted in many fights that left a small number of deaths, many injuries, and shooting incidents, some of which have been captured in police records and others never reported.

According to Ogden Gang Unit data, from 1995 to 2003 the number of gang members increased, with the most active gangs varying by year. By 1995 there were 950 listed gang members, with the most active gangs including OVG, Ogden Trece, 18th street, 8-ball Crips, Asian Boy Dragons, Yo Mama (YM), Q-VO, West Side Piru, 21st street, and Norteños. Stallworth (1995) argued that Salt Lake City had 288 listed gangs involving 3,104 individuals in a city of 181,743. Latinos constituted the majority of members (46 percent), followed by whites (24 percent), others (20 percent), and blacks (10 percent). The local gangs in Ogden and Salt Lake City are different even though some members move back and forth between both cities—a distance of thirty-seven miles. In 1997 there were 70 listed gangs in Ogden, 15 of which were considered the most active. In 1999 there were 1,600 listed gang members, with the most active gangs being 18th street, Ogden Trece, Ogden Compact Players, Titanic Crip Society, Asian Brotherhood Dragons, Dog Den, OVG, West Side Piru, 8-ball, and Natural Born Killers. The city is primarily dominated by Ogden Trece and 18th street. In 2000 the United States Census indicated that the city of Ogden had 77,226 residents.

While federal funding was devoted toward law enforcement efforts to suppress gangs, a different and much needed initiative focused on neighborhood revitalization. Starting in 1994 and lasting until 2005, Ogden received money from the U.S. Department of Housing and Urban Development as a result of being designated an Enterprise Community. This designation provided an opportunity for Ogden to receive ten years of federal funding ($2.95 million) along with tax incentives to revitalize the Central Business District and three surrounding neighborhoods (Ogden Enterprise Community 1997). These same three residential areas were identified in the 1994 Annie B. Casey "Kids Count" as three of the four most harmful neighborhoods for children in the state of Utah. These neighborhoods also contained some of the highest concentrations of Latinos and nonwhite racial groups in the city. The importance of neighborhood revitalization became twisted as Mayor Mathew Godfrey was elected in 2000 and focused on gentrifying the neighborhood by moving middle-class Mormons back to the downtown and creating more events for this population. He began pursuing the removal of individuals he considered socially undesirable, including poor and homeless people, and cracking down on activities considered condoning moral corruption, such as bars and strip clubs. During Godfrey's twelve years as mayor, the Latino community and non-Mormons in Ogden received little support.

Despite data indicating that the rate of violent crime in Utah was around half that of the rest of the nation, Utah began getting stricter with juvenile and adult offenders (Utah Commission on Criminal and Juvenile Justice 2006). Utah was perceived as a potential hotbed for crime because of the size of its population under the age of 17 and the fact that individuals at this age accounted for the largest number of gang members (*SE*, 1999). The Ogden Gang Project cited James Alan Fox when it reported, "Communities are seeing a growing number of juveniles with no-hope, no-fear, no-rules and no-life expectancy. A new class of vicious and remorseless young violent offenders is emerging" (Ogden/Weber Metro Gang Unit 1997:7). The Utah Legislature passed the Serious Youth Offender Bill in 1995, which automatically transferred juveniles into the adult system at the ages 16 to 17. It was reported that Utah experienced one of the highest growth rates of the prison population in the nation (State of Utah 2001). The Serious Habitual Offender Comprehensive Action Program (SHOCAP) combined agency resources to identify gang members and lengthen the average three-month probation sentence to one year. It provided closer monitoring of juveniles and enforced a "no gang association" restriction (Utah Gang Update 2001; field notes).

The suppression approach in Utah received tremendous support from the U.S. Department of Justice. In 2001 one of the first joint collaborations with the local community involved Weed and Seed, which converted a twelve-block neighborhood into a program designed to "weed" out crime and "seed" neighborhoods with revitalization efforts. According to Dunworth and Mills (1999), Operation Weed and Seed was first launched in 1991 to control violent crime, drug trafficking, and drug-related crime and attempt to provide safe neighborhoods by funneling $35,000–$750,000 a year into neighborhoods. Based on a study of ten areas, the results were mixed, with many factors listed as creating difficulty in attaining project goals. The Weed and Seed program in Salt Lake City led to slightly decreased crime and victimization, and the majority of respondents in 1995 and 1997 said the police were doing a good job (Dunworth and Mills 1999). In Ogden the data collected was inadequate to determine whether crime rates had decreased, but white residents reported feeling somewhat comfortable with the police or that the police presence in the area was adequate (Garza-Caballero 2005). Missing from both studies were detailed analyses of what impact weeding of a community was having on the overall community atmosphere and how it condoned racialized policing. Most of the respondents in both studies were white, with only marginal inclusion of Latinos and African Americans.

Two other strategies included the Department of Justice's use of the RICO Act and U.S. Immigration and Customs Enforcement's (ICE) initiative titled Operation Community Shield. Although RICO was used at a lower rate than in Denver, Salt Lake City officials increased their partnerships with federal attorneys to pursue several prosecutions after 2000: King Mafia Disciples, Soldiers of Aryan Culture, Tiny Oriental Posse, and Tongan Crip Gang. ICE participated in a local/federal collaboration that resulted in the arrest, deportation, and prosecution of 284 undocumented individuals throughout the state, many of whom were from Ogden and Salt Lake City.

In 2010 the U.S Department of Justice provided training and encouragement for the Weber County Attorney's Office to draft and secure a gang injunction against Ogden Trece. This was the first gang injunction in Utah and is probably the broadest gang injunction in United States history as it has been applied to the entire city of Ogden instead of a particular neighborhood. Moreover, the civil order is attempting to serve more than four hundred individuals. In other communities around the nation, maybe fifteen to thirty people are typically included in an injunction. The American Civil Liberties Union (ACLU) and several lawyers have challenged this court order, which has resulted in an upcoming review with the Utah State Supreme Court. However, since it appears that the court may not hear the case, a lawyer on behalf of a victim wrote a writ of certiorari requesting the U.S. Supreme Court to review the injunction. The gang injunction makes several legal activities illegal:

associating with alleged members, possessing legal firearms, drinking alcohol, and engaging in other types of constitutionally protected speech
and activities. The conservative *Standard Examiner* has supported the
gang injunction with its reporting, emphasizing every criminal incident
involving someone alleged to be a member of Ogden Trece, writing an
editorial offering their agreement, and providing articles (more like ad-
vertisements) in which law enforcement officials boast about the positive
reasons for an injunction. I received many complaints from members of
the Latino community reporting increased harassment.

Politics in Ogden and Weber County have remained conservative and
white. In 1993 Jesse Garcia was the first Latino elected to the City Council. As a resident of West Ogden and a youth and senior assessment
counselor, he helped bring a political voice to the issues of the Latino
community. Nevertheless, after sixteen years of service he too was targeted and ridiculed for being too closely identified with gangs, as the
concepts Latino and gang membership began to represent the same thing
to many residents of Utah (*SE*, July 19, 2007; January 2, 2010). Despite
Garcia's efforts, the Latino community since 2000 has become heavily
stigmatized as nativist fears since 9/11 have only encouraged residents to
demonstrate their patriotic loyalties against undocumented immigrants
and the Latino community in general, which is considered to be made up
of illegal residents. A disheartening trend is the serious lack or underrepresentation of Latinos in positions of authority or advocacy that could
challenge these events on a broader scale. The city of Ogden is definitely
experiencing a crisis in the twenty-first century.

Those considered nonwhite and non-Mormon have encountered many
obstacles in Utah. The framework of religion has tremendously shaped
the ideology of the state and the perception of non-whites as historically separated in time and given a stigma of darker skin. Members of
the Church of Latter-Day Saints in Utah have an awkward relationship
with cultural diversity and relating to individuals who were not blue-
eyed and blond-haired like those of Mormon European ancestry. Similar
to Mormons, Latinos came to Utah to pursue a better life, and their
historical ties to the area have helped shape it as a generational home-
land. Many Latinos in Utah have experienced relative economic advantages compared to other states. Nevertheless, Latinos have encountered
numerous forms of unequal treatment. As the Latino population grew
from less than 1 percent of the state population to 13 percent, with

Ogden (30.1 percent) and Salt Lake City (22.3 percent) containing even higher proportions of Latinos, one avenue chosen by some individuals for attaining self-protection and self-actualization became the gang. The choice of a small number of youth to organize under the title of gang, however, has resulted in a tremendous drive against all Latinos, blacks, Tongans, and Asians, who are considered to form the majority of gang members. For the first time in Utah's history, the early 1990s brought a war that has been legitimized and considered appropriate for targeting those considered nonwhite and non-Mormon.

The U.S. Department of Justice and other federal agencies have cultivated Utah's fears of individuals perceived as nonwhite, immigrant, and criminal. Residents who question these new tactics of enforcement or nativism are often ridiculed or demeaned. The decline of SOCIO has left a gap that currently has resulted in a crisis for the Latino population in the state.

CHAPTER FIVE

Negotiating Membership
for an Adaptation to Colonization
The Gang

Walking in the barrio is an intricate journey because there is always something emerging on the streets, from alcoholics, city workers, drug addicts, drug dealers, gangsters, police officers, and prostitutes to children, older people, and others going about their daily routine. The population density gives individuals little choice but to share space and negotiate encounters. Vehicles pass by of various styles, from those that barely run (buckets), to lowriders, to those at a higher end, with the music of choice often emanating from car stereos. Some of this interest compels individuals to sit on their front porch and hang out, observing people as they come and go. These social spaces are important in shaping daily activities, and if it wasn't for Frantz Fanon's analysis of colonialism things probably would appear normal and the way they are naturally designed. The neighborhood census tracts that include higher proportions of Latinos are very different from those with high concentrations of whites. Many individuals in the community recognize the visible differences.

In the barrio poverty shapes all options in life. Traveling down B Avenue in Ogden or Decatur in Denver, you realize that money affects life choices: from small homes, apartment complexes, and projects to clothes being dried in the front yard. The barrio struggles to have pride among its bars, jails, homeless shelters, and liquor stores. The police continually monitor the neighborhoods, looking for individuals to stop and investigate for criminal wrongdoing. As I walk the streets, I feel like an advocate for the betterment of my community despite all the conditions that try us and push us to feud with one another. I greet the people I pass with a "what's up?" I take out my video camera and record police stops. I move among the residents trying to develop the solutions that will set us free.

In the white neighborhoods there is quiet serenity that allows resi-
dents to stay behind closed doors with manicured lawns in a spectacle of
space that highlights an aura of elitism. I feel very out of place walking
these white neighborhoods. There are often no sidewalks for walking,
and if they do exist, the only individuals who are on these passages
are walking a dog or jogging. The homes are huge and the landscaping
is elaborate. Car and house alarms protect the property. There are no
police patrolling these streets looking for crime or criminals. The birds
chirp as I think to myself that the differences between the barrio and
suburbs easily explain whether an individual will be required to make
the decision of whether to join a gang. There are definitely white social
organizations that operate here, but the youth are not criminalized. They
do not have to fight for their survival. If needed, they can use the police
or other institutions to solve their problems.

The goal of this chapter is to determine how individuals in the barrio
negotiate the line between being an associate or member in a group created in response to colonization. Researchers have often argued that
only a small percentage of youth ever join a gang—anywhere from 4
to 14 percent. Thus even in the poorest neighborhoods most youth will
never join these groups (Vigil 2007). It is the context of different lived
experiences between Latinos and whites that influences the development
of a chapter focusing on the decision making involved in joining a gang.
I analyze four pathways for developing access to these groups: marginalized neighborhoods, family survival, gender socialization, and school
experiences. I also look at the associations and relationships developed
in each of these four pathways. Despite the different histories of Denver
and Ogden, as outlined in previous chapters, the youth adaptations to
discrimination and inequality in these cities are very similar.

Marginalized Neighborhoods

My ethnographic research and maps obtained by the police indicated
a concentration of gang activity in certain neighborhoods. Graffiti on
buildings, fences, signs, and walls supported these findings. The places
where people lived provided their first opportunities for and obstacles to
joining gangs. Experiencing the harsh realities of life in the barrio placed
Latino youth in a social world that required adaptations to a particular

area. The barrios of both Denver and Ogden brought together marginalized individuals who felt blocked from attaining legitimate opportunities. Most people in the neighborhood were law abiding, but everyone had to be prepared to manage difficult circumstances. Individuals who served as representatives of mainstream society (employers, housing officials, police, probation and parole officers, social workers, teachers) rarely lived in the barrio, and this often translated into social distance from and thus a lack of empathy and support for the Latino community.

Barrio neighborhoods are defined predominantly as being of Mexican origin, residentially and socially segregated, and often located near places of industrial employment (Camarillo 1979; Garcia 1981; Romo 1983). These three distinguishing factors were often intensified by the impact of continual immigration, concentrated poverty, and unequal treatment by society. The structural patterns in neighborhoods that contain gang activity have a long history in previous studies (Tannenbaum 1938; Thrasher 1927; Whyte 1943). In Los Angeles, Moore's (1978, 1991) and Vigil's (1988, 2002, 2007) research on gangs found that ecological problems have in many ways become spatial and visual reminders of Mexican Americans' marginal acceptance. Accessing public social control (Vélez 2001) and encountering the legal and judicial system (Mirandé 1987) became important issues for resolving conflicts or issues.

The number of Latinos living in both cities has increased significantly. According to the U.S. Census (1990–2010), Latinos in Denver increased from 23 percent (107,382) in 1990 to 32 percent (190,965) in 2010 and in Ogden from 12 percent (7,669) in 1990 to 30 percent (24,940) in 2010. In the barrios in particular, the concentration of Latinos ranged from 50 to 76 percent in 2000. The post-1990 increase in the number of first-generation Mexican immigrants moving into the barrio and fertility rates has helped to further enhance these concentrations. Despite the nationwide increase in the number of Latinos, a limited number of studies have focused primarily on barrios. Peterson and Krivo (2009) analyzed data from 8,286 census tracts across eighty-seven cities from the year 2000 to argue that blacks and Latinos continue to live in separate social worlds from white local environments, which are more socioeconomically advantaged, stable, and imbued with more external resources. Black and Latino neighborhoods were the most disadvantaged and bore the brunt of urban criminal violence (Krivo, Peterson, and Kuhl 2009). Logan and Stults (2010) utilized 2005–09 American Community Survey data to indicate that Latino isolation has remained the same since 1980. These authors also argue that whites live in very different social spaces from those of blacks, Latinos, and Asians.

The concentration of poverty limited economic opportunities for Latino residents. Wilson (1996) described "ghetto" neighborhoods as those in which at least 40 percent of the residents are poor. Peterson and Krivo (2009) identified high-poverty neighborhoods to be areas with 20–40 percent poverty. There were a few census tracts within Denver (1.5 of 16) and Ogden (2 of 5) that were in "ghetto poverty," but in the majority of the barrio poverty exceeded 20 percent (13 of 16 tracts in Denver and 4 of 5 in Ogden) and thus qualified as high poverty. It was rarer for a neighborhood that was primarily Latino to not be impoverished. The concentration of poverty limited economic opportunities for residents of Mexican descent. Latinos moved in search of employment and better circumstances for their children but faced employment constraints and obtained only marginal inclusion in wider society. The majority of barrio residents in Denver worked in construction, production, and service jobs (78 percent). In Ogden they worked in similar blue-collar occupations, such as manufacturing, production, and service occupations (84 percent). For Latinos over the age of 15 counted in the formal work force, 40 percent in Denver and 61 percent in Ogden were not working. Venkatesh's (2000) research in the Chicago housing projects found the existence of a thriving underground economy. Residents were required to create various hustles to ensure their basic needs were met.

D-loc, a 25-year-old former gang member, captured the barrio experience:

> Wherever you go in these poor communities, gangs plague them. Young people with nothing to do and you will find the same illnesses in all these communities that plague these children, like not enough funding for education, not enough staff, inadequate teachers to fill the school, not enough programs within the school to occupy a child's time. There aren't adequate health care services in the community to work with the kid that might have a disability or learning disability that might need medication to calm their nerves so they could sit and listen to a teacher. So a lot of these kids get displaced within the school—they're looked at as troublemakers, they don't fit in and they feel intimidated. They don't want to go to school. And so what is there within the community? The

rec centers are closed. A lot of rec centers charge money. A kid can't even afford to go to some of the rec centers. So what are these kids to do? How do they still find themselves as part of the community with young people their own age, with their peers, and they find that within gangs. So across the board, across the country, you see a lack of education in the Chicano and black communities, you see a lack of services for young people in those communities whatever that might be. Whether that be, like the library, the libraries in the hood they ain't hooked up with everything you need to know for your educational resources. We don't have the most advanced computers in our hood, we don't get the newest books, the latest magazines, we get all the kick downs from all the branches that have money and the facilities to hold those. We get the kick backs from them. Meanwhile in our communities, across the board, across the country, blacks and Chicanos [have] the highest rate of incarceration. We have the highest dropout rate. So this play of racism definitely comes to play on the street.

D-loc went on to explain that all these community problems only endorsed the gang as a solution. He thought people in the 'hood developed a feeling that there was no way out unless you hustled or joined a gang to get ahead because this was simply the way things were in the barrio.

The lack of legitimate opportunity in Denver and Ogden encompassed residential and social isolation that concentrated poverty, lack of education, and an inability to attain jobs for a wide number of residents. These conditions created a push for residents to seek both legal and illegal forms of economic improvement. Neighborhood structures such as parks and unique markers are important in shaping the territorial identity of gangs. Although the city is the property of the state, gang members' daily experiences result in a feeling that these locations are home. The names of several gangs are synonymous with the neighborhood or sections of the city. Occasionally gang members or associates from other areas of the country or nearby cities reside in a neighborhood or section, but it is the local gangs that dominate the scene. The second-class treatment, land separations, political disenfranchisement, and economic subservience created a firmly entrenched socializing agent: gangs. The land and gang names are protected to the fullest, for they denote something greater than the actual gang member—they constitute a living, breathing entity that is the GANG, or *mi barrio*.

Family Survival

Families tried to minimize youth involvement in disreputable activities. Respect was important in the family and community. Catholic and Christian beliefs served as a strong moral gauge of behaviors, and honor pervaded all public evaluations (Horowitz 1983; Mirandé 1985). Families lived by principles of how individuals should carry themselves. Families in Denver and Ogden did not preach gang membership. Working and taking care of family were important goals. Families were built on courage, honor, respect, and strength. However, attaining these family ideals within the barrio often required behaving in ways that were in conflict with conventional society's institutions and social settings. The neighborhood youth attempted to fill their place within the family and legitimate society, but most of the acclaim was accomplished by personal triumphs of overcoming various life obstacles.

Family was the primary loyalty that existed before people entered a gang, and it continued to be a central institution for Mexican American culture (Keefe 1979; Mirandé 1977, 1985; Sena-Rivera 1979). Familism offered economic, emotional, physical, and psychological support. Similar to Horowitz's (1983) gang study, I found most Latino families to be composed of a nuclear family within a single household with varying generations of relatives living nearby. Horowitz (1983:40) reported, "The common culture and support of kin outweighed all problems of the community." Entire extended families (cousins, aunts, uncles, grandparents) often lived within walking distance of one another, which increased physical and emotional support. Families faced employment constraints and marginal inclusion in wider society. Aunts, uncles, cousins, grandparents, and parents had encountered various forms of neighborhood obstacles for generations, and thus successful upward mobility (the American dream) was an aspiration that might never be legitimately attained. Several manufacturing jobs were relocating to other countries, yet a higher percentage of Latinos in Denver and Ogden remained working in some type of service job rather than facing unemployment.

Families living in the barrio had not attained upward mobility, but they made up for this by creating a community of friends, family, and common culture. The lack of opportunity was based on family exclusion from fully integrating outside the barrio community. The extended family often provided access into a gang, especially if the family had lived in the neighborhood for an extended period of time. Families learned to physically protect one another, and it was outsiders who saw this as a problem. Although none of the gang members or associates I interviewed reported that their parents had been involved in gangs, many had siblings, cousins, or even uncles who were or had been involved. Moore (1991) reported that half of gang members had a relative in a gang, but membership was not inherited. The majority of families in Moore's study and mine did not have gang membership passed down. For some gangs, the gang was not a substitute for the family but rather an extension. Lucita, a 25-year-old gang associate from Ogden, explained the importance of family for gang involvement: "I think you have to be a family member. Everyone is related to everyone. I don't know anyone who is just friends. Everyone is related to someone. So I don't know if John Doe could get in if he wanted to. Maybe they would use him to do all of the little dirty work, but as far as giving him respect, no."

The intertwining of two institutions, family and gangs, presented a serious challenge to the expectations developed from membership. A family that shifted protection from the nuclear to the extended family provided a wider umbrella for ensuring safety, but when gang injunctions or police made such interactions a crime, the law became problematic.

Overall, having a family member involved in a gang made it much more difficult to refrain from fighting when family members came home after being beaten, bruised, stabbed, or shot. Family members wanted to provide protection for one another. Seeing family members injured was one thing, but being included in an attack despite not being a member complicated reasons to stay away from supporting the gang. Lucita, the 25-year-old gang associate, described a confrontation with another gang in high school that made the line that separated members from associates very thin:

I remember an experience when we went to the mall [laugh]. My brother and I, my mom, and my brother's girlfriend, we got jumped. Two days later it was a Friday or Saturday, I don't remember, but they came back to the school and I was in basketball and we were training, getting ready for a big game and, ugh, next thing you know we see a whole bunch of gang members come from all doors and they had sticks and that's when I realized, dang. I'm a lot more involved than I thought I was. I don't know if it had to do with who I was related to, or I was really involved. Maybe I'm a closet gang banger. I don't know.

Lucita mentioned how she had first encountered gangs when she was 11 years old. She witnessed a cousin getting jumped into the gang and wondered if gangs would become a part of her brothers' or her life.

Having family members involved increased individual networks with gang peers and activities. Older siblings involved in the gang often appeared as role models. They presented an image of being tough, cool, and unafraid of life obstacles. Smokey, a 22-year-old Ogden gang associate, said:

> It made me feel like they were cooler than they probably actually are. It gave it more of a glamour that there probably wouldn't have been had he [my brother] not been involved. [And why is that?] Mmm, it just seemed like to me like he was always going out and having fun doing the things he was doing. I knew he was involved in that limelight, and I think it kind of made it a little glossy for me.

Despite developing an interest, Smokey never joined a gang. He struggled in school but developed other friendships that were more closely matched to his interest in the outdoors.

More than half of respondents said that their parents were strict, and close to half lived with both biological parents (nationally 35 percent of children lived with their biological parents according to the Bureau of Census 2001), yet most gang associates and members believed that those who joined gangs came from broken families and were given less structure regarding what time to be home and where they were going. In conducting my research, I was unable to confirm the prevailing belief in broken families and lack of structure or discipline among gang-affiliated youth. Members incarcerated in youth corrections, however, were more likely to follow the pattern of troubled homes based on incoming mail, phone calls, and number of visits received by the youth. Youth housed in group homes, treatment centers, and youth corrections appeared to have the most troubled families, but the majority of these youth were also not in gangs. A higher percentage of youth who attended ASAP and were living at youth facilities described their parents as abusive, neglectful, and uninvolved. These youth mentioned a higher rate of alcohol and drug abuse at home and in their own lives.

Latino families experienced conflicts between maintaining their work and their relationships and staying away from violence and drama in a cut-throat social environment. A felony record could impose an impenetrable barrier to attaining stable employment. Individuals with criminal records reported enhanced difficulties in finding employment, followed by people who lacked high school degrees or a GED. Incarceration, death, drugs, and deportation often removed family members from the household as well as leaving children to grow up searching for family love. D-loc the ex–gang member, mentioned how neglect extended beyond the family to include societal neglect:

> Every one of those kids say they weren't paid attention to, and when they were paid attention to they were picked on, pushed on, put down, disrespected, and belittled. That's what all these children say. Why? Because there isn't a focus on our children, there isn't a love of our children, there's only a love for the adult that is trying to capitalize and make money off somebody. That's the only one being paid attention to. The big-ass singers that are on TV with the videos, the president making a speech, the news broadcaster or the movie star. That's the focus, on the person that can make the most money for themselves and the riches and the glory themselves, not for our children or on what we can do as a whole for our community.

I am unaware whether there has ever been a generation in U.S. culture that has devoted itself toward its youth. Although white society may have enhanced resources, personal observations suggest its members also lack attention. White people continue to be overrepresented in the number of school shootings, mass shootings, serial killers, and white-collar offenses, which raises the question of whether they too feel love (Russell 1998). Such efforts of uplifting youth may exist in certain organizations designed to prevent youth from being corrupted by society.

Family members provided pressure for youth to stay away from gangs because of the consequences from rival gangs and the police. A family member involved in a gang could serve as an example for why not to join. Monique, a gang associate, described how having a family member involved in gangs led her to want to do something different:

> I think that made me hate them even more. . . . [How is that?] Just because seeing the stupid stuff that he goes through and all it's doing

is putting him in and out of prison and he is doing it all for a gang and a color. Also how they treat him. They would never be here [in a supportive role], you know what I mean, and it is never going to be his. He is doing it all for a gang.

This interview was conducted with Monique when she was 22 years old, yet during high school she had a hard time staying away from friends and associates who were gang members. The murder of her child's father through gang violence and the incarceration of her two brothers led her to attempt to negotiate a life, and the life of her three children, far from gangs.

Moore's (1991) longitudinal gang research with Mexican American gangs in Los Angeles found that two-thirds of the men and women reported that their parents were upset with their gang involvement. Smiley, a 23-year-old gang associate, described how he was more scared of joining a gang because of how his family would respond: "Personally I was always scared, myself, to get into a gang because of the influence of my father and of my brother too because they always told me that if I would ever get into a gang I would have to deal with them too. I was more worried about that than anybody else."

Jay, a 27-year-old ex–gang member, described how the depressing impact of gangs on his life made him want something different for his brothers and sisters: "I don't want them to go through what I went through because it's dangerous, you know? Crazy shit happens. So in that aspect, I guess, yeah, it changed the way I thought about it because I didn't want them to be put into some of the situations I was in, so, but you can't control what others do, you can only control what you do." Jay didn't want to see his family members get involved with gangs, but there was little he could do to alleviate the pressure they faced away from home. Cola, a 27-year-old ex–gang member, told me that even though his parents disapproved of gangs and illegal activity, no one could hold his hand when he left home, and he had to learn to take care of himself.

Immediate families living in the barrio often lacked the ability to launch their children into a social world of legitimate opportunities without the need for constant protection and support. By relying on extended family members and friends, safety was more far reaching. The stress families faced encouraged adaptations toward attaining respect. The historical and contemporary response was to unite with one another to provide defense, to find entertainment and friendship. Family or group support countered the primary emphasis in U.S. culture on individualism.

Gender Socialization

Socialization into masculinity and femininity was taught by parents and monitored by siblings, family members, and other youth in the neighborhood from an early age. Mirandé (1985) reported that Latinos did not adequately fit within Anglo conceptions of masculinity and femininity. Boys and girls were taught at an early age to value bravery, loyalty, perseverance, pride, respect, and strength. Boys were more ingrained with the obligation to provide protection, and girls were socialized to provide maternal support. Mirandé (1977:753) stated that "adolescent girls are much more restricted and sheltered than adolescent boys." Many family members tried to protect girls from excessive partying and receiving the bad reputations that often came through heavy gang banging. Horowitz (1983) found it was the male duty to protect family honor by ensuring the sexual purity of the women. Although both studies are more than twenty-five years old, women continued to struggle in opposing double standards during the time frame of my research.

Several ASAP meetings included young gang members criticizing young women who wanted to hang out with male gang members. For example, a 14-year-old Latina reported how her boyfriend who is a Sureño bought her a cell phone and she snuck out late at night to party with him and his friends. Several young men reported how they thought the 14-year-old was going to be raped, which led to some slight laughter among the group. A male probation officer who was attending the group verbally reproached this behavior, saying "You never lay a hand on women." The probation officer began telling the story of Brandy Duvall, who was raped by several members of a gang and then killed. The horrific story was recounted in *Westword* (Jackson 1999) and influenced me to visit the home where the attack began and then later the rocky cliff where her life was tragically ended. As a father of two daughters at the time, I was very upset by this story. The primary individual involved was given the death penalty but has since been given life in prison. The gang-involved youth at ASAP appeared to feel embarrassed when they heard this story after their role in teasing the 14-year-old attending the group. She was later removed from ASAP for fear that the group might only increase her contacts with gang-involved youth. The standards of chivalry and sexism continued to play a strong role in perceptions.

Many young women appeared to gravitate toward gang members and perceived the young men involved as "finer" or "cuter." Gang members had mystique and excitement. There was no peer organization or group that provided comparable opportunities, friendship, and status for males. Moore (1991) found that "75 percent of the women—especially the younger women—had boyfriends who were in the gang, and only 43 percent dated boys that were square (not in a gang)." Her respondents reported that guys who were not in gangs were too nice and boring. Although having a boyfriend in a gang increased excitement and the perception of protection, it placed girlfriends in the difficult role of being seen as a member of that particular gang. There were definitely risks associated with women from the neighborhood dating members of rival gangs. Anne recalled an experience at a party:

> I kind of was stuck in the middle of it. I didn't say I was [gang name omitted to provide anonymity], but I ended up getting in with a guy who got in with a gang that they hated. That really made it hard for me because I loved my boyfriend a lot and plus I was pregnant from the father of my child, yet the people I grew up with and hung out with, you know, they put me in the middle and it was really hard, even though I didn't gang bang it was still like I was or I did, like I had to choose: my childhood friends or the love of my life. . . . I think if they really were my friends they would have supported me because I wasn't in their gang, and I never got to the point where I would snitch on them for shit they did, or never told them stuff about [gang name omitted] or I would never tell him about stuff, you know what I mean? I don't think they should have treated me that way.
>
> I remember this one time me and two other friends, we went to a big [gang name omitted] party, a keg. . . . We went to the party for one of their birthdays and it was me and two other girls. We went and it was packed with guys and girls. . . . We pulled up, and I kind of had a bad feeling like, I don't know about this. [About you going to their party?] Yeah, because I had already had a couple problems, people talking shit, and she was like "No, it will be okay. We know all of the girls, you know? We know all of them," because her boyfriend hung out with my boyfriend. . . . And so it's jammed pack in there and everyone is drinking and smoking. So I'm really nervous, really really

nervous, like when you just get a bad vibe . . . and I was thinking I needed to watch my back and the girl at the door that was marking our hand [to get beer] was like dogging us too like mad. . . . We walked in where the kegs were in the back of the house, in the kitchen OK, so the room is packed and walking through and people are staring at us really bad, and then I could hear whispering "them bitches are [gang name omitted]." I told my friend, "We need to go. We need to go now!" I was like "I don't have a good feeling about this." She was like "No, no, it's all right, it's all right," and then I seen another girl I knew, that I've known a long time and that I used to work with when I was younger and she was like "What's up?" and she told me, "I don't think you should stay. There is a lot of people tripping on you because they think you are [gang name omitted]," and I told her, "But you know I'm not," "But you know that is what they think," and um it was just awful. I thought we were going to die in there. . . . I hurried and drank my beer; we are going to get jumped, these people are getting drunk. . . . We left and I think that was the last time I really went to a large [gang name omitted] party. But yeah, I was shocked because none of them had my back. [Your friends?] Yeah none of them, the girls I hung out with, not the ones I went with [to the party] but the other ones. I felt like I was alone. [You think you were the target?] Yeah, I think they felt betrayed. I think they thought I was there to spy on them or something. It was hard for me because I got thrown in the middle of it.

Anne's experience of negotiating the gang's expectations to conform to their rules of relationships was shared by many of the young women. Failure to abide by these expectations resulted in a form of group expulsion that often included the possibility of physical confrontation.

Rebellon and Manassee (2004) reported that peers learn vicariously to mimic risk-taking behavior when it is seen as increasing dating opportunities. Since young women were attracted to guys in the gang, it had an influence on young men considering gang membership. Smiley noticed how gangs attracted more women to the young men:

[How would the girls look upon those that would join and those that wouldn't?] Most of 'em liked them. They would like hang around the ones that got in gangs for some reason. I don't know. It would attract them. They would always have girls around 'em. Not all of them were like that, some just thought they were, but most of the guys. I would say the ones who join were more respected, more feared. When you are in gang, especially in middle school, the ones you see in gangs, they have a lot more respect. I don't know if it is out of fear, but they would have respect for them. The ones who did join would look at those that didn't like they were lower than them because they were scared or something or they did not have the guts. They would think they were better.

Negotiating this decision making was more difficult when the gang so easily tapped into preexisting forms of dating and increasing chances for developing relationships.

In both Denver and Ogden there were young women involved in gangs. The Denver Gang Unit estimated 10 percent of gang members were women, whereas Ogden estimated 6 percent. Although Gang Unit official statistics on gang members were often poorly gathered, and self-reports altered these numbers, young women were more likely to be associates than members. Larissa, a 17-year-old gang associate, described how she wanted to join a gang in the seventh grade because they were cool. However, she thought her hometown gang did not treat its women well. She mentioned how the rival gang treated its women better. Portillos (1999:239) reported, "Although the gang provides an escape from traditional notions of femininity and abuse, it cannot be described as a site of gender equality." Gang members spent the majority of time with their same-gender peers. However, gang parties and hanging out often included both boys and girls because there was an underlying interest in developing future relationships.

Gender roles are proper ways to fit in and are socialized into young females and males living in the neighborhood. Although these examples focused on how the gang influenced courtship, gender expectations and roles played a significant part in behavior and analyzing situations.

School Experiences

The impact of European education on individuals of Mexican descent has a troubled history (Espinoza-Herold 2003; Valencia 1991). Nationally in 2000, Latinos had the highest dropout rate in the country at 28 percent, four times higher than whites (7 percent) and two times higher than blacks (13 percent) (Kaufman, Alt, and Chapman 2001). The proportion of Latinos 25 years or older with a high school diploma in Denver's and Ogden's barrios (33–37 percent) was far below the state average of 87–88 percent (National Change Database CD 1970–2000). The lack of perceived opportunity in school was a major crisis for providing future educational or employment options and networks. Education has been found to correlate with higher wages and better occupations. Most of the parents were supportive of their children graduating and doing well in school despite their personal lack of knowledge about how to make this a realistic goal (Delgado-Gaitan 1988; Valencia and Black 2002).

The interviewees did not think that administrators or teachers cared ("didn't give a shit") whether Latino youth succeeded. Researchers have found that teachers' perceptual bias of students' overall success in the classroom can create a self-fulfilling prophecy where students of color become negatively evaluated (Farkas et al. 1990; Rosenbloom and Way 2004). Padilla's (1992) gang research in Chicago reported that teachers' negative evaluations only led youth to act out and create an oppositional behavior against what they perceived as unfair treatment. With all the problems in schools and the negative treatment of nonwhite students, investing self-worth in the curriculum was seen as odd. Rodney, a middle-aged African American Latino who was an ex–gang associate, said:

> I mean really, it all starts in school. It starts in the classroom when you stop identifying with the curriculum that they are teaching you and you look for something that makes you feel validated. Because the classroom alienates you and teaches you that you don't really exist or except as a slave or for a Latino a bean picker: a field worker. They don't really teach you that you exist. But I know you are sitting around in the classroom. You ain't doing nothing. [laugh] You look around and you see who ain't doing nothing with you right? [yep] But now you see Robert ain't doing nothing and Robert cool. He black, because you really start identifying anything that has to do with school as white. And it goes both the same way for blacks and Mexicans. You start identifying with school. If you are doing schoolwork you are a sellout. That's how you start looking at each other, and you start identifying who is not selling out, and you start clicking and you start hanging out. Next thing you know you are running around playing basketball, football, you are all doing everything together but you aren't doing any schoolwork together, and one day you say, "Let's give ourselves a name" [laugh].

Institutionally, most of the schools lacked proportionately comparable Latino teachers and a less Eurocentric curriculum. In 2003, 80 percent of Denver's students were nonwhite, and yet 76 percent of the teachers were white (Colorado Department of Education 2003; Department of Planning and Research 2003).[1] Ogden's administrators and teachers were less diverse in terms of racial and ethnic percentages than Denver's, and by the twelfth grade the number of Latinos attending Ogden's mainstream high schools continued to demonstrate these push-out patterns. Anne, the 24-year-old gang associate, noted: "I didn't like school. I didn't feel like there were a lot of opportunities because I was poor, or for minorities. Maybe it was because we didn't think it was cool maybe, and I got in trouble a lot in school." The students felt like a statistic. I asked Lucita about the schools in her neighborhood and she replied, "Um, you hear about good ones and bad ones but I think being a minority it is hard getting your foot in the door. It is just restricted. Being a minority getting in you are labeled or they offend you in a way and you just walk out the door. There is just restrictions. I think we are limited. It's not fair. There is a lot of racist people."

Sheets (2002) reported that teachers' and students' different cultural backgrounds and social positions created divided perceptions on appropriate forms of discipline. Students felt alienated and discriminated against for their different skin color, ethnicity, and clothing preference. Peguero and Shekarkhar (2011) analyzed a national data set of 7,250 students in 580 public schools and found no statistical difference between Latino and white student misbehavior. They did find that first-generation Latino students received similar outcomes as white males despite engaging in less school misbehavior, and third-generation Latinos were the most likely to be punished at school. In sum, Latino students were more likely to be punished in schools than white students despite engaging in similar behaviors as white students.

School discipline lacked consistency in matching the severity of punishment with the actual infraction. In Denver and Ogden, misconduct was no longer tolerated in high school. Urban schools enacted stricter punishments such as zero-tolerance policies for fights, gang activity, and gang-related clothing. The enactment of tougher policies began increasing dramatically in inner-city schools after several suburban and rural school shootings during the 1990s, including the shooting at the primarily white Columbine High School in Colorado. Newman (2004) conducted research on rampage shootings and found the punitive zero-tolerance approach was counterproductive because isolated incidents were shaping national policy, but these incidents resulted from a broader range of social issues. The majority of Latinos involved in gangs had been kicked out of mainstream high school before twelfth grade and sent to alternative schools. This opposition from the school, however, continued to allow gang membership to thrive and displace the hopelessness into the community. There were a few programs in place to deal with struggling students. Pregnant students were sent to a young mothers program at the alternative school to help them graduate. Anne and Larissa had both attended this program, but only Larissa finished with a diploma. The alternative schools were often more supportive of the youth in terms of finishing school, but the self-fulfilling prophecy of removal and the lack of individual resources were often enough to dwindle youths' chances.

In the Denver Public Schools, when a fight occurred, the youth were ticketed and had to go to criminal court (Advancement Project 2005). According to the Advancement Project, the number of referrals to law enforcement officials increased 71 percent between 2000 (818) and 2004 (1,401). Forty-three percent of these referrals were for violations of school codes of conduct, followed by 32 percent for drugs, alcohol, tobacco, assaults, dangerous weapons, and robbery. Students of color were overrepresented with tickets and arrests. In Utah students were suspended for a few days, yet no mediation was conducted between the students in order to resolve the issues that led to the fight. Nevertheless, security guards, resource officers, and cameras were the norm in the schools to monitor the behavior of youth. Although school oversight and enforcement was far-reaching, there was still a high rate of intimidation and bullying.

Certain types of clothing and colors were banned. Common examples included the colors red, blue, and light blue along with sports apparel, certain shirts, belts, and hats. The effectiveness of such clothing policies was not independently evaluated. Most students reported to me that they felt discriminated against and denied having any gang affiliation. A teacher told me how local gang officers came into her school and scared all the teachers into believing their school was encountering a lot of gang activity. The school reacted by imposing increased consequences. Most of my research found that these "gang infested" claims overdramatized and captured too much innocent youthful style of dress and behavior.

The pressure to belong to gangs intensified at school for many barrio residents. Klein (1995:168–69) reported, "The school is perhaps the main place where potential gang members, from the most innocent to active 'wannabes,' come into contact with street gang culture." Youth from different neighborhoods, backgrounds, and ages were brought together into school institutions that were ill prepared to provide protection for 800–2,200 adolescents. Hutchison and Kyle (1993:132) found issues involving gang recruitment and intimidation a serious issue for Hispanic students in Chicago and other cities. Padilla (1992) reported that during elementary and middle school, Latino youth could be marginally connected to the gang, but this all began to change in high school. In Denver and Ogden, the peer pressure began in middle school, and by high school the odds of joining a gang were the highest. When Jay, a 27-year-old, was asked who he saw primarily joining the gangs, he said:

> It was primarily around, I would say from seventh graders on up all the way to seniors in high school. They would get jumped into a gang because they wanted to, you know, you had to have your boys, you had to have your backup, so that's pretty much what it was all about, man. You had to be in the gang, 'cause if you didn't, you would be a loner, and if somebody would come up on you and if you didn't have your back up, you were screwed pretty much. So they pretty much targeted all of the juveniles. Anybody that wasn't in their gang they tried to get you in so they could, I guess, dominate the market.

Latino youth first focused on how they could survive socially without being picked on or intimidated. Those who joined were seen as having more opportunities, backup, and respect and were also more feared and seen as leaders. Akers (1990) reported problems with rational choice theory because people operated more on limited rationality, for often the information available was faulty or their assessment of a situation was incorrect. The perceived opportunities obtained through a gang in an intimidating school environment made sense for many youth. Nite Owl, a 17-year-old ex–gang member, said this when asked what the difference was between those who had joined and those who would not:

> I think the ones that didn't join was because they didn't have any problems or nothing like that. They didn't get into fights, no one picked on them or nothing like that. The ones that did, because they had problems or stuff, things like that. [How do you think they were able to stay out of not having problems?]. I don't know, by not saying

nothing, and all of that. By staying quiet. But some guys, they don't even stay quiet, like me. If someone talks shit I'll talk shit back to them. If some start talking shit some stay quiet and don't listen to them. But I don't. I'm different. Somebody talks shit to me, I'm going to tell them something back.

There were fights between rival gangs at school, but for the most part the buildings or campus became a place to increase tensions that were taken care of after school.

D-loc probably summed up this entire process of school pressures best when he said:

I think the pressure is still big when you are a young person. When young people start to consider gangs and getting involved is approximately middle school. They kind of get to fiddle around with it, play with it, pretend, dress the part, talk a lot of smack, and kind of get to run around innocently with the big O.G.'s or whoever the homies are that are running the streets. I think that pressure to at least look and be around it and play the part is big, but innocently those kids don't know what they're getting themselves into. I think in high school that's when the pressure really comes on to like, "All right now you make your decision, you've been messing around, you talk a lot of stuff, whatever." In middle school and in high school it's like, "All right, put up or shut up." You know? "Are you down or not?" And everyone starts siding up real quick in high school just because the high school dynamic of when a young person starts to mature and the shock of a young person entering high school with older youth and just trying to make status for yourself as a freshman compared to the seniors that have been there. They seem older, more mature, and more responsible that all of a sudden when you come in as a kid you want to have that immediately. And a gang gives you a false sense of that: of control, of status, of respect, of awareness. And so when you're a freshman and you're at the bottom of the pile, the bottom of the chain, and you seem to be the weakest part of the chain, gangs is definitely a quick solution to strengthening your own heart, your own mind, your own person within the high school culture. So gangs really take control of a young person, definitely in those beginning years of high school I think. In Colorado anyway.

Smokey, a 22-year-old, agreed that the pressures at school were challenging because the bullying led many to perceive gangs as a better road than being embarrassed publicly. He stated:

> I think in some ways there was a little more freedom if you didn't [join], but in other ways if you did [join] you would have all of that backup if anything was to happen, you would have more power and more respect. But if you didn't, you could associate with whoever you want. More of a freedom of choice kind of thing. But for the most part if you mess with someone who is affiliated, you would have a lot more to deal with.

Smokey was glad he didn't join a gang because he didn't want that path in his life. But he thought there were a lot of problems in some communities and was disappointed in how poorly minorities were treated.

Many youth were seen as being "out in the cold" if they didn't join and were sometimes perceived as or called a "chump," or "chicken." Thus while individuals who joined gangs were elevated in status, those who did not were lowered. Gang associates were somewhat able to buffer these negative pressures by being good friends to gang members. Nevertheless they could not consistently associate with a certain gang because of others people's perceptions of that person belonging to a particular group. Jay, the 27-year-old ex–gang member, said: "Those that didn't [join] were always looked at like busters, you know, they were considered pansies or pussies or whatever. Like you, if you were part of the gang you were down, you were one of the boys, you were equal. But if you didn't join, you were definitely lower, you weren't equal."

Associates' reasons for not joining included not wanting the consequences of gang life. The dangers of gang activity often became apparent when hanging out with gang members. Not wanting to engage in physical fights or possibly even the lack of interest in gang activities kept many from trying to join. Instead many youth attempted to negotiate a line of association with previous friendships but not get too close where the pressure increased to join. Lopez et al. (2006) reported how a fourth of students in their sample engaged in active strategies to avoid gangs, such as avoiding gang hangouts, ending relationships with friends, refusing to hang out, and moving to new residences. Higher-achieving students were more likely than low-achieving students to utilize these strategies. The majority of gang associates who hung around gangs thought that they were often treated as gang members by police, rivals, and those within the gangs, despite not formally joining. Although gang associates did not join, they were often involved in protecting friends from negative encounters. To them, the friends they grew up with or became close to were important enough to physically protect. Thus the ability to define a street gang can often be very ambiguous as street culture confused authority figures and residents in the community into assuming everyone potentially had ties to a group for self-protection.

In both Denver and Ogden, one or two gangs were often predominantly located at certain schools. Gang members from different neighborhoods were placed at increased risk for victimization. Gangs significantly affected fights, intimidation, protection, and status. Gangs made life hard for people who rubbed them the wrong way, but they lacked the number of members and institutional authority required to completely control the school. Most students unaffiliated with gangs did not bother gang members. Anne, the 24-year-old gang associate, described how the attraction to gangs remained strong:

> Everybody wanted to be part of the gang. Nobody messed with you, you know what I mean? Everybody wanted to be part of that, everybody was afraid of you, nobody messed with you. [Did the girls like that too?] Yeah, nobody messed with us, we were mean. We fought a lot. I fought a lot. I think it was more of a cool thing to do, trying to fit in, trying to be part of it.

Anne encountered a lot of difficulties with the school system and in the neighborhood because of her active involvement in aggression. She was suspended numerous times and eventually expelled from school. Only two months into attending the mainstream high school during her ninth grade, Anne and her cousin were jumped by several young women in older grades. Both Anne and her cousin were expelled despite being the victims.

A segment of Latinos in both cities were highly motivated and aspiring youth who made people aware that they wanted to go to college and that they had the grades to make this a reality. This group appeared to constitute a small but significant percentage of Latino students. Many of the members of Jovenes and Padres Unidos fit these criteria, as did the student leaders at Weber State University who participated in the student leadership group MEChA. For a student project in undergraduate school, I interviewed five of these leaders who came from similar backgrounds as some of the gang members but pushed themselves to excel with school instead of meeting the stereotype of dropping out or being pushed out. Three-fourths of the gang members I interviewed aspired to going to college or a trade school, but hearing many reports of not feeling "smart enough" affected their confidence in achieving these accomplishments.

Racially derogatory comments or treatment encouraged young people to join with peers who refused to tolerate abuse by teachers, administrators, or other youth. Ethnic solidarity was often the backbone for uniting. Mack-one, a 24-year-old gang associate, said, "Um, the only pressure I felt was due to racial pressure at my school. The school I was at, the majority was white, and you had the black students showing their Crip allegiance and the Chicano students, a lot of them, showed their Blood allegiance, so I felt a bit of pressure because of that, because there were few minorities, so I felt like I had to do that." Mack-one felt some solidarity in hanging out with Bloods. He was able to maintain a line of friendship but never went as far as joining.

There were also conflicts between first- and later-generation Mexicans. Vigil (1988) reported that much of the intraethnic conflict revolved around economics, competition, culture, and linguistic differences. Vigil found that Mexican Americans who he considered identified with a cholo style[2] denied being Anglicized but held a negative attitude toward Mexican nationals or immigrants. I found this pattern in Denver and Ogden. Some of the largest gang rivalries were between Mexican-born and United States-born Mexicans. Raul, an 18-year-old ex–gang member, said:

> The only things going on when I was young was going to school and just staying out of trouble. When I started middle school that's when it all started because that's when gangs started to come. [Were you feeling pressure to join?] Yeah, because being Mexicano and going to a middle school, and there is a lot of Chicanos, and being Mexicano, you were getting picked on by other people that were Mexicanos too, but they were just picking on other people because they didn't have anything else to do. [Why did you start?] Because other people were trying to pick a fight with us and calling us wetbacks.

Raul expressed the difficulty of negotiating the general cultural divisions that separated first-generation Latinos and those whose parents were born in the United States. Such divisions were expressed in the 1970s and 1980 interviews in Utah and in Denver.

Schools indirectly pressured Latino youth to join gangs by providing a neglected physical space to pursue peer and cultural acceptance. This neglect funneled despair and racism into marginal youth who wanted something better for themselves. The social, ethnic, and age distance between school administrators and teachers and Latino youth removed these authority figures from mediating the problems marginal youth were encountering.

Friendships

Living conditions, family survival, gender socialization, and school experiences shape daily routines that affect youth decision making, but despite all these ordeals most youth will still never join a gang. Vigil (2007) provides an important analysis when he seeks to answer why some individuals who live in the projects join gangs and most other youth choose another route. He found that gang-involved families presented some of the most significant pressures pushing youth to join gangs. He argued that macrohistorical and macrostructural forces were manifested in four classes: (1) agent effects—psychology; (2) push effects—something that drives a person to respond; (3) pull effects—effects that draw a person toward a behavior; and (4) interrupter effects—intervening events or individuals. My research found that family played a role in push, pull, and interrupter effects, but the key decision ultimately included the pull effects of friendship. Associations are the final critical pathway in whether someone will be more likely to join a gang or simply remain part of a group of friends.

Friendships include all the patterns of where you live, who is your family, how you are socialized in terms of gender, and where you attend school. There are a variety of social groups: clubs, ROTC, and sports. Gang youth were often the individuals who did not feel like they fit in in these traditional groups or were more socialized to pursue gang friendships. In the gang an individual's background in terms of race and ethnicity can often be very important. In Utah and Colorado most youth associated with their own racial and ethnic group or with individuals of a mixed background of various minority groups and marginalized whites. People who were not of the same race or ethnic group encountered difficulty in developing friendships. I researched primarily Latino gangs that mirrored my ethnicity, but there were black, Native American, and Asian members in several of these groups. Latino and African American past and present experiences with racism made it more difficult for whites to join these groups. Whites were perceived as having more opportunities besides gangs. There were exceptions, however, especially for individuals who adopted Mexican culture: these members could be of any racial or ethnic background.

Group Adaptations

Gangs in Denver and Ogden were organized around social and family friendships. Gang members in both cities primarily used two types of organizational recruitment similar to those outlined by Sánchez-Jankowski (1991): fraternity and coercive. A fraternity type of recruitment entailed positive images of gang life, and so the individual needed to prove his or her worth to the gang in order to be admitted. The coercive type of recruitment was based on increasing membership quickly in preparation for future battles with rival gangs.

Approximately 50 percent of gang members in both Denver and Ogden belonged to an established gang that had been present in the neighborhood for several generations and used a fraternity type of recruitment. This closely resembles Klein's (1995) traditional gang typology and Valdez's (2007) barrio-territorial typology. Established gangs were composed of young and old family members, were seen as "cool," and were secure in the community. They maintained pressure to join the gang but only to fully integrate individuals into the collective camaraderie. Females participated in the gang through auxiliary groups.

Established gangs also had a larger number of members and associates because their ties into the community were multigenerational. The gang was an institution within the neighborhood, almost in the same way as a school or church but without a defined building. There were individuals who provided both charismatic and experience leadership but were not a central leader. The gang was designed to exist beyond any one individual. Since the core group was stable, there was rarely a reason to physically force associates into the gang. People had to prove they were worthy of being included. Everyone was influenced by the gang, but being a member obligated people to follow the core ideals. Ralph, a 19-year-old gang associate, said, "Even though I wasn't in it, they [the gang] considered me the same anyways. A lot of them thought I was anyways and I never really said no I'm not; I'm not in their gang. I think it was pretty lucky I never got pressured, and I wasn't threatened, or felt like I had to."

These fairly large numbers of members and associates made it difficult for law enforcement to discern membership. Because of this law enforcement usually labeled both groups (members and nonmembers) as being gang involved. Family and gang social networks were important in determining the level of peer pressure received to join a gang, but friendships sometimes could mediate these demands. The law enforcement response of treating both members and nonmembers as the same often pushed individuals who were not involved in the gang to feel that they had less to lose in terms of a social stigma since they were already treated as gang members.

The second type of gang did not fully exist prior to the 1985. Most gang disputes were between different neighborhoods of established gangs. Since this period demographic and structural shifts within the barrio have created new forms of rivalries. Some of these changes include the impact of incarceration, demolition of barrio housing, freeway growth, gentrification, immigration, and moving between states to find employment. This new form of gangs was found to be "fractured." None of the typologies given by Klein (1995) or Valdez (2007) match this description. Fractured gangs were composed of two types: those that were well-known but not integrated into the barrio (20 percent of members in Ogden and 40 percent in Denver), and those that were composed of small groups of friends with marginal ties to a historic barrio or within newly created barrios (20 percent of members in Ogden and 10 percent in Denver). These proportions were based on identifying gang members and gangs from interviews and fieldwork. Fractured gangs were more likely to use coercive recruitment methods, including physical threats and psychological intimidation. Individuals choosing not to succumb to the coercive pressure faced getting regularly beaten up or harassed.

In Denver and Ogden the first form of fractured gangs came from well-known groups from Los Angeles. Sureño gangs developed into the biggest rivals of established gangs. They were more likely to include a larger number of first-generation immigrants who spoke Spanish compared to the established gangs, whose members primarily spoke a mixture of English and Spanish. Since well-known gangs were seen as more notorious in the national media, they often attracted impressionable or excluded members who were seen as too Mexican by the established gangs. Mexican Americans are by far the largest number of Latinos in both Denver and Ogden. Victor, an undocumented 18-year-old, described how he joined a gang:

> I was like 13, when I went to middle school. People would talk shit to me, and it was always like five or four guys and I was all by myself. So that was when I like started hanging around with some homeboys and we decided to get in Sureños. [Why would they talk shit to you?] Probably because how I used to wear my clothes, like they use to tell me "wetback" and why you dress all poor and everything. Who was pretty much doing all of that? The West Siders.

Members of these gangs were the exception to the local rule since many of them were able to establish a section of the barrio as their territory without being pushed out by rivals, and hence they were a large factor in increasing the number of disputes. California-type gangs such as Sureños and primarily black gangs of Crips and Bloods were more numerous in Denver, but in both cities these gangs were working hard to become established in the community. The gang members often reported ties to the original gang neighborhood in another state, but most had only a loose to nonexistent association. There were occasionally disputes between gang members from the original gang city and the local imitation gangs with the same name. However, none of the well-known gangs was composed of a hierarchy leadership that allowed for checks and balances to keep nonendorsed gang members from using the name. Females within these gangs were integrated into the broader gang and were not found to exist within an auxiliary group.

Well-known fractured gangs have also confused law enforcement since these gangs use the names of notorious groups in larger cities. Many Gang Unit personnel viewed well-known gangs as more organizationally developed. The criminal organization image was regularly reported at gang conferences, at community forums, and in the list of RICO indictments. Maxson's (1998) research found gang migration to be inaccurate. According to her research, most gangs were not connected to gangs in other cities, and the ties were often only in name or possibly involved only one or two members who had moved from this location with their families. My interviews and fieldwork with several members of these gangs did not find drug connections or military hierarchies as depicted by law enforcement.

The second type of fractured gang was composed of small groups of friends similar in age and excluded from the established gangs. These fractured gangs were occasionally more racially and ethnically diverse, often including whites, Asians, blacks, Native Americans, and Mexicans in one gang. Other times they were composed of a single race or ethnicity and built around this identity. It was also within this type of fractured gang that I encountered a few separately run female gangs. The many social divisions in the city of Ogden made gangs based on small groups of friends more numerous. Jay, the 27-year-old ex–gang member, explained how his group got started:

> Basically, just where you happened to live in Ogden, you know the 'hood I lived in it was who lived around me and the people that lived in my neighborhood. A few houses down the road were black guys and we hung out ended up playin' ball together whatever smokin' some Chronic and we just hung out and partied together. So that got started, we got drunk and one of 'em said you'll be part of the [gang name omitted], this that. They didn't really jump me in or anything, it was just you're down you're cool you're part of the [gang omitted] now. That's pretty much how that got started, just became friends you know, just became boys.

About half these smaller gangs only looked out for each other and offered membership to close associates. They were more defensive and often faded with that cohort unless they could create a niche by establishing greater ties to a section of the barrio or an area not claimed by an established gang. They attempted to minimize the threat posed by established and well-known gangs by either active recruitment or admission based on friendship. Some small clique gangs have transitioned through the support of prison incarceration into semiestablished gangs. A few of these gangs have been created in prison and have been found to continue a presence in the community.

The third type of gang organization included the unlabeled gangsters. These youth did not fit the typical pattern of poverty or being a member of a minority group. They were primary composed of white youth from various economic backgrounds, depending on the social group. In Adler's (1993) six-year ethnographic study of upper-level white drug dealers in San Diego, California, she found a group of individuals operating in a way that presented a nonthreatening image (i.e., forms of white privilege), which allowed them to sell large amounts of cocaine. Two dominant groups in Ogden were cowboys and preppies. Of the two groups, preppies were more involved in drug dealing, whereas cowboys became involved in more territorial fights. Both groups had a set standard of clothing, symbols, and group identity. Cowboys were more likely to come from rural backgrounds and greater levels of poverty, whereas preppies were more middle class and educationally successful. The Gang Units in Ogden and Salt Lake City monitored the primarily white groups Straight Edge and Insane Clown Posse and several motorcycle and car clubs as gangs. Despite these observations, white gang membership was considered to be only 28 percent of the total gang membership in Ogden, which was a significant underrepresentation.

Some researchers (e.g., Klein 1995) do not typically label groups based on Aryan supremacy as gangs, but such a closed definition fails to include a wide array of groups who operate in similar ways to gangs. Many of these groups have a presence in the neighborhood, school, and prisons and therefore should not be so easily dismissed. I was unable to find female gang membership in the unlabeled gang type. Several of these gangs developed in Utah prisons, including Soldiers of Aryan Culture and Silent Aryan Warriors.

This chapter provided an overview of the different pathways involved in gaining access to a gang. Various factors, such as place of residence, family survival, gender socialization, school experiences, and friendship associations, continue to affect key decisions that later increase the chances of joining a gang. The experience of walking this line between association and membership is a very important form of social negotiation, which makes it surprising that more individuals from the neighborhood do not join gangs. When pressure becomes overwhelming, the type of gang that is available for an individual to choose for membership is affected by a variety of factors. Gangs in Denver and Ogden are influenced by generational descent, race and ethnicity, friendships, place of residence, and school.

Contemporary barrio neighborhoods exist in separate social space from that occupied by most whites. The barrio experience is one of poverty, lack of opportunity, and greater pressures to handle things without involving mainstream institutions. Many of the mainstream institutions have a very poor record with the Latino community, leading to individuals and families solving problems on their own, and hence many of the intense pressures to create informal social groups to handle these issues.

CHAPTER SIX

The Only Locotes Standing
The Persistence of Gang Ideals

In life, I often wondered whether I could completely escape the impact of gangs. As a researcher I tried to remain on the fringes, but the events of July 24, 2002, reminded me that the reach of gang drama was never too distant from those around me. The events that transpired on this day, like so many others, made me realize why it was so hard to depart from gang survival techniques. My older brother had recently been paroled from prison, and excitedly I wanted to show him a good time. We decided on Salt Lake City since there are a lot more things to do than in Ogden. After partying at a club, my two brothers, one of their girlfriends, and I began walking a short distance to our car. I had parked in an apartment complex the parking lot at the club was full. As we were walking we approached a young man sitting on a cement wall that marked the entrance of the apartment complex parking lot. We didn't pay any attention as we passed this individual. All of a sudden he shouted "Fuck Red" to my younger brother, who was wearing a red shirt. My younger brother said reactively, "Fuck you too," and the vato let out a whistle. My older brother and I later discussed that if we would have knocked out this vato in the beginning we could have prevented the whistle that brought seven individuals running up to confront us.

I told the young vato who continued whistling that there was no problem and we didn't have any desire to fight. Another young vato with a bald head ran up to me shirtless, displaying his tattoos, and asked me what the problem was. I said we don't want any problems and we were simply trying to leave in our vehicle. I had perfected a nonviolent approach while working in juvenile probation, in youth corrections, and as an ex–gang member working with ASAP. Instead I was met with a fist in my face from the individual who had whistled. Instinctively I responded by throwing a punch back and knocking the individual to the ground. As I walked over to reduce his threatening actions, I was pushed to the ground from the back. I was attempting to get up when a fist clocked me in the nose, slamming the back of my head into the cement. I tried to get back up but started to receive several kicks to the body. As this was developing, my older brother, recently released from prison, tied his shoelaces and began fighting as if he was a gladiator. My younger brother also became involved in the fight. Eventually I got up and once again repeated, "Peace, we don't want no problems!"

Repeating the theme of peace bought us a little time to walk over to the vehicle and get everyone in the car except for one of my brothers. I reached into the interior of my trunk and grabbed my gun case, in case things got out of control. I took a couple more punches in the face after I did this and said, "We are leaving." My older brother had been surrounded and told me to pick him up a little ways down the street. As he ran, I gunned the engine in order to pick him up and used my vehicle to cut off the individuals chasing him. He leaped over the hood of the car and slid into the passenger seat. As soon as he closed the door he told me that he had been cut as blood began pouring down his shirt. At this moment I became enraged at my continual emphasis on nonviolence and how it resulted in the injury of my brother. I was totally absorbed in a desire to have shot those fools. I rushed around the streets of Salt Lake City looking for the hospital, running every red light that attempted to stop my progress. When we arrived at the hospital my older brother was placed in an ambulance and taken to the emergency medical unit, which was at another location. The doctors began surgery to save his life and said if the cut had been a centimeter deeper it would have cut my brother's jugular and he would have died. As my brother lay in a hospital bed, I drove home to rest my eyes. I was most likely suffering from a concussion as my head had hit the concrete, and I slept horribly. The next morning I washed all the blood from the front and inside of my car. I wondered how this situation got so out of control. I felt like a failure.

The police did nothing to make any arrests, and this event in my life really affected my thinking about how to prevent violence through nonviolence or whether self-defense was a better strategy. The strategy of self-defense made me feel like a survivor, whereas this stand of nonviolence almost resulted in the death of my brother. As gangsters, fighting aggressively was how we survived to live another day, but choosing not to fight resulted in a different form of defeat—one that kept us around to *live another day—but victims of being in the wrong place at the wrong time. My two brothers fought while I tried to keep the peace and successfully negotiate an alternative outcome. Although I responded directly after being hit in the face, my subsequent inaction left both of my brothers in harm. I was trying so hard to keep from going to prison, but the drama in the streets kept calling me to deal with these problems.*

The idea of a chapter on the persistence of gang ideals developed from my research studies to figure out what exactly was holding gangs together. What was the glue? Why did individuals stay committed despite negative outcomes? My initial interest in creating a theoretical understanding of what holds gangs together reflects my interest in the work of Emile Durkheim (1951, 1984). Durkheim devoted his career to outlining different forms of cohesiveness and integration into society and theorizing how changes in regulation and control may affect individual behaviors. My goal was to discover the unwritten yet strictly observed patterns of behavior for gangs of Mexican descent in order to provide a pathway toward an alternative of greater community empowerment.

I report and analyze four important core ideals of gang culture: displaying loyalty, responding courageously to external threats; promoting and defending gang status; and maintaining a stoic attitude toward the negative consequences of gang life. These core ideals perform important functions in generating solidarity and maintaining the group, they possess a coherent internal logic, and they are functional for group members in the sense that they address real and specific social needs. However, they do so in contradictory ways that have serious negative consequences for group members and the wider community. For very important survival reasons, gangs adhere to certain core ideals that guide and structure members' behavior. These ideals and behaviors are continually reinforced by state-supported suppression, pointing to the need for grassroots solutions. The core ideals can be found in other social groups, but the key difference is the way in which they are manifested. They are a direct response to a particular colonized social setting.

Subordinated groups adapt to these colonial conditions in a variety of ways. The social context of racial and economic oppression fundamentally alters human relations. Fanon (1963:52) pinpointed the problem: "The colonized man will first manifest this aggressiveness which has been deposited in his bones against his own people." The reaction described by Fanon differs from the Mexicano forms of resistance seen during the late nineteenth and early twentieth centuries (Rosenbaum 1981). During this period, Rosenbaum argued, resistance against Anglos was displayed in four basic ways: withdrawal, accommodation, assimilation, and resistance. However, identification with the oppressor and false consciousness, reflective of colonialism, pushed some groups away from external resistance and into self-hatred. The propaganda of self-hate was furthered when the United States began applying one standard of justice for Anglos and another for Chicanos after the Treaty of Guadalupe Hidalgo (Mirandé 1987).

As an adaptation to colonization, gang membership moves barrio youth into a new social arena of possibilities. The gangs' core ideals create internal cohesion and respect for their members. Joining a gang means shifting one's image from that of a victim who weakly tolerates affronts to that of a strong and courageous warrior who reacts quickly to perceived disrespect. The individual becomes part of a larger collective with informal rules to guide behavior and enjoys solidarity and other benefits denied to nonmembers.

Nonetheless, with these benefits come costs, and the outcomes of gang membership are contradictory. Involvement in gangs greatly increases the chances for being victimized by rivals. Perceived membership also increases harassment by employers, law enforcement, and school officials. Individuals who are tagged by law enforcement officials for gang membership experience sentencing enhancements and decreased ability to move freely through the community as a result of gang injunctions. Possibly the greatest consequence is the enhanced dangers placed on family members and friends with no gang affiliations.

In addition, gangs typically do little to advance gender equality. Young women represent an estimated 4–10 percent of all gang members, according to law enforcement, or 8–38 percent based on self-reports (Moore and Hagedorn 2001). I found that the gangs, and gang ideals, in Denver and Ogden were primarily male dominated, consistent with the findings of other studies (Moore 1991; Portillos 1999). Portillos reported that the gang "simultaneously liberates and oppresses women" (239). The core ideals outlined below emerged from interviews with both males and females and therefore are not seen as gender specific. However, Latinas reported that males were more likely than females to be pressured to attain and accomplish these ideals. In the following discussion, gender differences are included to bring greater attention to patriarchy and paternalism as manifested (and sometimes challenged) within gangs.

Displaying Loyalty

The first core ideal, displaying loyalty ("I got your back"), is formed through opposition and multiple marginality encountered over time. Before they even enter a gang, barrio youth experience mainstream white society's opposition to individuals of Mexican descent in the form of classism, nativism, and racism displayed by bullies, rivals, teachers, and police, among others. This solidifies their attachment to the gang and ensures a common cause among members. Most of the gang members I interviewed decided to join a gang in order to counter victimization and create their own internal cohesion. The gang demands faithfulness to its ideals because such loyalty is the foundation for the group's formation and its continued existence. Males and females uphold this ideal equally, yet the Latinas I interviewed were more likely to be associates than members.

The gang initiation process, which serves the important function of changing victims into protagonists, ironically begins with a victimization ceremony that symbolizes the beginning of a new persona. Undergoing this initiation is the most important way of proving one's loyalty. The most common way of joining a gang is to be jumped in. While Vigil (1988) found that only people who were peripherally or temporarily involved in the gang were jumped in, in Denver and Ogden 90 percent of gang members (70 of 77) entered this way. As in the study by Sánchez-Jankowski (1991), joining a gang was a two-way decision involving both established and prospective members. Mexican Americans who subjected themselves to an adrenaline-fueled beating affirmed their switch from gang wannabe (acting and dressing the part) to gang member by overcoming their physical and mental fears. Each gang's jump-in was different in duration, knock-downs, and opponents. The initiation occasionally broke jaws, noses, or ribs or knocked out teeth, but most recruits did not require hospital treatment. The demonstration of this loyalty is present in other socially organized groups, such as fraternities, military, and criminal justice agencies, but the difference lies in the form of validation.

Less common ways of acquiring gang membership include being "grandfathered in" or "sexed in." The former applied to a few people in Denver and Ogden who were active leaders (in some cases the original founders) of their gangs and had longtime involvement or family members in the gang, or both. Though they did not have to pass through an initiation, they should not be confused with gang associates, who also lacked initiation. Finally, there were a few fractured gangs that initiated young women by coercing them, often with alcohol or drugs, into having sex with the same number of gang members required for a jump-in. In the status hierarchy young women who were associates and members treated those who were sexed-in as much lower, and the latter were often despised (Miller 2001; Portillos 1999). The powerful negative labeling makes being sexed-in an infrequent occurrence, and none of the people I interviewed reported joining a gang through this type of initiation.[1] Latinas were more likely to report that family members expected them to be loyal to the gang but also pressured them not to join. Dominique, a 23-year-old gang associate from Ogden, had several brothers involved in the gang:

> I think my brothers did a good job of not wanting me to be a part of that, but at the same time I was supposed to back 'em up if a female came up to them, you know what I mean? They were like, "No, you stay away from it. No, don't go party with my friends." And they made sure that I didn't go into that environment, and they would always pressure me. "No, you are going to go to school. You are a female. This is not a thing for a female. Forget about everyone else involved, all the other girls. Be a lady, don't be a pig." [Did you see much difference between the males and females?] Either the females were going out or having kids with the males so the females have respect regardless of what actions they took so it didn't matter. I think they got respect within that group. [Were the women just as down as the guys?] Yeah, I think so, if not more vicious. They were the ones willing to pull out a screwdriver or a bat, you know what I mean. Jump somebody more than the guys. A guy would rather go toes one on one. [What was their role?] Maybe the backbone. The support. Everyone likes to have a cheerleader I guess. That's the way I look at it. Yeah, I think so, they [females] were there to just pat them [males] on the back—"Oh, you did a good job."

Dominique's two brothers were high-ranking gang members, and people in the barrio often assumed that Dominique herself was one of the active females within the gang. She was very loyal and dedicated to the gang despite her brothers' attempts to keep her away from this lifestyle.

Initiation serves a variety of purposes, from increasing solidarity, en-suring commitment, and proving toughness to warning onlookers of the consequences for anyone who attempts to challenge the gang. It con-verts an individual from a potential victim of the gang into someone embraced and protected by the group, and it obligates the new mem-ber to remain loyal to the gang despite possible consequences. Gang members—however they entered the gang—do not receive a membership card, plaque, trophy, or anything material to prove their adherence. Only fellow gang members can validate a successful initiation. Nite Owl, the 17-year-old from Denver, described how the gang's attitude toward him changed once he became a member: "They gave me more respect. I think when I was not in [the gang] they would tell me, come on get in it and everything. So now when I got in they respect me more. When I needed some help, they were always there for me and everything. They were like my brothers to me. I've known them since a long time ago." Nite Owl's description is consistent with the reports of many other respondents who described psychological and relational changes after joining a gang.

Gang members' overall experiences with violent victimizations and deaths led to the perception that the outcomes of conflicts are unpre-dictable, but that the best defense includes having fellow gang members present as often as possible. Members spend most of their time in small groups of close gang friends and associates whose loyalty is known and proven. Internal gang problems are defused through the maintenance of smaller groups that allow differences and special friendships to coexist within the gang. These smaller groups come together for large fights or parties. When members support one another it enhances cohesion, but when support falters, perhaps because of fear, a simple fight can get out of control. Although gang killings are infrequent, the rate of homicides greatly surpasses the general population in both Ogden and Denver.

The main punitive policies designed to eliminate gangs have only enhanced gang loyalty. Suppression tactics used by Gang Units, zero-tolerance gang enforcement, and gang ordinances stigmatize the entire Latino community as gangsters and criminals and reinforce perceptions of opposition and exclusion. This serves to perpetuate gangs. The major-ity of gang bonding takes place in response to external opposition, but gang members actively seek each other's company to prepare for future conflicts and to challenge second-class treatment. Ritualized initiation achieves the initial break with the recruit's previous identity and shifts him or her into a new level of friendships and experiences. Loyalty to the gang builds over time, but certain events help solidify the attachment Latino gang members share with each other. During criminal investigations, law enforcement agencies particularly attempt to disrupt this solidarity for their own gain, which leads to internal gang feuds and punishments enacted against violators.

Displaying loyalty leads to what I call "entrenched solidarity," a stronger form of social solidarity than described by Durkheim (1984). Durkheim focused on social solidarity in the context of a just and equal society that maintains a collective consciousness shared by everyone. Specific changes in societies can place pressure on cohesion and solidarity, leading in turn to egoistic, altruistic, anomic, and fatalistic adaptations and responses (Durkheim 1951). The opposition by the state to the Latino community continually demonstrates injustice that serves to split one collective identity into various fragments. Such experiences match more closely the fatalistic adaptation, which Durkheim considered rare in the late 1800s. According to Durkheim, "fatalistic" is defined as the social solidarity created in response to "excessive regulation, that of persons with futures pitilessly blocked and passions violently chocked by oppressive discipline" (1951:276). Such a definition matches more closely the colonial situation and how individuals facing such overwhelming obstacles need to create greater forms of resistance. Entrenched solidarity demands that gang members display loyalty despite instances of wrongful and shameful behavior from some fellow members of the gang.

Responding Courageously to External Threats

Responding courageously to external threats ("putting in work") has two strategic purposes: to control situations with aggressive behavior and to take advantage of punitive actions by the state to provide status enhancement opportunities for individual gang members. Part of this strategy manifests as pressure among peers to contest second-class treatment. The suffering endured by Latino youth in the barrio pushes some to hide their internal pain and inflict pain on others. Through gang activity, Latinos begin to challenge the degradation imposed on the barrio by mainstream society. The gang members' ability to dominate their peers and community symbolically proves that they are not inferior or controlled by others. They can do whatever they want.

Socioeconomically disadvantaged neighborhoods experience not only higher rates of interpersonal violence (Krivo and Peterson 1996; Krivo, Peterson, and Kuhl 2009; Kubrin and Weitzer 2003; Phillips 2002; Sampson and Wilson 1995) but also increased aggressiveness and violence from agents of the criminal justice system in the forms of brutality, deadly force, and punitive controls (Rodriguez 2003; Wilderson 2003). Such violent settings are not conducive to efforts to heal one's own pain and suffering. Gang members with troubled families, or those raised in state institutions, often lack hope for an alternative future. Victimization changes people's perceptions and beliefs about others in society, highlighting the predatory potential of others (Fischer 1984; MacMillan 2001). Witnessing violence increases aggressive behavior and depression (Gorman-Smith and Tolan 1998; Moses 1999). Rodney, a 34-year-old former gang associate from Denver, reported:

> A lot of people that end up in gangs they don't see no hope, no opportunity, no future. That usually starts in the home. I first moved in here and moved into the projects. It's easy to lose hope living in the projects. It's not easy to see yourself getting up out of that situation and so you live day to day. For those individuals who maintain themselves outside of it, [it's] only because of that positive influence at home. Then, different dispositions you know. Some people are inclined toward violence. I was. I had a lot of anger; you know what I'm saying, from my childhood and what was going on in my life, especially with my father. That really pushed me to become involved with gangs and drugs. Anything that was criminality was a lure to me. The police, they enforce the law, they kill my dad, then I am going to break the law and antagonize it. So you get somebody who has been in them situations and circumstances, I could see them avoiding, but if I looked back on my middle and high school years, I would say a small percentage can avoid the gang violence altogether. I would say most of them are either bookworms or athletes.

Cyclone, a 25-year-old former gang member and ex-con from Ogden, said:

> Fourteen, 15, I got locked up in Vegas for strong-arm robbery and I went to jail, and that's when me and my parents started conflicting

more and they started noticing what I was doing at that age. And I mean it was just hard for them to see why I was doing what I was doing, but at the same time it was hard for me to see why they weren't involved in my life. So I wanted a new life, I didn't want my parents anymore. I totally rebelled and just continued to screw up. Everything I was doing was more or less to hurt somebody or to take from somebody or to hurt myself in a sense also. I've seen and done almost everything that people watch on movies or hear about. I used to think hurting people would be fun. Just to see if I could hurt them or if they could hurt me, and when you are young and you think you're that tough you start testing it.

Both Rodney and Cyclone felt a sense of anger and confusion at the reality of their situation of troubled homes, drugs and alcohol, police violence, and incarceration experiences within the barrio. They shared a growing rage with no clear opponent to combat. Gang membership would later create targets that allowed them to deal with this internalized suffering.

Most gang members I interviewed combined gang activities with alcohol and drug abuse. This helped alleviate internal pain, fear, and questioning. Ehrenreich's (1997) research on war found reference to the use of drugs and alcohol in many cultures to impel people to fight. Alcohol, the most frequently used drug, is known to increase violent behavior and reduce inhibitions (Moore 1991; Parker and Auerhahn 1998; Sánchez-Jankowski 1991; Vigil 1988).

The ability to control situations and their subsequent consequences is a motivation for showing a courageous response to external threats. Several researchers report that inner-city residents' involvement with interpersonal violence relates to issues of honor, respect, and status (Anderson 1999; Horowitz 1983; Hughes and Short 2005; Luckenbill and Doyle 1989; Sánchez-Jankowski 1991). In Denver and Ogden achieving these values requires gang members to actively pursue status-enhancing interactions. To get respect, gang members said, one needs to be a "badass," "fight anybody," "gain control," "hold their own," "make money," "outdo everyone else with negative," and "show dedication." The more gang activity, the higher the status of the individual and the more elevated the position of the collective gang. Rodney, the former gang associate from Denver, reported:

> Gangs run the streets, man. The politicians and the lawyers, and teach-
> ers, and all that mess, they run society, but gangs run the streets, and
> either you respect them and survive, or you end up a victim. If you
> think that you don't have to deal with 'em [you're] a fool because there
> is a whole different set of values and norms within a certain section of
> the community that identify with the gang bangers.

Rodney was superconfident when he described the power of gangs. I
agreed, as I had never before seen a group within the barrio that could
generate such a whirlwind of power and destruction.

Black (1983) pioneered the idea that responding to grievances through
violence or illegal behavior may be a form of self-help. He argued that
individuals who are denied equality under the law attempt to pursue justice by different means. Consistent with this, Anderson (1999) found that
inner-city residents' lack of faith in mainstream institutions and negative
treatment by the police and judicial system creates a "code of the street."
These residents organize informal social control mechanisms in order to
gain respect despite the lack of mainstream institutional support. Felson
and Steadman (1983) reported that homicide victims are more likely to
display a weapon, to be intoxicated, and to be more aggressive in conflicts, which makes offenders more violent in response, and they argue
that responding violently can often be a strategic move to defend against
victimization. In Denver and Ogden the biggest targets for confrontation
are rival gang members. Rivals can be anywhere, since gang neighborhoods often border or overlap one another. Valdez, Cepeda, and Kaplan (2009) found most gang homicides in San Antonio were between
members of gangs bordering the same neighborhood. Since rival gang
members adhere to the same core ideals, both groups understand that
whoever acts first can gain the upper hand in a confrontation.

Street skills, such as surveying the field (to look for distinguishing
clothing or people), monitoring demeanors (to ascertain when a fight
might be about to happen), and being prepared to fight greatly enhance
gang members' odds for living another day. Gang members in a group
are likely to feed off friends in picking up cues of disrespect that could
justify a group attack. The core ideals hold that situations that are demeaning, in the eyes of the gang, require a response. Physical retaliation shuts people up most effectively and provides closure to perceived
episode of disrespect. People perceived as unaffiliated with the gang are

often given more in defusing volatile encounters, but, consistent with findings by Horowitz (1983), sensitivity is especially keen in public situations, and how people respond reflects honor or dishonor on the gang. Gang members are constantly required to define their situations and the social relations between themselves and those they encounter, and they survive by accurately assessing the potential threat of places and people. J-Dog, a 25-year-old ex-con and prison gang member from Denver, reported:

> You got to not be a bitch and let people disrespect you. You go get at 'em or your boys are goin' to get at you, and let you know, because it makes you guys look weak if someone is talking shit to you and you don't do nothing or say nothing, then that makes your whole team look weak. [What if you let it slide?] If it happens once it is just going to keep going like that, you know what I mean. People are just going to start diggin' at you and word gets out. Ahh these fools are weak, they don't even back their shit up.

Six months after this interview J-Dog was back in prison for stealing cars. He had lived a large part of his life shuttling back and forth between juvenile corrections, jail, and prison, with only brief periods of nonincarceration. He never was able to hold down a steady job, and he lacked close relationships with his immediate family.

The core ideal of putting in work shows interesting gender differences. Aggressive male behavior aids survival (Vigil 1988), but as my research found, aggressive female behavior and preventing unwanted pregnancies also aid in survival. Young women are actively engaged in controlling situations. Males and females often attempt to enhance their gang status within and outside their own gender group. If Latinas join males, it is usually as a driver or lookout, but rarely as co-collaborators in gang pursuits. Gang-involved women usually confront other young women more so than young men. This does not mean women were afraid to challenge young men, as I occasionally observed. However, males are socialized to protect women, and thus women are not viewed as targets for physical violence but rather as potential interests for short-term relationships. Young women seemed to target their rage against other women, as demonstrated in the following observations. At ASAP, tensions were often high since the group brought members from rival gangs together in one room. Rosa, an 18-year-old woman who had been attending the group off and on for three years, reported that one weekend a group of North Siders rolled up on her and they all got out to jump her, but her homie pulled a couple of girls off her, and she began "fucking" them up. She said the male members of the rival gang simply sat in their car and watched. She said she always had love for her gang (Sureños) and was trying to change her behavior, but that some people were just asking for trouble. Shortly after Rosa described beating up some North Siders, Cindy, a 15-year-old member of a North Side gang, announced that she was not afraid to shoot someone. She didn't care about the consequences that such behavior could have for others. She reported that she had chosen a gangster life rather than a life of getting pregnant and having kids like her friends. Both the young women and young men at this ASAP gathering constantly asserted that they could not allow anyone to disrespect them and that the way to resolve this issue was through violence. Jones (2004) reported that similar to their male counterparts, young women in inner-city social environments perceive violence as a tool to mediate the physical vulnerability they experience within their own lives.

The second way of responding courageously to external threats is by credentializing prison. Incarceration—the main state response to crime in Colorado and Utah—proves that a gang member has put in work. Males are more likely to experience incarceration than females. Both males and females who enter prison are temporarily removed from their urban social environment and placed in a confined setting where they are separated from family and friends. Inmates must learn how to operate in another social world, one where issues of respect and intimidation are just as salient as they are on the street. In addition, prison intensifies racial and ethnic rivalries. Latinos make up a higher proportion of the prison population than whites or blacks in both states and are seen as having the most power. Many gang members continue their gang membership in prison and even increase their networking with other members of gangs. Incarceration also pushes people who were not previously members of a gang to join one in order to not be on their own. Felipe, a 17-year-old youth incarcerated in a secure facility, described to me his gangsterism: "I ain't no wanksta. I be dropping fools [he makes the image of shooting two handguns]. A lot of these fools out here try and act like they are a gangster but they haven't shot nobody, they have no clue what it's about. They haven't been locked up. You can look at my record. I'll be a Damu [Blood] until the day I die." Felipe learned to manage himself during his incapacitation. His tough bravado prevented others from bullying him.

D-loc made the following comment when I asked what effect prison has:

> Prison makes gang members. I know a bunch of people that are goin' to jail, detention, prison. They weren't even gang members when they went in, but they're coming out gang members, they're coming out hard-core. I remember a lot of the kids that went to detention and shit when I was a teenager or younger, they went in for some stupid little shit and came out full-fledged gang members. So the prison, one thing that is networking and happening in the prison, is prisoners using and abusing each other. It's not like the prison is rehabilitating them or trying to make better human beings or making them healthier or anything, trying to educate them to be profound or outstanding leaders, or civic community organizers in the society. They're housing them like cattle.

Based on my interviews with incarcerated youth and adults on parole, prison was exactly as Felipe and D-loc described it. In the social environment of the prison, physical force was valued above the ability to retreat or negotiate through words. Prison was making better gangsters.

People who had been incarcerated were respected for putting in work, and they also were perceived to have underworld insight into how to organize and take the gang toward higher levels of sophistication. The core ideals of gangs were reinforced by the convict mentality that called for honoring obligations and not snitching. Rodney reported:

> I think it [gang lifestyle] is more powerful now because it is organized. Back then our generation partied. The 35- or 40-year-old, maybe 45 years old, back then was a teenager [or] a young adult and didn't have the same cognitive abilities to actually organize and put things in order. It was sporadic. [What are some of the big gangs you see out here now?] The Mexican gangs are the biggest thing going. GKIs [Gallant Knights Insane or Gangsters Killing Incas], who runs the prison, runs the streets. In the prisons in Colorado the GKIs are it. [How do you think they got to that level?] Murder. And murdering each other. They are the biggest cut-throat gang there is out of all of them. If you

cross them they will kill you quick and if you don't cross 'em they will kill you quick.

Although the majority of gang members who left prison simply wanted to achieve a conventional lifestyle, the gangs that were seen by inner-city residents as the most notorious became this way because they were able to link the streets with prison. All the gangs that received federal racketeering indictments in Denver had intertwined prison and street life. The racketeering charges were significantly targeted against several gangs' involvement in drug distribution networks.

Howell and Gleason (1999) found that their law enforcement respondents believed that 43 percent of drug sales in their jurisdictions involved gang members, of which the majority were primarily at a lower distribution level. Gangs responded to the poverty that most members experienced by figuring out ways to make money. Drug dealing was often perceived as a way to accomplish this. However, the fluctuating highs and lows made drug dealing primarily an individual pursuit rather than a gang activity (Klein 1995; Vigil 1988). In Denver and Ogden drug dealing was not a gang enterprise, yet gang members were able to access a broader social network of users and suppliers along with increased protection. Gang members and non–gang members reported very mixed opinions as to which individuals were more involved in drug dealing. Based on the entire interviews, only 24 percent of these individuals reported having been known to sell drugs at least one time. Field observations demonstrated that there was a 50/50 split as to whether they were a gang member or not a member. Of sellers in Ogden, only 35 percent (9 of 26) had devoted a year or longer to selling. Thus only 12 percent of Ogden gang members or gang associates (9 of 77) had devoted a year or longer to selling drugs. The individuals who distributed drugs were overwhelmingly male, with only one female drug dealer who sold drugs for longer than a year.

Many gang members tried to sell drugs, but not everyone was good at dealing. Some gang members used too much of their drugs, which reduced profits. Some gang members ripped off drug dealers when loaned a small portion of drugs (i.e., fronting), which eliminated the possibility of future business. Gang members with connections to drug dealers outside the country had the potential to make more money and attain an elevated status. Drug connections with the border towns in Mexico were important. Sporadic drug dealers occasionally spent the quick money from drugs unwisely on flashy cars, clothes, jewelry, and so forth. Drug dealing required good money-management skills, but factors outside gang members' control often had a significant impact. The high-crime neighborhoods increased the chances of gang members getting robbed or their place of residence getting burglarized. Moreover, the police were often a constant presence whether the individual of interest was engaging in legal or illegal activity. The racial and ethnic stereotypes in conjunction with criminal justice surveillance were not conducive to the distribution of drugs.[2]

Responding courageously to external threats has a counterproductive side. The perceived threat to the gang becomes not structural racism but the *ese* or *loca* on the other side of town. Individuals who are encountering the same struggles in dealing with barrio colonization are led to believe that they are each other's enemies instead of feeling united in confronting a common adversary. The early military tactics of divide and conquer and subduing an enemy without fighting (Sun Tzu 1963) are both hastening the downfall of the Chicano community. The manifestations of structural racism and advanced colonization allow the state to reign with supremacy.

Promoting and Defending Gang Status

The third ideal, promoting and defending gang status ("representing the gang"), is lived daily by glorifying and protecting the gang's symbols and status. Representing is encouraged by members and spoken about with pride. Group affiliation often entails embracing the external signs of the group, such as cars, dress, graffiti, kinesics, nicknames, parties, speech, and tattoos (Vigil 1988). According to my research, putting in work is fairly infrequent compared to representing, which is constant. Living the representation of the gang emphasizes a gang member's courage to stand alone and be a constant symbol and spokesperson.

Representing the gang means different things depending on the age of the member. For gang members in their teens or early twenties, representing means exhibiting the gang's symbols proudly—by wearing certain clothing, hitting people up (throwing up gang signs or calling out gang names), spraying graffiti, and getting tattoos. This can be provocative, bringing increased police oversight as well as hatred from rivals. Garot (2010) devoted his entire book to understanding the rituals by which youth demonstrate and perform their gang identities. By the time young members grow to adulthood, their focus often transitions from representing to defending the gang's image and status (Horowitz 1983). Image defenders do not intentionally provoke violent situations, but they expect others to respect their personal space. Sampson and Laub (2003) reported that even the most active criminal offenders reduce their levels of offending with age, particularly by the middle adult years. In Denver and Ogden, by the time Latino gang members have matured out of the prime gang-banging years (14 to 24), representing entails a more calculated form of promotion since they no longer desire undue attention. D-loc commented:

> So in all of our communities these people that are unrecognized found an avenue to be heard. And the gang movement made people be heard. It gave our children [a way] to be heard. It might not have been heard in the best way, but it was a cry for help. It was a cry for attention. It was a cry that there was a problem here in our community. And if it wasn't for our young people, our children killing and shooting and blastin' motherfuckers, our community wouldn't get heard, and we're only heard when these things happen. . . . Those kids don't know what they are, they don't know exactly why or how it is that they came to be in the position that they're in now—facin' prison, facin' their legs being cut off, facin' living in a wheelchair, having a colostomy bag hanging off the side of them that they take a shit in for the rest of their life. They don't know why all of these things are happening around them, they don't know why they're being pushed out of school, why they're dropping out of school, why they're getting pregnant, why they're using drugs. . . . They don't know why these things are the way they are in their community, but when they start shootin', and showing their fear and their hurt, and their pain and their depression, well then someone hears about it in our community.

D-loc described how putting in work can take on a life of its own after the fact in the form of representation. Gang members and associates can describe with pride and strategy the wars that have been fought. Violence and self-destruction have become the only voice that receives a response. Representation is reflected in shows such as *Gangland*. A varying number of incidents are dramatized and etched in stone to create an overall threatening image of particular gangs.

Differences between males and females are often displayed in relation to this core ideal. Young men strictly maintain gangster attire, whereas young women might simply dress in tight-fitting clothing. Both males and females use gang signs and markings on notebooks, but males are more likely to spray-paint graffiti on walls or buildings. Young women occasionally have gang tattoos, but none I met had tattoos on the face, head, or full arm, as was common with male members.

As with all the ideals, prison changes these expectations. Maintaining honor and respect becomes even more important in prison. Incarcerated gang members often acquire a very intimidating demeanor through injuries (stabbings and gunshot wounds, as long as not debilitating), size (bodybuilding), and tattoos. Olguin (1997) suggested that tattooed brown prisoners' bodies symbolically challenge the experience of domination through peonage, proletarianzation, and mass incarceration. Tattoos create a material and symbolic link to the prisoner's community and to his people (*la raza*). In Denver and Ogden, these tattoos reference the gang, barrio, culture, or religion and highlight the struggle for survival. The tattoos and scars that mark gang members' bodies attest to the pains of life. The more battle scars, the more an individual has been physically tested. Scars are a living record of the drama of victimization and perpetration.

Older gang members often say, "I don't bang anymore [or "put in work"], but I'll always represent" [or "be down for the gang"]. In Denver and Ogden the older gang members are known as the OGs or *veteranos* and are admired by the younger members. But they are still required to maintain face, and issues of disrespect are watched closely. Gang members must always stand up for themselves and put their lives on the line to maintain their honor. Tone, a 28-year-old ex-convict, emphasized that demeaning comments require a response:

> [Even the words stuff would tear you around too huh . . . not just being beat up?] Oh yeah, people remember things . . . like if someone was to call another person a rat, or a punk, that's like the two worst things you can say to a person. And if that person doesn't do nothing, then that's what people consider you are. [What are you supposed to do about it?] You gotta fight . . . you got to stand up for your name.

Life in prison and within the gang established a reputation known to very few outside these social networks. Tone had a very well respected name inside prison that allowed him tremendous respect and reverence, but on the streets this deference to his status was unknown. It is for these reasons of status that young gang members often attempt to steal the reputation of OGs and *veteranos* in an attempt to rise more quickly up the ladder.

A policy that takes advantage of this core ideal will seek to reduce the image promotion of the gang and substitute promotion of cultural pride. The core ideal of representing the gang involves symbolic expressions of allegiance to a group that has encountered enormous external opposition, and thus members weathered the storm by taking events and circumstances and inscribing them on their bodies through scars and tattoos. Once obtained, these markers remained until death.[3] It is understandable how attempts to reduce image promotion can prevent increased opportunities to "put in work." Several antigang policies have attempted to reduce or eliminate gang clothing or colors, but this is usually viewed as another example of mainstream society enforcing its values on barrio residents based on the actions of a small number of gang-involved individuals. Although this may have a situational or short-term impact for strangers, it does not remove the root cause of resorting to such image promotion. Gangs can always improvise and create new identifiers. Status symbols may be expressions that are part of human nature and thus difficult to disrupt or alter, and therefore efforts designed specifically around this core ideal appear more futile. Gang-member perceptions both real and unreal often shape encounters with perceived rivals, and once such actions are set in motion, face saving requires acting as if the perception was real, which often can result in individuals outside gangs becoming a victim.

Maintaining a Stoic Attitude Toward Gang Life

The fourth core ideal, maintaining a stoic attitude ("smile now, cry later"), recognizes that the excitement, adventures, and rewards available to gang members now will lead to negative and often unintended consequences in the future. The "smile now" ethic is surprisingly unexplored in the gang literature. What is traditionally referred to as originating from Greek theater highlights the duality of life, blending itself into the teaching of the Catholic Church and its version of fatalism. For barrio youth, gang membership is a more powerful and alluring identity than he or she previously enjoyed, and this pushes youths to trade up to a more prestigious persona by shunning people and roles from their pregang lives. Indeed, this process evokes the "gloried selves" described by Adler and Adler (1991) in connection with college athletes. According to these authors, the reputation, status, and fan worship accorded players lead them to form a centralized identity blindly narrowed toward one set of expectations: an engulfed self. Once this identity had been shaped, it is hard to shed.

In the gang world the media attention and street respect accorded gang members lead to a gloried self that includes feelings of importance. Gang members report overcoming obstacles and doing things denied to the majority of people from their background. Their lifestyles might include material possessions such as cars, money, and guns. The respect and fear they command on the street brings power.

There is a downside, however, as gang members taking on these gloried aspects experience what Adler and Adler describe as self-immediacy, self-detachment, and diminished awareness. Individuals who develop a gloried self may lose future orientation as they are swept up in the intensity of their present excitement, importance, and respect. In Denver and Ogden this present orientation is exacerbated by the bleak prospects for urban Latinos. Gang members seize the moment because in these socioeconomically deprived contexts there is little hope for living conventional lives as legitimately employed workers.

To smile now means appreciating the good life through barbecues, birthdays, quinceañeras, parties, picnics, and other social get-togethers that bring together gang members and associates and people from the larger community. Barrio residents are the primary support group for the gang. The image of the gang is constantly shaped by activities, rumors, and police or media attention that establish gang members as local celebrities. This celebrity also helps male gang members attract women. Rebellon and Manasse contend that "delinquency increases dating outcomes by making the delinquent more attractive to prospective mates" (2004:382). In short, gang members enjoy a sense of accomplishment, prestige, and belonging that contrasts to their life before the gang, when barrio residents of Mexican descent were virtually invisible. Smile now often creates a sense of attraction for nongang members: a perception that this lifestyle can improve life chances.

The other side of this ideal, "cry later," refers to the consequences of gang life. The gang members I interviewed averaged two to three years of active gang involvement. The expected outcomes of this lifestyle include pain, prison, and death. The pain comes from fighting and from being unable to change one's impoverished and victimizing surroundings over time. The gang wars never cease, and the drama never abates. Gang members victimize their own communities: stealing from people who are already poor, shooting people who are already disadvantaged and stigmatized. Gang members rationalize this behavior by creating differences between their gang and rivals: "they wear an ugly color," "they're scandalous," "from the wrong neighborhood," "wetbacks," and so forth. Still, most gang members' consciences eventually begin to bother them because victimizing other barrio residents was not the original purpose of joining. But they face a dilemma because there is no comparable social arena in the barrio in which to maintain the gloried self. In many ways, improving life chances requires ensuring the downfall of others in same social setting.

Gang members expect prison for their criminal or delinquent activities and for challenging their status in life, yet they find it difficult to do time and watch family members suffer. Mateo, a 17-year-old gang member serving a year in youth corrections, told me that being good (assimilating) was just not for him. He was a member of one of the country's largest Mexican gangs. I tried to help him, as he was outgoing and a leader and had a lot of potential. He felt proud of being considered a potential OG at the lockup facility but humbly said that he was unsure whether he wanted all the attention. He showed me around his "house," a four-by-seven-foot room with pictures of friends and family on his desk and a little metal bed on the side of the wall. He rarely received mail or visits, though he sent many letters out. He was alone. His life was similar to so many others that I observed.

While individuals in gangs vicariously learn the consequences for being caught for violating the law, the damages brought forth through criminalization are rapidly changing and becoming more punitive than in the past. Many individuals believe they will shed their criminal identity once they have served their sentence or completed their court-ordered therapy. The majority of the crimes committed by gang members do not receive a life sentence, but as misdemeanors or felonies they remain a constant stigma etched upon members' lives. A criminal record influences employment and housing options and treatment by law enforcement. In reality, ex-convicts find that it is impossible to completely overcome criminal labeling: the stereotypes remain for life.

As prisoners hone skills to deal with intimidation in a correctional facility, they lose the skills needed to survive outside prison walls and fit into mainstream society. Cyclone, the 25-year-old ex-inmate and prison gang member, said:

> I did five years altogether in prison and if I could take back some of the things I would. It is pretty hard when you think about it. I have been off parole, out of prison for a few years, and yet it still is hard for me to maintain a job without getting looked at funny. It's hard for me to be around people now because I am so confined to myself because of prison. . . . They told me I was guilty when I defended myself so I realized, oh yeah, I am guilty, but what they are guilty of is more or less taking my soul, my pride. They took me from me my family, everything. I was misrepresented. I didn't know nothing about the law. Now it's weird because they make you do all of these programs so when you get back into society [you] adapt, but they don't think about the mental stress that it causes somebody. How much hurt, how much pain, or the people's family, or what goes on. Yeah you committed a crime, but sometimes that crime was necessary. I mean if you have to defend yourself you are going to do it. I lost my family because I defended myself and ended up in prison, and that's where I became affiliated with gangs, and that was my new family. It felt like I had lost everything. It makes it hard. You have friends but you lose. You lose your friends that are not locked up because they look at you like you're a bad person now, they don't want to be around you, or it's hard to be around your family because they don't know if you are going to hurt them or be gone, or if they are going to have trouble at their house, if their house is going to get shot at, or if you're going to end up dead. It's hard for me to be around my kids, it's hard for me to be around new people that I have never met, big crowds. I walk out my door and look both ways like crossing a street.

Several years have passed since these original interviews with Cyclone. Negotiating a life outside the barrio and gang proved an overwhelming challenge for him. Moving away helped for a period of time, but one day upon his return to the barrio he and some friends allegedly became involved in a dispute with another man. The man was severely beaten and almost died. The label of "criminal" was something Cyclone couldn't escape in attempting to create a new path of opportunity. I consider

Cyclone one of my best friends, so it is very disappointing to hear about these unfortunate circumstances.

Although most gang members who join and remain in a gang know the typical consequences of involvement, very few recognize the dangers faced by members of their own gang. The gangs in Denver and Ogden operate under informal behavior codes that are discussed and that all members are expected to follow. Many of the rules are prohibitions: against associating with or dating rival gang members or associates, disregarding a directive, not spending enough time with the gang, talking bad about the gang or its members, appearing soft, lacking in courage, exhibiting weakness, not representing, and many other infractions both real and imagined.

Anne, the 24-year-old former gang associate, reported that girl gang members have their own behaviors that violate gang rules:

> Girls don't like to be talked about. Especially from our friends, who we think are our friends. [Like good or bad things?] I think both good or bad. We just didn't like to be talked about. The guys, I think, there was a lot of things they could get in trouble for, you know, hanging out with, or being seen with someone else, or they needed you to go to them for something and you didn't go. I think there is a lot more things with guys than with girls. [What would happen then if somebody would disrespect one of the girls in the gang?] They, we, would confront them. I remember this one time, this girl was talking about a couple of girls behind their back and they were hearing about it and so they confronted her. You know they went up to her, confronted her, and she didn't deny that she was, but she didn't admit to it either. She was like, well people are going to talk, whatever, and they just confronted her and if they heard it again that there was something, that it was going to be dealt with, you know, it wasn't something they weren't going to let go. . . . I knew better to talk about nobody, I didn't want to get an ass kickin'.

The longer Anne participated in the gang lifestyle, the more she struggled to break away. Internal feuds among women because of boyfriends make it difficult for gang-associated girls to maintain a strong allegiance with one another. Young women who become emotionally close to actively gang-involved men often experience the quick demise and destruction of their boyfriends by way of victimization, incarceration, or death.

Additionally, dating relationships within the barrio occasionally bring young women into conflicts with their own gang for dating rivals. Most of the young women interviewed reported that they and their girlfriends did not want their kids to join a gang.

Scott (2004) articulated best many of the contradictions of gang life, noting that gangs form to fight oppression and end up reproducing and inflicting that same oppression on their members. When I was a gang member I endured many instances of disrespect and abuse from within my own gang for perceived infractions. I was threatened several times as a warning to maintain an exclusive relationship with my gang, and I was shot at several times when I was thought to be hanging out with a rival gang. A fellow gang member attempted to jump me out of the gang because he was trying to create a new gang. In all, I had just as many fights with my own gang as I had with rivals. It is precisely for this reason that gang members associate mostly with their closest crew, as the larger gang brings together many different members with their own agendas. It is these contradictions that allow ex–gang members the opportunity to create more empowering forms of group associations that can serve as attractive alternatives.

One can smile now and attempt to enjoy life, but the crying later is inevitable. Some gang members I interviewed noticed the contradictions within the gang and got out, while others remained locked into the glory and belonging that the gang provided. It is hard to leave gang life, especially after prison, which disrupts employment opportunities and family life. Many gang members have been lucky, finding a steady job, marrying, having kids, and breaking away from the gang world. It always has been troubling to me to think about the next generation of barrio youth and how they will experience gang life. It is for these reasons that former and current gang members are essential actors in efforts to rechannel the energy of gangs.

This chapter explored the glue that holds a gang together. Each ideal provides room for individuals to develop success. The inherent contradictions that continually develop when facing external oppositions create many internal conflicts that alter gang dynamics. Looking back at the numerous stories of those I interviewed and my own experiences brings to light how the gang itself is unable to alter the social context of the barrio or the daily routine of subjugation. Another group is needed to accomplish this goal.

Since I studied gangs that were primarily Latino with varying degrees of other racial and ethnic groups included, I am interested in whether predominantly Asian, black, or other racial and ethnic gangs have similar ideals. Walter Miller (1958) argued that lower-class culture contained six focal concerns (trouble, toughness, smartness, excitement, fate, and autonomy). His primary thesis was that individuals developed conformity to immediate group values. Anderson (1999) developed a similar argument of a "code of the streets" originating where the law failed to provide protection. I have attempted to provide an argument that gangs have created an adaptive response to the conditions and experiences they have encountered in the barrio. Although most of these youth share similarities with other groups in society, their criminalized nature makes them different, as does their historical experience with racialized oppression. The ideals emphasized in this chapter are present in many other social groups; the major difference is in how they are manifested. Most individuals will fade away from their active involvement in a gang because the expectations for rule conformity are difficult to constantly uphold. Providing an overview of the core ideals is not done for the purpose of demonizing gangs but rather to offer an overview of gang survival. Similar overviews could be provided for many other social groups.[4]

CHAPTER SEVEN

Barrio Empowerment as a
Strategy for Transcending Gangs

*In ASAP I listen while young men and women who are primarily Latino,
black, and Asian describe their experiences of gang life Denver. D-loc
runs the group with the assistance of other former gang members and
a medical doctor, prosecutor, and teacher. Every Friday we meet at the
courthouse, where everyone is required to pass through a metal detector
before entering a room in the basement. The chairs are organized in a
circle to provide space for the three-hour discussion. As individuals start
entering the room, there is a feeling of anxiety as youth wear various
colors and styles reflecting their group identity. The youth are at different points in their gang careers: some are in the active stage of wanting
to promote the gangster life to the fullest, whereas others have begun to
consider alternatives or are actively involved in forging a new path for
themselves. Previous delinquent charges and court appearances are often
the norm before attending the ASAP program for ten weeks. A trend
begins to develop, and that is that the longer the involvement in gangs,
the more likely it is that individuals will begin to speak about pursuing
alternatives. The difficulty for all of these young men and women is
staying out of the juvenile or criminal justice system and finding a more
promising alternative than the gang.*

*D-loc starts every meeting the same, by first asking for a moment of
silence to acknowledge all the dead homies and the individuals locked
up who cannot be here. Most participants attempt to keep to themselves
during the group meetings, and as long as no one "trips," the meetings
run smoothly. I listen to the youth tell their stories and see them struggle
to comprehend death or prison as a possibility for their lives. D-loc ar-
ticulates other options and choices being available but also wants the
homies to understand the seriousness of their chosen lifestyles. He knows*

many previous members, and some ex–gang member volunteers, who at-
tended the group and have gone to prison or been killed.

D-loc is not ashamed to look like a gangster; to him the image of a
gang member is not the problem. One Friday D-loc gets into an argu-
ment with a gang member in his mid-twenties, a Sureño from Los An-
geles, over colors. D-loc reminds the man that this is Denver and argues
that colors are not the issue, but rather using cultural pride against one
another. "My grandfather dressed like a gangster but he wasn't one.
There is no reason we cannot have pride in the way we dress. I don't
care if everyone got all tatted up and dressed to the fullest. This is not
the problem. The issue is these youngsters taking it further and making
it a problem." The vato from Los Angeles appears unflustered despite
a moment of tension that develops by how D-loc responds to the ques-
tion. The vato says nothing more but seems unconvinced in continuing
to dress like a gang member and not being treated as one by rival gangs.
Several times while attending ASAP meetings I wondered whether a fist-
fight could occur, but every Friday came and went without incident. In
fact, I only heard of one situation in two years where two youth had to
be separated. The prevailing view was that members of rival gangs could
not be in each other's presence without fighting, but ASAP accomplished
this goal twice a week for more than a decade.

D-loc describes to me after the meeting about how we need to con-
front the central issues to reduce the conflict between gangs. He states
that many groups confront clothing, but to him exposure to a cultural
identity can change the gang scene by making individuals look past
colors. As mentioned previously, he totally despised the mainstream re-
sponse to gangs captured in chapter 2. Every year D-loc encourages the
youth to participate in the All Nations–Four Directions March and vari-
ous activities designed to expose youth to conscious-raising organiza-
tions and activities. Despite most of the youth knowing very little about
the activism in Denver during the late 1960s and 1970s, they are being
exposed to present-day activities that are attempting to accomplish a
similar goal of increasing awareness and changing the conditions in the
city. Each year that I participated as security or as a participant in the All
Nations March against Columbus Day, I was mesmerized by the power
of walking through downtown Denver with around seventy-five other
people as cars remained stopped, with no choice but to allow us to pass.
All four corners met in front of the capitol to demonstrate against hav-
ing Christopher Columbus as celebrated via a national holiday. Little did

I know at the time, but I was also undergoing a transformation that I never could have imagined in Utah.

From the inception of gang studies, researchers have offered suggestions about how to transform these groups and reduce their level of delinquent and criminal activities. In 1927 Thrasher argued that attacking the problem required taking the boy out of the gang by moving the member to another neighborhood or by providing meaning to life, allowing ambitions and dreams to become significant. Over the years many responses have developed focusing on prevention, intervention, and suppression, or a combination of all three. Suppression has been the most funded and favored approach since the 1980s. ASAP would be described as a form of grassroots local community mobilization. The group began in response to violence in the early 1990s and developed into a nonprofit organization. The energy and mission of the group may have been slightly co-opted to be more mainstream with the inclusion of the medical doctor, prosecutor, and teacher, but the overall goal was the same: to utilize former gang members in helping not only to transform but to reduce violent conflict. Who could speak more about what it is like to be a gang member and offer strategies to move past this lifestyle than a gang member? It is a philosophy that is shared with Alcoholics Anonymous and organizational training programs worldwide: those who have knowledge can share their wisdom to help others achieve success. As I attended ASAP for two years, there were definitely many conversations that increased the reflective experience of the youth to think directly about how membership in a gang and participation in violence alters the life course.

Spergel reviewed various responses to gangs and reported the following about community youth organizations that included former gang members working to transform current gang culture:

> These community movement and social action efforts should not, therefore, become a basis for sustaining gang structure or attachments to the gang over the long term. As a rule, the gang—committed to violent and criminal activity—cannot be redirected through its own structure to legitimate and effective organizational activity, despite claims to the conduct of a legitimate enterprise. The gang's rationale for survival and development over time would cease thereby to exist. The gang system itself, because it is largely dependent on threat, intimidation, and violence would be destroyed. (1985:287)

Spergel reported how such organizations may only increase fragmentation and work to arouse the ire of police and established political, agency, and community leaders. Klein (1971) became a critic of gang intervention, as he found an increase in delinquency and solidarity in the two street-worker programs that he evaluated. He argued that cohesiveness within the gang was produced externally. In this book I have argued against Spergel's and Klein's foundation of youth gangs as being committed to violent and criminal activity. In continuing this disagreement, I will outline why and how transforming gangs by utilizing former gang members and encouraging cultural resistance can fundamentally alter gangs and the communities where they originate.

Early Forms of Grassroots Mobilization

Responses to colonization have existed in many forms. The various strategies of survival for African Americans and Latinos in the United States have received excellent coverage in previous publications (Acuña 2000, Franklin and Moss 2000; Meier and Ribera 1996). Rosenbaum's (1998) historical research on the protest and violent resistance of Mexican American residents in the United States from 1846 to 1916 in the Southwest offered three types of resistance: withdrawal, accommodation, and violence. Gómez (2007) outlined how Mexican strategies for survival required adapting to double colonization. The racial projects of countering racism were slightly different in each local and state context. The main point was that counterpower was present in all forms of domination (Castells 2009).

Actions around the world in fighting colonial powers served to spark interest. Fanon (1963) described the Algerian revolution against France. He argued that the lumpen proletariat, the dangerous class, deserved the freedom movement's greatest attention because they always answered the call to rebellion (Fanon 1963; Macey 2000). They were the most abused percent of the population. Fanon argued, "The lumpen proletariat is like a horde of rats; you may kick them and throw stones at them, but despite your efforts they'll go on gnawing at the roots of the tree" (130). Fanon, along with many other anticolonialism scholars, recognized the difficulty in creating consciousness since the leaders of colonialism had often used members of the lumpen proletariat against one another (Anderson 1997; Brown 1992; Cleaver 1968; Haley 1964). Many liberators of colonized countries attempted to disrupt the false consciousness of the colonized, the identification of the oppressed with a system that oppresses them, and provide a liberation. Che Guevara attempted to create unity in the Americas by encouraging armed resistance to the state (Anderson 1997). He also believed that revolution began on the ground by working with the oppressed to create change.

In the United States the civil rights movement of black, Latino, Native American, and white activists to improve the conditions and treatment of the oppressed developed rapidly. The 1960s and early 1970s urban Chicano responses included challenging legal repression in the form of nonviolent protest along with militant action that incorporated self-defense (Haney-López 2003; Montejano 2010; Muñoz 1989; Vigil 1999). During this time the Black Panther Party encouraged black gangs to unite, as captured in David Dawley's work in Chicago (1973). Dawley described how in 1967 the Vice Lords evolved from street fighting to a viable community organization. The gang started in 1958 in St. Charles Reformatory and became notorious over the years. Over time the group was the only thing happening, as many of the residents felt hopeless over the social conditions in which they lived. The gang received a grant in 1968 and 1969 and developed several programs that helped provide services to the people living in the community (including Art & Soul, Beautification, Management Training Institute, Partners, Simone, Street Academy, Taste Freez, Teen Town, Tenants' Rights Action Group, The African Lion, The House of Lords, West Side Community Development Corporation, and Youth Organizations United), but with Mayor Richard Daly's war on gangs the funding stopped by 1970. The criminal charges against Jeff Fort and the funding received by the Black P. Stone Nation contributed to this downfall.

Daly's involvement in repressing black gangs that were transitioning toward community self-help is interesting, as research evidence has outlined how the mayor was involved in a gang during his youth that helped establish his political career (Hagedorn 2008). His acceptance of racism may have inspired his desire to prevent blacks from gaining mainstream political power. William Whyte (1943) outlined how clubs in Boston provided an outlet for poor Italians to organize and develop political support. Thus many historical examples exist for how marginalized groups have transitioned from gangs into socially mainstream organizations. Groups such as the Ku Klux Klan in Colorado and the Mormons in Utah were able to use this foundation for political and social power.

Contemporary gang members, while often characterized as criminals, demons, or the enemy—and the actions of some members definitely merge
with this image—cannot easily be essentialized into such category of
hopelessness. Gangs include a broad array of members, many of whom
have worked to transition out of a crime lifestyle and thus are potential
allies against racism because they were created from racial oppression.
Many individuals are caught in a trap of destruction by rival gang members and the state, but there are numerous examples of countering the
inequality of a colonized status. Creating such an organization of political uplift and changing the conditions in the barrio are central in shaping
gang transformation. Two home-grown organizations in Colorado and
Utah are particularly noteworthy.

Denver's Crusade for Justice

The Crusade for Justice in Denver during the late 1960s and 1970s
serves as a model for rechanneling the dreams of youth toward community empowerment. According to Ernesto Vigil, "the Crusade for Justice,
for a span of 15 years, was the most powerful and effective organization to fight for the rights of people of Mexican descent in the state of
Colorado in this century" (1999:381). Ernesto was born and raised in
Denver, a city where gangs of Mexican descent had been present since
the early 1940s, and during his young adulthood he became active in the
Crusade for Justice. He recounted how this political organization helped
shape and develop youth organizations such as the Brown and Black Berets that decreased the popularity of gangs. When I interviewed Ernesto
about gangs, he described how the Crusade impacted Latino youth:

> My orientation is always political. Once these youngsters are orga-
> nized and socially conscious they became a base of youth advocacy.
> Who else can lead youth and organize youth except youth? It's simple.
> I don't see why some people don't see it and act on it. It has been done
> here before, youthful organizing from 1969 to 1979: through political
> organizing and creating social consciousness of youth, and incorporat-
> ing them into different types of community organizations. There was
> no gang violence in the Chicano community for ten years. The cops
> didn't do this. The teachers didn't do it. It was the community organiz-
> ing itself, and it can be done. By and large the institutions that claim

that they work with youth never recognized this accomplishment. They never gave credit for it happening. It was like off their radar screen. [Why you think that is?] Specifically because the organizing that went on was considered radical. Politically radical, but look at what it did. It ended the gang phenomenon. It became, anyone who wanted to start a gang or be in a gang was considered a little bit backward. "Why you want to do that? That's knuckle head kind of stuff." And this is other youth that were telling them that.

Ernesto went on to recall numerous incidents at public parks where fights were mediated to provide an overall better atmosphere in the community. He described how the Crusade for Justice quickly drew a following for its active advocacy on behalf of the Chicano community because the organization challenged the inequalities that existed with the police and schools. Ernesto recalled that the activism encouraged youth to create groups to aid in this struggle:

A youngster who had gone, let's say 1969, a youngster who had been going to West, North, or Manual [High School] and would have seen gangs and during the 1960 walkouts that was city wide: and it extended even into Adams County, Commerce City. Students walked out, and they formed their own leadership. They had some dynamic leadership, and since these youth were from the streets, by and large, they were not gang members. There might have been some on the fringe. Some guys were gang members who became politicized, and the group that comes to my mind right away was the East Side Brown Berets. They used to be the Curtis Park Boys and they became politicized and became Brown Berets. They came from being a gang into being a youth organization. The East Side Brown Berets and people consciously put gangs behind them. "Why are you always fighting each other? You know you shouldn't do that. We need unity: the East Side, West Side, and North Side. We are all brothers. We are all the same people. We have the same enemies."

That was the rhetoric, but it was also true. So gangs became irrelevant—they became like passé, and youth by and large were like, "This is backwards stuff. We don't need that stuff. That's backward, you know? What kind of trip are you on?" And so this whole social scene sprang up where people went from barrio to barrio and partied and had boyfriends and girlfriends and parties and socializing and different activities, and that whole thing about gangs and neighborhoods was put on a shelf and new leadership arose. A lot of the youngsters that participated in the high school walkouts were the same element that gangs would come from. Some might have been gang members, but most of them weren't, but they are also street savvy. They could handle themselves. They had all the same leadership qualities that guys in the gangs would have, and they displaced gangs and so people quit and walked away from their gang involvements because it was a much better social scene, right? Because if a big part of youth activities is the attraction between males and females you would have a broader array of young women to chase after, you know, when you have this theme of unity and all the communities unite and go to many more parties than just the ones in your own neighborhood. So, ugh, gangs had just faded. You could go back and read the papers.

Ernesto stated that after 1979 the new cohort of youth came into a situation where the barrio conditions were relatively the same but grassroots community organizing had begun to fade away. Ethnic pride was on the downhill while political repression increased.

These activities and connections that were considered radical led the FBI in 1967 to create an ongoing file on Corky Gonzalez and the Crusade for Justice for being considered a threat to the internal security of the United States (Vigil 1999). Vigil described how Corky and the Crusade were placed on the "Rabble Rouser Index" and "Security Index." Donner (1980) reported that these files had included information regarding private lives, financial resources, and day-to-day activities with the goal of forming a penetrative investigation. During this time the FBI was running counterintelligence programs designed to target dissident groups (U.S. Senate 1976). The groups considered dissident had challenged the status quo of capitalism and racial hegemony or were pushing for social change. The FBI, in conjunction with local police, politically repressed the Crusade for Justice and the Chicano movement in several ways: death, prison, and psychological warfare.

Vigil (1996) estimated that the volume of FBI intelligence documents on the Crusade for Justice and its key figures numbered tens of thousands of pages. He reported that Corky would always say, "If you get involved in the Movement, the only thing you have to look forward to is a long prison sentence or a bullet in the head." COINTELPRO utilized techniques the FBI used against foreign agents on domestic threats.

The techniques went far beyond investigation to include actions to neu-
tralize "hostile" agents that ranged from trivial to dangerous activities.
The FBI's trivial activities included creating propaganda that was sent to
newspapers, media, and groups to discredit individuals or groups and
destroy their character image. Some of the coercive activities that led to
violent outcomes included blackmail, encouraging gang warfare, falsely
labeling people as police informers, and instigating feuds between groups
(Donner 1980; U.S. Senate 1976).

The Senate committee (1976:12) argued that negative media attention to covert intelligence gathering ended COINTELPRO activities, but
the committee also noted that COINTELPRO existed for years on an
ad hoc basis before the formal programs were instituted and, more significantly, COINTELPRO-type activities may continue today under the
rubric of "investigation." According to the Senate's Select Committee to
Study Governmental Operations with Respect to Intelligence Activities,
COINTELPRO activities were concentrated on five perceived threats:
the Communist Party USA; the Socialist Workers Party; the "White Hate
Group"; the "Black Nationalist-Hate Group"; and the "New Left."
Donner (1980:212) reported:

> With its 360 [FBI] operations, the Black Nationalist-Hate Groups pro-
> gram was second in size only to the COINTELPRO-CPUSA [Com-
> munist Party], and considering its short time span, was the most in-
> tensely pursued of all, involving nearly 100 operations a year between
> 1967 and 1971. . . . In contrast with the Klan program, it [Black
> Nationalist-Hate Group program] was comprehensively directed
> against an entire movement, including groups that had rejected vio-
> lence but were labeled as "Hate" because they opposed institutional-
> ized racism.

Some of the biggest targets included the nonviolent Southern Christian Leadership Conference (SCLC) led by Martin Luther King, Jr., as
well as more activist groups such as the Black Panther Party. Gutierrez
(1996) argued that while Attorney General Peterson did not elaborate
beyond the five basic threat groups, he did admit to two COINTELPROs
not under this umbrella. One of these was the Border Coverage Program,
which included over a dozen FBI COINTELPRO tactics conducted in
Mexico that raised serious concerns about the handling of international
affairs during the years 1956 to 1971 (Gutierrez 1996, n.d.; Vigil 1996,

1999). The other actions targeted Chicano organizations such as Corky Gonzalez (Crusade for Justice) and Reies Lopez Tijerina (Alianza Federal de Mercedes).

Donner (1980) emphasized the problems inherent in governmental intelligence gathering and how it created a grisly irony: turning law enforcers into law violators. Donner argued, "Moreover, the history of the modern state reinforces the prospect of planned provocation of violence to justify repression in the United States and to increase dependence on the 'defensive' and 'preventive' security role of a political police force" (463). The FBI's involvement against groups fighting institutionalized racism led to unprecedented changes in control that disempowered the Latino community. This coincided with the importance of incarceration and gang suppression. Sutton (2000) reported that imprisonment rates rose fourfold during the two decades following the mid-1970s.

The national opposition to the Chicano movement and its internal problems increased in Denver after a 1973 shoot-out between police and Crusade members. Sixty people were arrested, one person was killed, several people were shot or shot at, and a dozen officers were wounded, four with gunshots. After this time several other high-profile incidents led to the decline of the Crusade and the Black and Brown Berets. These included several deaths in Boulder in 1974 (Los Seis de Boulder), many arrests, and movement members being incarcerated. Despite these setbacks, the Crusade for Justice continued to operate until the late 1970s. Although this organization is no longer present in Denver, its ideals continue to shape the consciousness of the community.

Utah's Spanish-Speaking Organization for Community, Integrity, and Opportunity

Ogden does not have the same level of activism or resistance as Denver. The problems with police and schools were definitely present in Utah, but the ability to organize and develop unity never achieved the same level of success. As outlined earlier, SOCIO began working along the Wasatch Front in 1968 to create a path for justice. In contrast to the Crusade for Justice, SOCIO desired to work with the system to create change. Iber (2000) argued that from 1968 to 1986 the group worked to achieve better treatment for the Latino community while reducing disparities and promoting ethnic awareness. SOCIO was primarily composed of middle-class men who had social and political ties to institutions in the state, and thus the group did not achieve the same level of barrio involvement or cooperation with the Brown Berets. The Mormon Church did not take direct action to support these efforts and continued to primarily focus on the betterment of its members. Thus SOCIO's assimilation stance never challenged the power foundation of the state.

For eighteen years SOCIO worked to transform the status and treatment of Latinos in Utah, but its demise came about unexpectedly (Iber 2000). Iber reported that as the group became more mainstream, it lost membership. Moreover, since funding was obtained from outside agencies, group membership was no longer as important and its forms of advocacy more restrained. A divide was created between those obtaining new opportunities in education and employment and those who continued to be left out of this inclusion. Iber reported:

> During its eighteen years of existence SOCIO operated throughout the state of Utah and established programs that fostered ethnic pride as well as academic and economic opportunities through active cooperation with state, local, and corporate entities. The group started as a voluntary association but soon became bureaucratized and almost wholly dependent upon outside funding for survival. This change in managerial structure, without corresponding alterations of reward structures (to maintain interest and loyalty), destroyed SOCIO. (2000:114)

The major differences between SOCIO and the Crusade for Justice highlight why SOCIO did not have the same level of impact on the barrio community or youth in helping to create resistance and empowerment. SOCIO was not able to competently address the needs of barrio youth. The conditions that remained allowed gangs to develop, and the presence of an activist organization to alter gang membership remained nonexistent. Another key difference is that because of SOCIO's more mainstream approach of advocating for reform, it did not encounter, to my knowledge, federal and local law enforcement opposition. If the organization had been affecting gang–involved youth, the question remains whether it too would have been targeted. The lack of activism is very significant in Utah as the media, criminal justice system, and political decision making reflect a lack of concern for meeting any of the interests of the marginalized.

Designing Contemporary Solutions to Gangs
Based on Opposition to Colonial Rule

The reemergence of gangs in the early 1980s could have been prevented by the Crusade for Justice or similar organizations if it were not for the tremendous opposition from the local and federal government during the 1960s and early 1970s (Vigil 1999). The pre-1980s demise of the civil rights era approach of directly challenging discrimination and inequality (Haney-López 2003; Muñoz 1989; Vigil 1999) coincided with the post-1980s increase in aggressive policing, criminal records, and mass incarceration (Bass 2001; Human Rights Watch 1998; Mirandé 1987). SOCIO, on the other hand, never developed the grassroots membership or appeal because it operated in a more conventional approach of developing reform rather than actively forcing change. In the absence of marginalized group resistance, gangs have become easy targets to oppress the entire minority community.

Despite the increasing number of obstacles working to prevent black and brown empowerment in the United States, the actions of several organizations have encouraged these efforts to change communities from within rather than from the outside. Scholarly works have captured some of these efforts with street gangs, including Brotherton and Barrios (2004), Esteva Martínez (2001), Hagedorn (1998, 2008) Hayden (2004), and Montejano (2010). Contrary to Klein's finding of numerous problems with gang intervention, Hagedorn (1998) argued that determining "what works" might be the wrong question and instead we should ask "who" is doing the "working." Hagedorn argued that former local adult gang members were the best individuals to develop a strategy of co-opting gangs. Esteva Martínez (2001) agreed when he discovered how the specialized knowledge of street activists allowed them to develop rapport and insight in encouraging political consciousness. Hayden (2004) argued that the local community inventions of peace by utilizing current and former gang members were important in reducing the madness. Brotherton and Barrios (2004) discovered a gang that was socially transforming itself from a street gang to political organization. In continuing to empirically demonstrate the post–civil rights efforts in this struggle, I analyze Denver and Ogden outcomes. As a departure from academics who simply observe conditions and write the results, I have taken an active role in creating three strategies that can transform gangs, which are outlined below in the spirit of critical race theory.

One of the challenges faced by the Chicano movement was the lack of promoting both male and female leadership and strategies for creating change (Haney-López 2003; Montejano 2010; Vigil 1999). To prevent replicating this error, many of the groups that were organized sought to include both genders and perspectives. Thus the strategies offered seek to accomplish the same goal.

Strategy 1: Cultural Empowerment and Promoting Gender Equality

Developing cultural consciousness and ensuring gender equality were essential for empowering the community. Decolonizing the mind was essential in these endeavors. Several organizations in Denver and Ogden worked to attain this goal. Knowledge of self, history, and the Chicana/o struggle formed an identity that encouraged personal success but also, and more important, contributing back to the community. Although most Latinos in the United States are of Mexican descent, there was active involvement from individuals born or descending from other Latin American countries to expand the discussion of Latino identity. These efforts also took the role of attempting to unite individuals of different generations and aligning with both the colonized and indigenous ancestry. In Denver efforts were also established to bridge divisions between the Latino and black community.

D-loc, the 25-year-old former gang member, captured his transformation by learning about his culture and the Chicano movement. He worked to help the younger gang members leave the life of gang involvement by way of cultural and political consciousness. The youth looked up to him because he did not sell out his culture or its struggle. He did not assimilate to go straight. In one of our many interviews, he reported the importance of the land:

> Now I'm from the Southwest, so I don't know anything about the East Coast. I don't know about no Puerto Ricans or Cubans, and Haitians, and all of that kind of stuff, but I bet it's pretty similar to how we feel. But Chicanos in the Midwest, we're big out here, we're a huge percent of the population out here, always have been. We've always been undercounted, undocumented, underrecognized for a long time. Now

they're barely saying, "Oh there is a Hispanic invasion that is coming over, a Latino invasion," but how can that barely happen overnight if we weren't already over here in millions.

This land, the mountains, the rivers are named after what our people called them in our language, whether it be in Spanish or in other indigenous dialect. . . . And so there is a strong rooted foundation here, and I think that's where gangs get their sense of "hey we got to fight for this, this is ours" because though we don't own a house on the block, we don't own anything on the block, but it's called Villa Park, you know Paco Sanchez Park, Martinez Park, all around here. This is our barrio, so this is our community, this is our land, this is entrenched in us. But society throws this blanket over it and calls it something else, but we're trying to hold on to it, that's what these kids are fighting for, to be recognized, to been seen for who they are, respected for who they are and where they came from, and what they've seen and what they've known and just understand that and respect that and help them move forward from that.

No one wants to stay in depression, no wants to stay in a state of disrespect of being belittled and spit on, and desecrated, derogated, no one wants to live that way, but no one wants to acknowledge the brutality that has happened in the past, the brutality that continues to happen towards our community, the racism that continues to happen to our community.

D-loc saw the problems inherent in gang involvement but recognized the lack of social institutions in the neighborhood that provided status and empowerment.

Rodney, the middle-aged African American Latino who was an ex–gang associate, reported to me how gangs started with good causes but changed after the 1970s:

Gangs were really formed in the beginning to be pro-black, pro-Chicano, but you could see that this gang thing was getting bigger and being formulated to be anti-black, to be anti-Chicano, and so I didn't want nothing to do with it. I didn't participate in it because I seen it as we are killing each other off when we should be getting together to get our piece of the pie together. The rest of us have been so blinded with the drugs and the gangs that they don't see a clear picture. [Yeah, so they are fighting each other]. Yeah, and sellin' drugs to each other.

That's great! Ku Klux Klan ain't got to kill you no more. They ain't got to do nothing to ya. You do it to yourself, but as soon as you become aware of that's what you do, they target you. . . . We got to bring back pro-black, pro-Chicano organizations and groups that aren't ass kissers. That aren't talking about nonviolence. They are ready for self-defense. Until we do that we are not going to combat the lure that gangs have for young kids growing up in a violent society. America breeds violence. That is the American way. This place was founded and built on violence so from the day a kid is born you receive messages of violence. That violence has to be channeled, and for most of our kids right now it is channeled through gangs. So the only way to channel that is through a gang.

Rodney wanted to see the activism that was produced during the black and Chicano movements start again. He countered the hypocrisy of the government's proclaiming of nonviolence when violence was used in the control of this country. Both D-Loc and Rodney emphasized the violence that had been inflicted upon their community, overtly and covertly, historically and in the present. These two respondents sought to empower the people who were considered hopeless.

Contemporary urban street activists stressed the ongoing racism and inequality in society and struggled to provide an alternative to gang membership. They had not proposed assimilation, but rather cultural acceptance. They argued that the government ignored the root problems in the barrio, and thus the community had to provide the solutions. In their eyes, many people in white society did not want them to succeed. Cultural empowerment originated from education of self and working in the struggle for creating change. This involvement in the struggle in many ways demonstrated in a nonviolent way Che Guevara's argument that participation in revolution created a heightened form of consciousness. Thus the various types of activities during the Civil Rights movement may reflect this enhanced knowledge through praxis. For example, my own participation with my family in the immigration marches of 2006 was definitely a transformative experience. An estimated 150,000 people marched to the capitol protesting the anti-immigrant rhetoric and policies. Unity beyond nationality divisions was displayed.

In terms of gender and educational uplift, the Movimiento Estudiantil Chicano de Aztlán (MEChA) organizations on college campuses required both a male and a female leader. Although Latinos continued to be severely underrepresented in Colorado and Utah colleges, the group attempted to provide both support and advocacy for college students and encouraged members to give back to the community. Some of the most active and vocal leaders during my time at universities in both states were women. For example, two Latinas whose family was from El Salvador pushed for at the national conference for MEChA to accept and appreciate not only members of Mexican descent but broader representation from all of Latin America. These two sisters obtained their college degrees and continued to serve as role models in the community. I remember being too shy during a discussion at the national conference held on the University of California Los Angeles campus while serving as cochair. When this Latina stood in front of the crowd of several hundred people and made a passionate argument, the audience and I were amazed, not only because of the error in our thinking (our primarily Mexican and indigenous emphasis), but also from learning how women were often providing better leadership and understanding than their male counterparts. The women used their voice and presence to share their ideas and provide outreach into the community. The women in this organization and in the youth group that worked to reform the schools definitely broadened the consciousness of everyone around. A significant part of the education MEChA provided in college allowed members to pursue their own creative interests and degrees within the institutional framework of encouraging members to maintain a relationship with the community. In the words of the MEChA philosophy (available at http://www.nationalmecha.org/philosophy.html), "Advocating an educational revolution, we recognize that our bullets are our books and our victories are an increase in Chicana/Chicano graduates committed to our people's progress."

Since most women did not join gangs, this may have affected their decreased role in serving as street activists in the same way as D-loc. Nevertheless there were gang-involved women who left gangs and served as models for the younger generation to stay away from this lifestyle. Most of the women I interviewed wanted to continue going to school, get married, and raise children. They desired to create a life for their children different from their own experiences. Cultural empowerment and gender equality remain important ideals in galvanizing the community to push for solutions.

Strategy 2: Challenging Police and Mainstream View of Gangs

In Denver, a small number of black, Latino/a, Native American, and white community members were outraged about biased police behavior and showed their frustration in several ways: by challenging Gang Unit knowledge, by observing police conduct, and by developing an audience to share insights with. These post–civil rights leaders created self-help groups to offer alternative futures to gang–involved youth beyond incarceration and a cycle of violence. As the criminal justice system became a primary source of difficulty in the post–civil rights era, these institutions of control became a central point of critique with regard to many of the problems occurring in the barrio.

Gang lists were an important point of critique because they highlighted the racist assumptions about gang membership and the improper role of law enforcement in defining the gang problem. The number of people in Denver and Ogden publicly reported to be on the gang lists fluctuated greatly since their inception, and with no one from the outside to provide oversight or checks and balances, the lists of reported gang members continued to reflect the desires of the individuals collecting the information. In their eyes, black and brown youth were gang members and a threat.

In November 2003 a police sergeant reported that there were 17,000 gang members in the city of Denver. A longtime historian and activist in Denver, Ernesto Vigil, organized a group of street community workers reflecting the black, Latino, and white communities. At this meeting it was brought to the attention of the group that these inflated numbers had been critiqued in the past. In 1993 the city of Denver was challenged for the racial and ethnic implications of the Gang Unit's gang list (*New York Times*, Dec. 11, 1993; *DP*, Dec. 5, 1993). At that time, according to a study that compared the Gang Unit numbers with the census, two out of three black males would have to be gang members. Some 6,500 individuals were listed as gang members. The NAACP and the ACLU were outraged, and the *New York Times* covered the story. At the meeting we strategized whether we could replicate this study while using the 17,000 number and exploring what current patterns may be in place. Since I had regularly received data on the number of gang members from the City and County of Denver Department of Safety and also used census data, I began crunching the numbers to determine the outcome.

When the 17,000 number was compared to the number of male Asians, blacks, Latinos, and whites in Denver between the ages of 12 and 24, the following patterns were found: two out of three black men (66.4 percent), one out of two Latinos (53.2 percent), one out of four Asians (24.9 percent), and only 1 out of 57 (1.76 percent) non-Hispanic whites would have to be involved in gangs for the data to be accurate. After learning these numbers, we sought an opportunity to educate the community and provide a critique of how the Gang Unit was operating. We participated in several community forums and met individually with City Council members. We even pursued the media to create a broader audience. Although the findings did not receive nationwide attention as the numbers did in 1993, our efforts did result in a local newspaper, *Westword*, covering the story on its front page. My efforts to study gangs and our group's efforts to critique the gang list were highlighted (June 3, 2004a, b). In response to this information, residents held several demonstrations and community forums protesting the racial profiling effects of the Denver Gang Unit (*Westword*, June 3, 2004a, b; *RMN*, Mar. 18, 2004; *DWN*, Jan. 29, 2004; *Metropolitan*, Mar. 11, 2004). The Gang Unit responded by reducing the 17,000 number to 9,213 gang members and associates since it was reported that the other 7,000 or more members were dead or in prison. As of 2008 the Colorado Bureau of Investigations estimated 8,800 gang members in seventy-eight gangs (*DP*, June 14, 2009).

In Ogden my final interview with a member of the Gang Unit resulted in being escorted out of the police department after I inquired whether I was on the gang list. Nevertheless the data I received from the Gang Unit between 1991 and 2003 allowed me to conduct a study similar to the one in Denver. In Ogden the number of gang members fluctuated from a low of 250 in 1993 to a high of 1,569 in 1999 (Ogden Police Department 2000). In 2000 this number was reduced to 300, but to better improve the odds of receiving federal funding the number has since risen to 1,210 as of February 2004 and then to 1,600 since 2007. Latinos were overrepresented in terms of the number of gang members reported by police. Two-thirds (63.4 percent) of the people on the Ogden/Weber Metro Gang Unit gang list were identified as Latino, whereas Latinos were only 12.7 percent of the county population. Whites consistently remained undercounted in terms of gang membership despite an Ogden Task Force member's claim that the Ogden area had been "flooded" with white supremacist gang members (*New York Times*, April 4, 2003; *SE*,

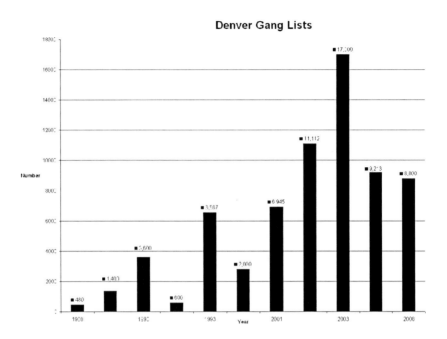

FIGURE 7.1 Denver, Colorado (fluctuating gang lists)

April 5, 2003). Whites represented only 27.8 percent of the people on the list despite representing 82.8 percent of the population. A comparison of the number of Ogden gang members with the census numbers for Asians, blacks, Latinos, and whites showed that the numbers were not as skewed as in Denver but still indicated disparities. For men between the ages of 12 and 24 the comparison is as follows: one out of five black men (21.1 percent), one out of five Latinos (20.64 percent), one out of twelve Asians (8.54 percent), and only one out of fifty-eight (1.74 percent) non-Hispanic whites.

I then tried to replicate the Denver strategy in Ogden by going through the similar process of sharing this information and advocating for a change in how it was collected. These patterns did not receive any local media attention beyond my letters to the editor (SE, April 11, 2004; July 26, 2007). In my efforts to help Ogden's Latino residents I started a local group that monitored the police, modeled after the POP group that I worked with in Denver. The group involved several community members. We quickly arranged a meeting with police administration before documenting stops. The police and local newspaper looked upon the

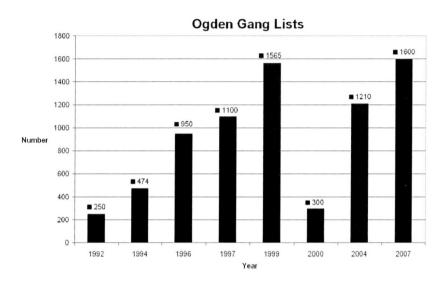

FIGURE 7.2 Number of reported gang members in Ogden

group negatively (*SE*, July 10, 2004), but after seeing the coverage on the news, many members of the community appeared interested ("Group Plans to Monitor Police Stops," *Channel 5 News*, July 9, 2004). The group faced obstacles in developing leadership to maintain a presence as I returned to Denver every August for school. Every year from 2004 to 2010, I attempted to challenge the Gang Unit by working with the local media, and I received an opportunity in 2007 for a front-page story on the issue (*SE*, Aug. 12, 2007; Aug. 13, 2007a, b). Despite this effort to create change, the news stories continued to portray the dominant perspective of the law enforcement community and of individuals living outside the barrio, shaped by the socially constructed panic.

In both Denver and Ogden, I worked with groups that gathered data and utilized this information to create change. In Denver the reception was overall positive as a number of activist organizations and more open-minded thinking worked to produce change. In Ogden resistance from the mainstream community and the lack of active organizations pushing for transformation ensured that no structural changes were accomplished. As of 2010 Ogden was waging a war against its Latino residents in the name of gang injunctions, ICE raids, and "immigrant lists." Such a war against the Latino community pushed me to write an op-ed in 2010 (*SE*, Sept. 14, 2010). Several other individuals have also subsequently written letters to the editor and have faced a racist and nativist backlash from the online responses. Voices of dissent are pushed into silence or ridiculed for speaking out against these anti-Latino agendas, and white supremacy remains strong.

Strategy 3: Designing a Gang Program

Creating cultural consciousness and gender equality and working to transform perceptions were great at creating change, but the third strategy works to directly transform gang members' lives. By participating in several organizations and working in agencies that focused on changing life chances, several of my interviewees provided enhanced insight into developing a gang program that could legitimately alter gang life.

I asked D-loc what his strategy would be if he could design one to decrease gang violence. He first stated that he needed a larger staff that included full-time counselors who were female, Spanish speaking, Asian, and black to serve the various communities in Denver. He thought the youth needed a place to go where they were safe and could receive various types of support. He said:

> So there is a lot of things you know. I just see a lot of these social illnesses that plague our community. A lot, half of this stuff we could take care of on our own. You know? Raza, the Indian community, the black community, Asian community. Whatever community you come from. I think a lot can be done ourselves. Without the system's help, without the system's money, without the system's dictation, without the system's court, without the system's policeman and probation officers and ankle monitors. I think we could do [it] ourselves.
>
> I think this is a very good time for community leaders to start to evolve again. Like we had Martin Luther King, like we had Huey Newton, Corky Gonzalez, and Cesar Chavez. This is a very good time to start that community activism and create those community leaders that inspire the nation to change because it has to come from the root level, the community level. Nobody knew Cesar Chavez, but they knew he was real because he came with the spirit of the people and the spirit of the land. Martin Luther King came with that same spirit of the land, of the people and its history. Nobody knew that Martin Luther King's parents were slaves at some time. No one knew Martin Luther King

grew up poor. No one knew Martin Luther King grew up oppressed, but when he spoke with clarity and understanding of the problems that plagued the society and our nation, motherfuckers listened and shaped up. And that's what can happen now. Because there is such a hunger and need for it, and it's a prime time because no one else is doing shit in the streets for real.

It's starting to happen though. It's definitely starting to happen as the new generation of social organizing or civil rights. So in small pockets it's happening; it's just getting it to a level that relates to to-day's generation. For a while that old movement started getting stag-nant, old, and repetitive, but now new ideas with another generation bringing a new clarity with what needs to be done.

D-loc wanted to get youth involved with adult mentors in the commu-nity who were in professional occupations to help reduce the stigma of these occupations to help youth see they are people. He thought classes could be arranged depending on what level of gang member: those pre-contemplating to those actively involved. He thought mixing youth at different stages, from those who don't recognize the dangers of gang life to those looking for a way out, was a bad combination because those wanting to bang only brought down those trying to fade out.

When I asked Ernesto the same question, he thought most social ser-vice agencies were bureaucracies that saw the youth as a number on a checklist, and that gangs were assumed to be a problem 100 percent of the time, but that this was inaccurate. He thought police were the worst individuals to address gang issues, and he didn't really think teachers were the best individuals for the job either. If Ernesto had his program, this is what he would do:

What I would do, and this is a hypothetical, I would go out and find people of the same ethnic background and primarily I would employ more men than women because the gang phenomenon is overwhelm-ingly male. In picking the people that I would hire, I would pick people who have shown that their heart and their head are in the right place. Not all folks are effective when working with youth. There is a real close friend of mine who is actually ill now and his name is Tony. He has a nickname because he is real tall—people call him Big T. He worked nearly a decade in parks and recreation. Never moved out of his neighborhood, and through parks and recreation he really worked well with youth. He knew the neighborhood. A lot of people respected him, so he would know what was going on in different parts of town. . . .

There was another guy that I went to school with and his name was Paul. And Paul in his own era had been a gang leader. He worked with a variety of service agencies and parks and recreation and funded programs for a long time, but he also had that right kind of personality. He likes working with youth. He likes working around youth. He knows the neighborhood. He knows the phenomenon. He knows how to deal with the situation, and so these would be the folks that I would hire. One to go out and do the outreach: make the contacts, figure out who are who, who are the gangs, where do they hang out, who the leadership is, what their issues are, what their wants are, what their needs are.

After that assessment, let's hypothetically play this out. So I would have my twenty-some staff members and they would be working in the field. Not expecting people to come to some institutional office, these folks go out to the neighborhoods, to the hang-outs, to the schools, to the parks, and it would have to be a yearlong thing. In two years the gang problem in the Chicano community, the problem could be solved. The first thing would be to identify the leadership, and once you identify the leadership you establish those bonds. A lot of gang leadership don't know who to trust, and they will be leery of certain adults. The individual[s] I am talking about [are] Big T and Paul. I know what folks like them are capable of doing, and one of the things that they have is a person of certain personality type, but these are the type of guys that young gang members could easily establish a feeling of trust [with]. Ugh, and once that is done through the leadership you can then have access to the followership. . . .

I have always felt, and I have said it repeatedly, that gangs give an opportunity for certain youth to exert their leadership, and these youngsters tend to be very, very sharp, and part of joining a gang is a phenomenon for these youth who have justifiable reasons for feeling resentful. This allows them to exert their leadership and to be assertive. And it is not necessarily a negative thing that is going on. . . . But if I was to have this staff, you know there are a variety of agencies (school programs, programs for single mothers, programs for single fathers), and this hypothetical team of twenty people would figure out which agencies would provide such services.

Certain social service agencies are notable by their dedication and their competence, and others are people just picking up a paycheck and being inept. So, upon assessing the needs of these youngsters, this hypothetical staff would also check out all the different agencies: city agencies, county agencies, nonprofits where these youth could have their problems addressed by the appropriate agencies. Then another thing to do is to the bring the group rivals into some type of social contact with each other where the potential for conflict is controlled because what will happen is that those youth will eventually make friends with each other. And that will work to eliminate the rivalry and the violence.

Ernesto believed that most youth will outgrow gangs as they grow up, but it was important to create better conditions for something else to do with their energy. He stated that gangs were a result of the social conditions of oppression and that people had vested interests in maintaining the status quo, but that looking at the issue historically, change was inevitable.

By incorporating both D-loc's and Ernesto's insights with years of working to transform gangs provides us insight that a gang program will need several things:

1. Individuals who are current or former gang members or with street connections are needed to provide a model for change. Father Greg Boyle serves as an excellent example of someone who is connected to the community and providing outreach to it (Boyle 2010; Fremon 1995). Gang members themselves have served as leaders, as I have come to learn about the actions of Lil Monster and Cle Sloan. The documentary *Bastards of the Party* captured this passion.
2. The group will require emphasis on cultural consciousness and gender equality.
3. The group will require outreach into the community to reach out to gang-involved individuals rather than waiting for these individuals to come to the program.
4. The program will need to provide a resource to the community and its participants by improving and enhancing education. The group will focus on training individuals to create empowerment. The group will address the problems that exist in the community.

5. The program will need networks and allies in the larger community to help sustain and advocate for change.

In summary, there are opportunities to change the lives of gang members for the better, but until racialized oppression is eradicated the best solutions require challenging this racism at its roots. Although it has always been my dream to create a program that could meet all of these needs, I have been impressed with the work of several groups, including Homeboy Industries, Homies Unidos, and CeaseFire. The local groups I worked with in Denver were also amazing or caught my interest, including Copwatch, Gang Rescue and Support Project, the gang group, Jovenes and Padres Unidos, MEChA, Open Door Youth Gang Alternatives, the Prodigal Son Initiative, and Youthbiz. As law enforcement officers around the nation hold gang conferences, so too should gang workers to share knowledge and insight and to encourage independent forms of program evaluation.

The contemporary response to gangs needs to be modified. The warfare approach does more harm than good. The overextension of the deviant and gang label to every member of the community engenders alienation, criminalization, hostility, and victimization. Erikson (1966:14) observed that "deviant forms of conduct often seem to derive nourishment from the very agencies devised to inhibit them." He suggested that this labeling creates a one-way street into deviance for individuals' lives. The police are particularly culpable in this area. If the police worked humanely and effectively within these inner-city communities, they might be provided with more assistance and tips from residents. By viewing the entire community as criminal, they effectively push the criminal and noncriminal elements together.

In terms of policy, focusing on the collective set of ideals maintained by the gang through entrenchment or engulfment can provide a wide array of solutions. Mexican American loyalty is formed through external opposition and victimization and internal support. Mediating the external opposition and victimization from agents of the state (I am particularly referring to schools and the criminal justice system) and mediating disputes among the oppressed will profoundly reduce the pressure to form a gang loyalty. Putting in work serves as an outlet to the troubled background and subjugated standing of people in the inner city. Instituting conventional ways for inner-city Mexican Americans to obtain respect is paramount.

Creating barrio empowerment as the strategy for transcending gangs can provide a pragmatic strategy for reducing violence and creating alternative social organizations to address the problems in the neighborhood. An activist approach is required to help transform gangs. The Crusade for Justice serves as an example of how such organizations can improve communities. However, rather than romanticize what the Crusade was able to accomplish, we can also learn from its history and its mistakes. We can understand how gender equality is an essential foundation. Moreover, the era of gang suppression and sending individuals to prison was born with the demise of the Civil Rights movement. Thus countering the system can no longer entail actions that result in increased criminality, although recognizing how to walk this invisible line remains unclear. Gangs are created in response to colonization, which has allowed for racial oppression to continue unabated. Transforming gangs will require changing the conditions by which they originate and providing an outlet for youth to grow as human beings into a society that has sought to restrict life chances. Looking at gangs as receptive to social movement responses that seek to challenge colonial conditions pinpoints the importance of incorporating gang-involved or -influenced individuals into groups that can help empower them.

Conclusion

I am beginning to prepare for Friday May 12, 2006. This will be the day on which I will be hooded and awarded my doctorate in sociology. The event is scheduled to be held at the University of Colorado's football stadium. My family is preparing to drive from Utah in several vehicles to be here for this moment. My wife and children are anxiously waiting for the time when all the hard work will pay off. After all the years my family has seen me attending school, studying, and working full time, the finale is moments away.

Persevering through graduate school was not easy, and every year I felt like quitting despite wanting to complete a doctoral degree. Both my undergraduate and graduate universities contained only small percentage of students of color. Blacks and Latinos made up less than 8 percent of the student body, which demonstrated underrepresentation compared with the Denver metro area and Wasatch Front. I am one of the few individuals in the entire school who came from the lifestyle of gangs. Thus learning to navigate these social environments was definitely a hurdle, but the expectations pushed me to rise to the challenge. This book is a reflection of that training.

Everyone I know thinks I'm a little bit crazy to have stayed in school for this long. But I continually tell them that completing this degree will be worth it. Friends see me and ask, "You're still in school?" with great perplexity as to why I have given school my entire attention. They remember when I had barely started college and I was embarrassed to carry books because it didn't look gangster. Now I have wall after wall of books. My brother tells me, "You are holding a winning lottery ticket," and he's proud to see me finish. My wife is so thrilled because we came from the same struggle and she's happy to see me become a leader and father worthy of admiration. I take my kids with me to the college campus and expose them to life beyond our barrio while at the same time instilling in them the joy and pleasure that comes from continuing to live in the neighborhood. I encourage them to stay in school, and I run my own "daddy college" to help prepare them for when it will be their chance.

The pressure to finish was intense. I had already accepted a tenure-track position in southern New Mexico, forty-five minutes from El Paso, Texas, and Ciudad Juárez. During my visit I was fascinated by the border and was in awe to see the fences, border patrol, and socially constructed separation between two countries. I watched in astonishment as a man and woman spoke to each another separated by a fence while the border patrol watched with binoculars. It reminded me of seeing family members behind bars, and it sparked my curiosity about these forms of social control not observed in Colorado or Utah. My family has lived in New Mexico for centuries, and I am drawn to an area where my children will not have to feel discriminated against for the color of their skin, last name, or ethnic background. I am excited to begin teaching at a university where the students will share my background and personal ambition as a first-generation college graduate.

Graduation day arrives and my family and I arrive in Boulder. On this sunny day there are thousands of people receiving degrees and quadruple the number of family members excited to see their loved ones receive their awards. We feel rushed in finding a place to park and the logistics of where to sit. The hot sun tests the patience of everyone, including my father, who is in a wheelchair after suffering a stroke several years ago. I am one of the small number receiving doctoral degrees, and I am caught up in the moment of happiness. Afterwards we attend a reception at my family's Mexican restaurant in Aurora, and I'm surrounded by family and friends who have always been there for me, encouraging me to succeed. I have made my family proud, and no one can take this day from me. For all the people who looked at me like I was trash and told me I would fail, this story is for you: the haterz—the ones whose negativity I learned to use at a young age as energy to push myself harder to prove people wrong. A story about gangs is not only a story about getting jumped into a gang and facing the outcome of death or prison; it is also a story of graduating with a Ph.D. It is also a story of writing a book on these experiences and the research that followed. And in my effort to give back to the community, these credentials have launched me onto a whole new level of commitment for which I can continue giving back in the form of advocacy, research, speaking, teaching, and writing in an effort to share the voices of all those who helped me to be here today.

This book has presented evidence that gangs originated as a response to racialized oppression that will require a social movement to alter membership affiliations. My insider status and comparison of two different southwestern cities allowed me to reach several conclusions.

Gang Paradigms

Joan Moore, one of the longest-engaged researchers on Latino gangs, argued in 1978, "If Chicano gangs are going to be taken seriously, the current theories of gang behavior must be drastically modified" (51). The focus on crime in the most popular and widely cited gang literature ignores the role of racism in creating unequal communities and giving rise to adaptive responses among some inner-city residents (see, e.g., Cohen 1955; Decker 1996; Klein 1971, 1995; Miller 2001; Miller 1958; Sanders 1994; Scott 2004; Short and Strodtbeck 1965; Spergel 1995; Yablonsky 1962, 1997). Scholars who have encouraged the mainstream ideology of criminalizing gang members without considering the root causes of structural inequality have allowed law enforcement efforts to grow without criticism. This has narrowed the scope and vision of proposed solutions.

My research seeks to expand this literature by creating a space in which to contextualize race and ethnicity within a broader structure of racism manifested through colonization of the barrio. This book has outlined some of the adaptive strategies that support the institutionalization of the barrio gang. Heightened control by the criminal justice system combines with neglected social and environmental conditions to create drastically different life chances for people of color. My conceptual focus on colonization and critical race theory most closely follows the model outlined by researchers such as Almaguer (1971), Barrera (1979), Barrera, Muñoz, and Ornelas (1972), Blauner (1972), Delgado and Stefancic (2001, 2005), Fanon (1963), Freire (1970), Krisberg (1975), Memmi (1965), and Mirandé (1985, 1987). These researchers describe unequal living conditions, negative treatment by powerful and privileged colonizers, and unequal enforcement of laws. In addition, they describe the hegemonic ideology created to maintain the colonial mentality and prevent the oppressed from altering their situation.

Historically Informed Insight on Gangs as an Adaptation to Racial Oppression

This book highlights the many historical changes that have brought about the current gang situation. It reflects the vast differences of enforcement, resistance, and gang development between two cities in separate states. In Denver for many years Latinos have been considered a minority population, with all the disadvantages and long-standing definition as a problem population. The city's ideology of white supremacy grew from membership of its leaders and community in the Ku Klux Klan. Gangs developed in the 1940s, and immediate efforts to control this new "Spanish Surnamed Problem" were instituted (Walsh 1995). These included criminal penalties and changes within the police department as well as gang (i.e., social) workers. In the era of the Chicano movement (in which the Crusade for Justice was very strong in Denver), many gangs were deflected into groups like the Black and Brown Berets, and gangs as a "problem" tended to disappear, only to reemerge as the movement momentum waned (Vigil 1999). In later years the institutions of control were strengthened, largely in response to various moral panics against gangs such as the Crips and Bloods, but such institutions also were counterinstitutions within the barrio. This is the context within which Denver gangs operate today: a very long history of control and countercontrol measures.

By contrast, gangs arose in Ogden only in the 1970s, and it was not until the creation of a Gang Unit in the early 1990s that control efforts increased along with media coverage. The flight of the Church of Latter-day Saints from religious persecution formed a community that built off an ideology that supported white supremacy. Over time the increasing Latino population faced obstacles that were shared with other communities in the Southwest, but also some that were different owing to the religious base of Mormonism and the suppression of advocacy groups. SOCIO combated inequality and sought to provide Latinos with a stronger base of advocacy, but it failed to reach the lower-income groups in the community. These control efforts were made easier because the structures were well in place nationally, so legislation and police administrative tactics were easy to mimic. The creation of Gang Units and injunctions brought about the institutionalization of control of gangs and inner-city minority youth. Lacking was a long history of community response.

Combined, the differences between emergent and traditional gang cities appear to be more than a distinction between gangs. Of greater distinction was the number of controls and countercontrols used to shape current gang politics. In Denver and Ogden the dominant group labeled Latinos as criminal, illegal, immoral, lazy, involved in gangs, having bad parents, and in need of more control. The push for greater control of the subordinate groups was supported in the 1940s by reports made by the police and emphasized in the media tying these groups to attacks on women, innocent people, and servicemen. Since the 1980s the killing of "innocent" victims has received the most outcries, particularly when these involved members of the dominant group. This supported the assumption that subordinate groups were a threat to the dominant culture. When the Latino community opposed enforcement, it resulted in a temporary removal of control, but later a few violent incidents were used to enhance and argue on behalf of new forms of repression. Both socially militant and urban youth were targets. Gang activity fluctuated with enhanced control but dissipated with increased countercontrol. Denver had strong countercontrol, but after the late-1970s it struggled to achieve the same dissipation hold that was present in the past. The eclipse of the Chicano and Black Power movements ushered in a new era of Mexican American political disempowerment and a growth of grassroots responses to urban ghettos that have resulted in an increased likelihood of gang membership. Ogden was never able to accomplish a strong resistance movement, and thus gang activity has risen and fallen with different cohorts. Despite such cycles, the criminal justice strategies developed since the early 1980s are clearly more institutionalized than in the past. Gang legislation and prosecution expanded. Incarceration rates boomed (Mauer 1999). Federal and multijurisdictional agencies worked together to combat gangs. Prosecutors used grand juries to indict large numbers of people. Nevertheless law enforcement continued to claim that the number of gang members and associates was growing. Since September 11, 2001, there has been an increase in labeling of gangs as domestic terrorists or as undocumented immigrants.

Members of the dominant group *not in power* questioned the mobilization against Latinos and their negative portrayals as a subordinate group. These people appeared to be Catholic Church leaders, teachers, and possibly a higher percentage of whites who had a close relative or friends who were members of the subordinate groups. There were also a small number of professional blacks and Latinos who spoke out against racism and galvanized the community, but they were the exception. Most minorities did their best to not be pushed out of their jobs.

These mostly white dominant group members *not in power* held meetings and conducted research that emphasized the harmful impact of discrimination. They argued that the subordinate group was poor and faced many obstacles in their lives, such as low education and poor housing. They attempted to reform the subordinate group to integrate them into the dominant group by emphasizing assimilation. They urged the dominant group *in power* to not discriminate, but to provide opportunities. They argued that the subordinate group had rights. Nevertheless they were unable to generate the power and number of people to fully counter the claims of the dominant group *in power*. The dominant group *not in power* won a few battles on a case-by-case basis.

Most of the Latino youth in this study grew up in socially disadvantaged neighborhoods that offered little mainstream opportunity. They were segregated unto a social environment that contained high poverty and joblessness. The youth watched their parents work hard for minimal pay, or they watched their parents unable to find employment because of limited education or criminal records. In response to the mainstream conventional society that cared little to integrate marginalized racial and ethnic groups in society, some youth created a social group that did appreciate their belonging. Youth joined gangs as a result of the conditions in the neighborhoods, and since many of their family members had lived in the area for a while, this created networks of a broader kin-support network. Most marginalized youth chose not to join gangs, but for some school pressures, a neglectful social environment, and opposition from mainstream society resulted in joining with others who were going to physically ensure their own survival.

Entering a gang transforms people's mentalities so that they are no longer victims. For the first time in their young lives, adolescent gang members are respected. Collective existence requires adherence to core ideals to hold the group together despite all the negative outcomes. These ideals develop over time and come to supersede both laws and external criticism; they take on a life of their own. Criminal records and incarceration—markers of stigma in conventional society—become status enhancers. The gang, socially constructed and formed in response to neglect and opposition, develops core ideals to maintain its longevity, just as many colonized groups have developed their own forms of resistance. Nevertheless, for meeting short-term needs the gang reigns supreme. No other group in the barrio offers such excitement and celebrity status. No other group shields its members from widespread bullying and victimization. Only rivals can engage gang members; other would-be assailants cannot.

Most inner-city residents shied away from involvement, but a larger number developed some ties to the gang who ran the strength of the peer networks and community protection. No current group within the barrio could compete with the gang to provide support when so many intuitional practices and ideologies were implemented to deny people of Mexican descent equal treatment. Nevertheless the gang increased criminal labeling and victimization, felony disenfranchisement, and prison chances that further enhanced the presumed superiority of the dominant group and their strong morality.

Gang members attempt to defy subordination, yet they contribute to their own group's oppression. The loyalty of the gang is sometimes only as strong as the people standing alongside each other during a confrontation. The senseless and planned violence against other Latinos ensures that gangs never gain majority support in their communities, and some of these actions definitely reflect this victimization of lost lives and injuries due to violence. Their actions lead other barrio members to condemn them as hurting the community. The lived experience of active gang members often perpetuates a colonial self-hatred, and the behavior of a small number of gang members fosters the larger group's self-destruction by providing dominant-group members a means of legitimating oppression.

As I compiled the reasons why Latinos join gangs, I found that they were not based on criminal inclinations as depicted by law enforcement, but rather on people's adaptations to their social environment. The number of people who joined gangs was small, and membership was often temporary. Most people in the neighborhoods were law abiding. The gang, socially constructed and formed in response to neglect and opposition, developed core ideals to maintain longevity. These ideals were not foreign or profound; many were characteristic of other groups as well, particularly fraternities and sororities. The major difference was the social environment in which the groups were responding. Gangs were not operating in the pristine settings of college campuses; they were in impoverished neighborhoods of violence and victimization. The various branches of the military also share similarities. Social groups created from friendship, from work, or for purposes of accomplishing a goal are not entirely different from street gangs; human beings learn to adapt to their surroundings.

In colonial U.S. society, the oppressed battle among themselves to fight off dominant-group ideologies and the dangers imposed by others encountering oppressed circumstances. Fanon (1963), Che Guevara (Anderson 1997), and Malcolm X (Haley 1964) all recognized the power of this subgroup if channeled toward revolutionary means. In the barrios gangsters make the rules and have the power to transform people from victims into strong warriors, but it is often channeled into destructive ways that can often perpetuate a cycle of oppression.

Toward a Theory of Racialized Oppression

Academic disciplines of criminology, psychology, and sociology have all used various theories, including biological, classical, conflict, control, feminist, social disorganization, social learning, and strain theories, in an attempt to explain gang behavior. A problem with many of these is that the concept of racism is not central to them and is often ignored. Only critical race theory and studies of colonialism have focused on this theme, and thus carving out such a focus is necessary before completing this book. The work of Blauner (1972), Krisberg (1975), Ladner (1973), and Mirandé (1987) is particularly influential in this endeavor. Politicians and wealthy people do not enter the barrio to shoot and kill gang members, but they play a role behind the scenes in manipulating what services are available and shaping how society thinks about these issues. Carmichael and Hamilton (1967:5) reported:

> "Respectable" individuals can absolve themselves from individual blame: *they* would never plant a bomb in a church; *they* would never stone a black family. But they continue to support political officials and institutions that would and do perpetuate institutionally racist policies. Thus *acts* of overt, individual racism may not typify the society, but institutional racism does—with the support of covert, individual *attitudes* of racism.

The racial structure of U.S. society plays a significant role in creating the conditions and the ideologies that are being challenged in this book. If we view gangs as not dependent on criminality and utilize current and previous members in reform, it requires a new approach toward integrating people deemed unworthy and criminal into the larger society. It emphasizes greatly needed structural reforms that will allow the possibility of new cultural adaptations (Brotherton and Barrios 2004; Hagedorn 1988, 2008; Horowitz 1983; Moore 1978, 1991; Padilla 1992; Page 1997; Perkins 1987; Sánchez-Jankowski 1991; Vigil 1988).

Racialized oppression is imposed on subjugated groups. Excessive regulation is central to this argument. In a footnote, Durkheim (1951:276) described excessive regulation as "persons with futures pitilessly blocked and passions violently choked by oppressive discipline." He argued that "it is not enough for rules to exist, for occasionally it is these very rules that are the cause of evil" (1984:310). Durkheim conceptualized this as fatalism, the opposite of anomie, and in his worldview it had little relevance so he did not expand on this concept. Control theories have primarily argued that if attachments to society are strong, then delinquency and criminality are lessened, but increasing the attachment to a society that does not value or deem equal marginalized groups means that such a connection is part of the problem. Colonial theories and critical race theory have critiqued the racialized hierarchies of the United States. In using many of these ideas, I will attempt to set forth a theoretical framework that is bigger than the topic of gangs.

First, the process of control begins with power differences between people. The people who will be excessively regulated first need to be defined or socially constructed as unequal and less deserving of the same rights and opportunities as the dominant group. Society hierarchies of class, gender, nationality, race, and religion will be socially constructed as important and thus worth reinforcing. Second, once identified and tagged for separate treatment, marginalized groups are pushed into land areas that offer different opportunities. The social conditions in these segregated areas will be conducive to subordinate group self-destruction, and the dominant group will respond by maintaining oppression. Third, since most subordinate-group members will resist self-destruction, the dominant group utilizes infrequent attacks by members of the subordinate group on the dominant group to legitimize increased control, that is, legitimated oppression. Despite encountering legitimated oppression, the oppressed group responds by various forms of countercontrol. In this section I will discuss each of these components in more detail.

Socially Constructing Power Differences

Defining the threat requires socially constructing certain groups of people as different. The dominant group will not argue that we are all human beings. They need to create a hegemonic worldview that justifies its negative and hostile treatment of members of the subordinate group. They will argue that some people are inferior and unworthy of enjoying the privileges. This will be done in a subtle manner by using code words. For the dominant group to legalize and garner support for a war on people of color—war on crime, drugs, gangs, terror—they needed to operate with language that was not seen as racialized. These wars had to gain support from both the dominant group and the oppressed group in order to dispel question. Making a public argument that Latinos deserve unequal services is illegal and violates the Constitution and Bill of Rights; however, if they can be redefined as criminals, domestic terrorists, drug dealers, illegal aliens, or gang members, then any subsequent infringements on equality are easily removed. In the *Art of War*, Sun Tzu (1963:41) reported, "All warfare is based on deception. A skilled general must be master of the complementary arts of simulation and dissimulation; while creating shapes to confuse and delude the enemy he conceals his true dispositions and ultimate intent."

Colonization automatically placed one group in power and subjugated another group. Mexican Americans began their relations with the United States by the conquest of Mexico (Barrera 1979; Murguía 1975; White 1991). The land obtained by the United States became known as the Southwest (Acuña 1972). The disputed takeover led to several protracted conflicts over time (Rosenbaum 1981). Since that time, U.S. ideology has supported the idea that Mexican Americans have only recently begun immigrating to this country. Multiple generations of European descendents and their increasing power helped formulate by law and common sense the people who were labeled white and nonwhite, and how they would be treated in U.S. society (Durán forthcoming b; Haney-López 1996; Roediger 1991).

There was nothing illegal about marginalized groups uniting in an effort to provide for the psychological and physical needs of the community. Mainstream society's definition of the inner-city Latino community as deviant leads to its disempowerment. Tuggle and Holmes (1997) have suggested that in moral entrepreneurial struggles, powerful groups use the deviant label to enhance their status and legitimacy at the expense of those they label and treat as deviant. By defining groups as deviant, they expand their social power and position. In this situation, the dominant group used extreme tactics of social control to degrade community members and thereby upgrade themselves. Their "war on gangs" is aided by defining the entire Latino community as a dangerous group (Reinarman 2001), scapegoating them for all of the violence and crime. Agents of the state do this to enhance their own power, position, and funding.

Agents of the state, recognizing that most people in low-income communities were law abiding, had to support the myth that people of Mexican descent encouraged illegality to condone excessive regulation. Agents of the state were able to formulate their own overregulation (i.e., mores, policies, and laws) to ensure that those who adapted unconventionally directly felt the additional punitive controls. Although the majority of the Latino community refrained from criminality, they were still treated as criminals. Reducing labeling required assimilating as much as possible to the dominant culture in characteristics such as dress and skin color, beliefs and mannerisms, and economic standing. Assimilated individuals were used as examples of how things have improved and how racism is gone. They were tokens, however: the majority of oppressed people will not experience these benefits (Murguía 1975). Tokens were used to pacify the masses and provide the mirage that racism was no longer a factor (Bell 1992). The tokens who achieved positions of power were consistently persuaded to keep change minimal or were threatened that they would be replaced by someone more eager to serve that role. Even economic and professional assimilation did not guarantee that discrimination ceased or no longer affected their lives (Acuña 1998; Bell 1992; Feagin and Sikes 1994).

Critical race theory has been critical of both liberal and conservative politics (Bell 1992; Delgado and Stefancic 2001). Both Colorado and Utah were Republican-dominated states, but there is no evidence in my data to suggest that Democrats were more progressive in responding to the needs of subordinate groups. Denver offers a case in point. Under the leadership of democratic mayors Federico Peña (1983–91) and Wellington Webb (1991–2003), gang control measures were at extremely high levels. George (2004) argued that Webb's terms as mayor highlighted how deracialization served the strategy of racial accommodation and tokenism and was unable to meet the needs of poor and working-class people in communities of color.

De Facto Segregation

Once a certain group of people were socially constructed as different, the markers of class, culture, and skin color helped to easily point out those who were to be considered undeserving. Ensuring subordination required different starting points, laws, and institutions that accelerate accomplishments for the dominant group and block success for the subjugated group. The control of space concentrated undesirables into segregated geographic landscapes.

This separation was accomplished institutionally and on a day-to-day basis by historical patterns that have not been removed. The ideology that condones inequality and maltreatment has become so taken for granted that Haney-López (2003:127) argued it has become common-sense racism: acting in a discriminatory manner, following certain scripts, has become so ordinary and pervasive that few people give it any thought: "Common sense is so integral to racism in the contemporary United States that I suggest a new definition: racism is action arising out of racial common sense and enforcing racial hierarchy. I specifically include the requirement that racism enforce hierarchy in order to preserve 'racism' as a term that describes actions that perpetuate racial status inequality."

The lack of legitimate opportunities served a wider purpose: to ensure that these barriers would prevent the majority of marginalized groups in the barrio from becoming a political and socioeconomic threat to the current stratification of these two cities. Durkheim (1984:1v) argued that "so long as there are rich and poor from birth, there can exist no just contract, nor any just distribution of social status." In segregated areas of disadvantage a controlling process swept over the community. Living life in such a social environment is psychologically and physically destructive. From the beginning families were positioned in communities that experienced high poverty, unemployment, and misapplied forms of social control.

The predecessors of critical race theory first outlined that communities of color remain disadvantaged because they serve a wide variety of psychic and material purposes for those in power (Blauner 1972; Carmichael and Hamilton 1967; Fanon 1963; Hechter 1975; Memmi 1965).

The dominant group argued that the best solution involved the criminal justice system. Quinney (1975) argued that crime was defined by the dominant class and formulated to be enforced on the subordinate class primarily to protect the interests of the rich. This process included an ideology that rationalized crime legislation for a segment of the population purported to be a dangerous class (Reinarman 2001; Shelden 2001). The dangerous class has overwhelmingly included blacks, Latinos, Native Americans, and immigrants along with poor people. The dominant group had no intention of drastically improving the lives of members of the oppressed group and their neighborhoods. The criminal justice system contributed to the harm imposed on the oppressed. The structural problems in the community were ignored, and their misery and failure were blamed on themselves. The dominant group claimed that to stop these issues they simply needed heavier oversight. The kids were reported to need consequences, and their bad parents more punishment. The dominant group wanted to scare the subordinate group straight by showing stricter consequences. Law enforcement swept aggressively over the oppressed group to help them realize their weakness and the error in their ways. People were given additional punishments, including probation, prison, and parole. Marginalized groups responded to the opposition from the criminal justice system as they did with school officials: they internalized frustration. They were made to feel different and unworthy of integration.

The increasingly excessive regulations imposed after legitimated oppression leave me to question whether marginalized groups living in the barrio may be approaching life comparable to a total institution. I am thinking particularly of Goffman's third type of total institution, which "is organized to protect the community against what are felt to be intentional dangers to it, with the welfare of the persons thus sequestered not the immediate issue: jails, penitentiaries, P.O.W. camps, and concentration camps" (1961:5).

Resistance

The tactic of violence as outlined by Rosenbaum (1981) may have been deflated in the contemporary movement, but the new tactics of urban resistance geared toward criticism, self-help, and the subtle threat of mass demonstration continued to challenge the ever-increasing powers of the criminal justice system. In addition, Rosenbaum (1981) outlined how Mexicanos in each state (California, New Mexico, and Texas) responded differently to Anglo hostility. In Denver and Ogden barrio residents re-acted differently to gang enforcement. The historical Chicano activism in Denver made resistance integral to the barrio experience, whereas Ogden remained silent in response to the overwhelming overt and covert racism and religious persecution.

Durkheim argued, "We need to introduce into their relationships [people's division of labor] a greater justice by diminishing those exter-nal inequalities that are the source of our ills. . . . Such a task cannot be improvised in the silence of study" (1951:340). As an oppressed group in the United States, inner-city Mexican Americans cannot change their treatment without external civil rights protection, institutional policy changes, and subordinate group members' collective opposition to legiti-mated oppression. I have focused on four areas: the war on gangs, ne-gotiating membership, core ideals, and transforming gangs, all of which have been framed historically and set in a longitudinal perspective of law and order.

Latinos did not receive media attention about why, as a subjugated group, they were having difficulties in Denver and Ogden. There were a lot of negative portrayals by agents of the state that bombarded people to continue thinking that subjugated groups were a threat (Russell 1998). If Latinos were allowed to enter dominant-group institutions, they were often blocked from creating major change. To meet their needs, Lati-nos created their own groups to attain more equal rights, such as the Catholic Workers Protective Alliance, Crusade for Justice, and SOCIO. Chicanos countered that they were not subordinate, they were oppressed (Acuña 1972; Blauner 1972). They emphasized their rich culture and his-tory. They rejected the images of them presented by the dominant group in power. In order for Chicanos to mobilize against the dominant group, they needed to emphasize their cultural pride and form an ideological opposition with visible and public displays of strength (in the form of either militancy or nonviolent suffering) and unity (Haney-López 2003; Vigil 1999). They questioned the discrimination, inequality, police bru-tality, and biased education and laws.

The neighborhoods where Latinos lived were conducive to the for-mation of gangs (Moore 1991; Vigil 1988). This made it more difficult to combat dominant-group ideologies. Oppressed groups often came to internalize these negative perceptions about who they were (Fanon

1963; Haley 1964). Mexican American gang members battled Latinos from other neighborhoods and over generational descent. The people involved in street culture perceived others similar to themselves as the biggest threat to their life chances. The violence in the barrio created an endless cycle of victimization that left oppressed group members blinded to solutions. The structural process of segregation will maintain inequality for ascribed others to remain oppressed. When those with ascribed inequality challenge this hierarchy outside of the provided framework, they will be given additional punishments that will further legitimize their subordination. Marginalized individuals who responded to racial oppression with a street culture further victimized the community and gave the dominant society the evidence to respond to the problems in the barrio with additional controls, thereby contributing to their own oppression. D-Loc eloquently described how gangs made the inner-city Mexican American community heard along with the problems being encountered. Conventional suburban society has responded to gangs by imposing increased law enforcement and incarceration to reduce the ability of gang members to put in work. However, if we looked at this issue in terms of a total lack of governmental support in helping the community obtain empowerment, we can see more long-term improvements than waiting for residents to resort to violent and criminal reactions. It almost appears as if this cycle of violence remains tolerated in many inner-city communities for the exact purpose of maintaining strong outside control. Sánchez-Jankowski (2008) likened such an experience to a term used by Everett Hughes, a "bastard institution." This idea was also advanced in the documentary *Bastards of the Party*. Although gangs are not sanctioned by the dominant society, they have become profitable and essential in maintaining the panopticon level of criminal justice enforcement in barrios and inner-city neighborhoods across the country.

Our society has no reason to remove excessive regulation for it has become so routine that it is not seen as wrong. The oppressed have every reason to collectively organize and oppose the current hegemony and unequal stratification. Gang representing emphasized that gang members had found a niche, and applied policy should focus on creating an organization that serves the needs of the community while redirecting how these ideals are manifested. I am particularly advocating the creation of activist organizations that pursue community empowerment, as with the Crusade for Justice and the Black and Brown Berets in Denver (Vigil 1999).

Dawley's (1992) research found that fighting stopped among Chicago gangs during a period of time when they received community funding to develop cultural and community empowerment. Brotherton and Barrios (2004) have also charted how the Latin Kings have worked to transform themselves from a street gang into a group for empowerment. Sadly, mainstream society will most likely attempt to repress the development of such groups, if the mid-1960s to mid-1970s Black and Chicano movements serve as precedent. Moreover, the current push by the dominant group to divide, conquer, and incarcerate members of the Latin Kings who have preached transformation means that the dominant group fears and cannot tolerate these challenges. Gang members should continue their perseverance toward transformation and include people who hold positions in the dominant group's institutions. This can be the time when tokens who the dominant group attempts to use as pawns can inflict internal damage by being the cogs in the wheel of this framework and push for social justice.

The last thirty years of gang policies, focused on punitive consequences for perceived gang membership, have only contributed to the persistence of gangs. The solutions to gangs can be found within the communities in which they form. The approach should be twofold: opposing antigang policies and drawing current and former gang members into socially empowering groups. An example is Denver's Crusade for Justice, which incorporated gang members in the 1960s and 1970s and drew on their energy to help the larger Chicano community (Vigil 1999). Pushing for the social inclusion of gang members does not condone gangs but acknowledges the broader structural inequalities of racism. Involving gang leaders in positive empowerment efforts should be a priority for culturally and politically oriented groups working in the barrio. Inner-city communities across the country can benefit from solutions that intertwine both local and structural patterns for creating empowerment. Such solutions require intertwining broader Chicano/a movement themes of empowerment with localized organizing and programs. For example, the organizations I worked with in Denver may not operate the same in Utah or New Mexico, but the key principles can be tinkered with until solutions are obtained. As a member of the Crusade for Justice told me, "Bricks in mortar are bricks in mortar. If it can be done in one setting it can be done in another setting. And it can be done!"

Notes

Introduction

1. I have chosen to use the term "Latino" to describe the people interviewed in this research unless specific origin is known, in which case I use Mexican American, Mexican, Puerto Rican, and so forth. The interviewees identified themselves as Hispanic, Mexican, Mexican American, Chicano, and Mexicano. Acuña (2000:462) reports, "Throughout Chicano history the question of identity has consumed a lot of time and space, which is natural given the legacy of colonialism. Even before the Chicano student movement of the 1960s, activists argued as to what to call themselves." The lack of political and educational access for the majority of the people interviewed prevented me from using the term "Chicano." For more discussion on this topic, see Muñoz (1989). Although national data indicate that most Latinos consider themselves as racially white, none of the respondents in these inner-city neighborhoods identified with this racial group. Rather, they considered their ethnicity as a race. I use "white" to denote people of European descent who do not have a Hispanic ethnic background. Black and African American are used interchangeably.

2. My colleague Alex Alonso is finishing a doctoral degree in geography at University of Southern California, and Victor Rios, an associate professor at the University of California Santa Barbara, recently completed a book on the criminalization of youth (2011). I have also learned of Douglas Thompkins, an assistant professor at John Jay College. These three individuals are, to the best of my knowledge, the only ones besides me who have come from gangs and are now in academia.

3. From 2007 to the present I have conducted research on gangs along the United States–Mexico border, including the communities of Anthony and Las Cruces, New Mexico, and El Paso, Texas. It is my desire to turn this research into a future book.

1. Researching Gangs as an Insider

1. "Locote" are crazy homeboys or homegirls willing to defend the barrio—crazy in terms of bravery.

2. I never claimed an ex–gang membership role in any of my state occupations. I only emphasized that I knew the streets. I still believe such an ex–gang member role suffers a huge stigma, and I could include many stories on how the police fear gang members infiltrating their institutions.

3. The most tragic of such recordings included the aftermath of a shooting of an unarmed young male Latino by a police officer in front of my apartment complex. I helped gather witness statements for the man's family and released my videotape to them. This officer shot another unarmed Latino six months later. The officer was commended as a hero by city's chief of police and was not criminally charged in either case. I am currently writing several research reports regarding police shootings in Denver from 1983 to 2008.

4. None of Ogden's neighborhoods was more than 50 percent black.

5. I hope to publish this work in the future, and I have given several research presentations on the topic.

2. The War on Gangs in the Post–Civil Rights Era

1. To date I have come across only one gang that matches this status in the cities I have studied.

2. On March 2, 1998, six pounds of cocaine were discovered missing from the property room of the Los Angeles Police Department. This led to the arrest of a CRASH officer, who later entered into a confidential plea agreement and received a reduced sentence on drug charges (*Los Angeles Times*, Sept. 21, 1999). The testimony of this officer would later lead to the overturning of one hundred convictions of alleged gang members and others arrested by the LAPD. Nine officers were prosecuted, and more than a dozen were fired or resigned, for behavior including beatings, killings, framing people, selling drugs, and engaging in various types of crimes while investigating and pursuing gang members (*Los Angeles Times*, Aug. 23, 2003). Many victims claimed their beatings were in retaliation for complaining about the officers' behavior (*Los Angeles Times*, Feb. 14, 2003). This scandal cost city taxpayers more than $40 million to settle claims by victims (*Los Angeles Times*, Feb. 27, 2003). A good overview of this scandal can be found in Kaplan (2009).

3. Racialized Oppression and the Emergence of Gangs

1. Of interest is how the South went from Democratic, anti-Republican, and anti-Lincoln to become Republican by the mid-1930s. Blacks also switched par-

ties; thus the early association of the Ku Klux Klan with the Republican Party in Denver was reflected the changes shortly to develop. See Franklin and Moss (2004) and Sitkoff (1978).

2. Two additional tracts contained people who were considered nonwhite but were in a different tract than the Spanish population. Thus, nonwhite races were more likely to be integrated with the Spanish-surnamed population.

3. For example, Cameron Smith (age 18) was shot and killed by Elliot Javay "Hollywood" Raiban, also known as Javay Richardson, an alleged Crip gang member; and Delontay Carolina Norris was killed in a drive-by shooting by an alleged Blood gang member named Darrell Wilson.

4. Demonizing Gangs Through Religious Righteousness and Suppressed Activism

1. Non-Mormonism seems to be typical of many of the minority gangs in Utah, with the exception of Tongans, who seem to have higher family involvement in the LDS Church.

2. The issue of illegal entry is ironic since residents of Utah enacted an immigration enforcement law that attempts to copy Arizona's legislation. The American Civil Liberties Union of Utah sued to block Utah's "Show Me Your Papers" law in 2011 and has been joined by the U.S. Department of Justice. http://www.acluutah.org/immigration.shtml.

3. For example, the lynching of George Segal, a 27-year-old Japanese immigrant, on April 20, 1884.

4. Further research is needed to investigate this period of time and whether there were any groups similar to gangs operating during this time frame.

5. Much of this early history can be enhanced when the *Standard Examiner* and *Salt Lake Tribune* make their news archives available and searchable for the years of 1970–1990.

5. Negotiating Membership for an Adaptation to Colonization: The Gang

1. To some extent, it may be possible that the administrators and teachers of color fell into the school policies or internalization of white ideology by maintaining the ongoing racism against students of color. A similarity was also found with police of color. I think because both groups were a small proportion of the overall number of police officers or teachers, they felt obligated to fit in or be replaced with a more willing control subject. It is always a trade-off: tokens can reach more people and influence the dominant group, but at the same time they often encounter losses to their dignity in putting up with common sense racism.

2. Vigil (1988:177) defines cholo as "A Chicano street style of youth who are marginal to both Mexican and Anglo culture; also used historically for cultural

marginals and racial hybrids in Mexico and some part of Latin America." This includes a distinctive style of dress, speech, gestures, tattoos, and graffiti that developed in a process of underclass and street exposure.

6. The Only Locotes Standing: The Persistence of Gang Ideals

1. Estimating the exact number of women sexed in to a gang is difficult. Several times I witnessed male gang members proudly proclaim the number of women that they had sexed into the gang, but much of it sounded like just talk. Most of the gangs I studied did not have this form of initiation.

2. For additional information on this topic, see my article in *Latino Studies* titled "Gang Organization" (2010), which provides a case study of Cola, an individual involved in drug distribution from his beginnings to his rise to his downfall.

3. Many gang intervention programs have begun providing tattoo removal to allow gang members to remove gang symbols and identity and begin anew.

4. For example, I have often provided a critique on academia because many academics act in similar ways to gangs in how they pursue power and attempt to dominate knowledge creation. Of interest with this topic could be the study of old-boy networks and how they continue to dominate university settings and professional conferences. In my view, academic gangsters are just as dangerous, if not more so, than street gangs because a lot of this jealousy is in the form of back-stabbing and using networks to keep certain people out, similar to a country club. They cite each other to rise in prestige, and it is presumed to correlate with their scientific merit regardless of the quality of work. Malcolm X made an interesting comparison of racism in the South and how it differed from the North. In the South racism was direct, known, and in your face, whereas in the North things may have been actually worse because the smile and handshake hid the knife that was about to enter your back. In my social world, gangs were direct about the issues, whereas academia attempted to utilize old-boy networks to make you learn your place. Derrick Bell (1985) offers an excellent critique of minority scholars presenting a challenge to the status quo. It is all good when the dominant group is perceived as helping you earn an opportunity in its social world, but quite another story when you are successful at it, because then you are a threat. "The more successful I appeared, the harsher became the collective judgment of my former friends. . . . The influx of qualified minority candidates threatened, at some deep level, the white faculty member's sense of ideological hegemony" (53). I find it interesting how most the so-called gang experts would never be caught in the company of those they write about.

References

Acuña, Rodolfo. 1972. *Occupied America: The Chicano's Struggle Toward Liberation.* San Francisco: Canfield Press.
———. 1998. *Sometimes There Is No Other Side: Chicanos and the Myth of Equality.* Notre Dame: University of Notre Dame Press.
———. 2000. *Occupied America: A History of Chicanos.* New York: Longman.
Adler, Patricia A. 1993. *Wheeling and Dealing: An Ethnography of an Upper-Level Drug Smuggling Community.* New York: Columbia University Press.
Adler, Patricia A., and Peter Adler. 1987. *Membership Roles in Field Research.* Newbury Park, Calif.: Sage.
———. 1991. *Backboards and Blackboards: College Athletes and Role Engulfment.* New York: Columbia University Press.
Adult Education Council of Denver. 1938. "The Youth Problem in Denver." *A Report by the Youth Survey Committee of the Adult Education Council of Denver* 14 (2). In clippings file, Denver Public Library.
Advancement Project. 2005. "Education on Lockdown: The Schoolhouse to Jailhouse Track." Washington, D.C..
Akers, Ronald. 1990. "Rational Choice, Deterrence, and Social Learning Theory in Criminology." *Journal of Criminal Law and Criminology* 81:653–76.
Allred, Alma. 2004. "The Traditions of Their Fathers: Myth Versus Reality in LDS Scriptural Writings." In *Black and Mormon,* edited by N. G. Bringhurst and D. T. Smith, 34–49. Urbana: University of Illinois Press.
Almaguer, Tomás. 1971. "Toward the Study of Chicano Colonialism." *Aztlan* 2:7–21.
———. 1994. *Racial Fault Lines: The Historical Origins of White Supremacy in California.* Los Angeles: University of California Press.
Anderson, Elijah. 1990. *Streetwise: Race, Class, and Change in an Urban Community.* Chicago: University of Chicago Press.
———. 1999. *Code of the Street: Decency, Violence, and the Moral Life of the Inner City.* New York: Norton.
Anderson, Jon Lee. 1997. *Che Guevara: A Revolutionary Life.* New York: Grove Press.

Arps, Louisa, W. 1998. *Denver in Slices: A Historical Guide to the City.* Athens: Ohio University Press.

Atkinson, Paul, Amanda Coffey, Sara Delamont, John Lofland, and Lyn Lofland, eds. 2001. *Handbook of Ethnography.* Thousand Oaks, Calif.: Sage.

Barrera, Mario. 1979. *Race and Class in the Southwest: A Theory of Racial Inequality.* Notre Dame: University of Notre Dame Press.

Barrera, Mario, Carlos Muñoz, and Charles Ornelas. 1972. "The Barrio as an Internal Colony." *Urban Affairs Annual Review* 6:465–98.

Bass, Sandra. 2001. "Policing Space, Policing Race: Social Control Imperatives and Police Discretionary Decisions." *Social Justice* 28:156–76.

Battin, Sara R., Karl G. Hill, Robert D. Abbott, Richard F. Catalano, and David J. Hawkins. 1998. "The Contribution of Gang Membership to Delinquency Beyond Delinquent Friends." *Criminology* 36:93–115.

Bayley, David H., and Harold Mendelsohn. 1968. *Minorities and the Police: Confrontation in America.* New York: Free Press.

Bell, Derrick. 1985. "The Supreme Court 1984 Term. Foreword: The Civil Rights Chronicles." *Harvard Law Review* 99 (1): 4–83

———. 1992. *Faces at the Bottom of the Well: The Permanence of Racism.* New York: Basic Books.

Bernard, Russell H. 1988. *Research Methods in Cultural Anthropology.* Newbury Park, Calif.: Sage.

Biernacki, Patrick, and Dan Waldorf. 1981. "Snowball Sampling." *Sociological Research and Methods* 10:141–63.

Bjerregaard, Beth, and Carolyn Smith. 1993. "Gender Differences in Gang Participation, Delinquency, and Substance Use." *Journal of Quantitative Criminology* 9:329–55.

Black, Donald. 1983. "Crime as Social Control." *American Sociological Review* 48:34–45.

Blauner, Robert. 1972. *Racial Oppression in America.* New York: Harper & Row.

Blauner, Robert, and David Wellman. 1973. "Toward the Decolonization of Social Research." In *The Death of White Sociology*, edited by J. A. Ladner, 310–30. New York: Vintage Books.

Bloch, Herbert A., and Arthur Niederhoffer. 1958. *The Gang: A Study in Adolescent Behavior.* Westport, Conn.: Greenwood Press.

Bogardus, Emory S. 1943. "Gangs of Mexican-American Youth." *Sociology and Social Research* 28:55–66.

Bonilla-Silva, Eduardo. 2003. Racism Without Racists: Color-Blind Racism and the Persistence of Racial Inequality in the United States. Boulder: Rowan and Littlefield.

Bourgois, Philippe. 1995. *In Search of Respect: Selling Crack in El Barrio.* New York: Cambridge University Press.

Boyle, Gregory. 2010. *Tattoos on the Heart: The Power of Boundless Compassion.* New York: Free Press.

Bringhurst, Newell G. 2004. "The 'Missouri Thesis' Revisited: Early Mormonism, Slavery, and the Status of Black People." In *Black and Mormon*, edited by N. G. Bringhurst and D. T. Smith, 13–33. Urbana: University of Illinois Press.

Bringhurst, Newell G., and Darron T. Smith. 2004. *Black and Mormon*. Urbana: University of Illinois Press.

Brotherton, David C. 1996. "Smartness, Toughness, and Autonomy: Drug Use in the Context of Gang Female Delinquency." *Journal of Drug Issues* 26: 261–77.

Brotherton, David C., and Luis Barrios. 2004. *The Almighty Latin King and Queen Nation: Street Politics and the Transformation of a New York City Gang*. New York: Columbia University Press.

Brown, David J. 1991. "Preprofessional Socialization and Identity Transformation: The Case of the Professional Ex-." *Journal of Contemporary Ethnography* 20:157–78.

Brown, Elaine. 1992. *A Taste of Power: A Black Woman's Story*. Anchor.

Browning, Katherine, and David Huizinga. 1999. "Highlights of Findings from the Denver Youth Survey." U.S. Department of Justice, Office of Justice Programs, Office of Juvenile Justice and Delinquency Prevention.

Browning, Sandra Lee, Francis T. Cullin, Liqun Cao, Renee Kopache, and Thomas J. Stevenson. 1994. "Race and Getting Hassled by the Police: A Research Note." *Police Studies* 17:1–11.

Bushman, Richard L. 1984. *Joseph Smith and the Beginnings of Mormonism*. Urbana: University of Illinois Press.

———. 2005. *Joseph Smith: Rough Stone Rolling*. New York: Knopf.

Camarillo, Albert. 1979. *Chicanos in a Changing Society: From Mexican Pueblos to American Barrios in Santa Barbara and Southern California, 1848–1930*. Cambridge: Harvard University Press.

Campbell, Anne. 1984. *The Girls in the Gang*. Cambridge, Mass.: Blackwell.

Carmichael, F. L. 1941. *Housing in Denver*. Denver: City and County of Denver.

Carmichael, Stokely, and Charles Hamilton. 1967. *Black Power*. New York: Random House.

Castells, Manuel. 2009. *Communication Power*. New York: Oxford University Press.

Cleaver, Eldridge. 1968. *Soul on Ice*. New York: Dell.

Cloward, Richard A. and Lloyd E. Ohlin. 1960. *Delinquency and Opportunity: A Theory of Delinquent Gangs*. New York: Free Press.

Cohen, Albert K. 1955. *Delinquent Boys: The Culture of the Gang*. New York: Free Press.

Cole, David. 1999. *No Equal Justice: Race and Class in the American Criminal Justice System*. New York: New Press.

Coleman, Ronald G. 1996. "Preface: Book Two, African-American Community." In *Missing Stories: An Oral History of Ethnic and Minority Groups in Utah*, edited by L. G. Kelen and E. H. Stone, 67–69. Salt Lake City: University of Utah Press.

Collins, Patricia Hill. 2000. *Black Feminist Thought: Knowledge, Consciousness, and the Politics of Empowerment*. New York: Routledge.

Colomy, Paul, and Laura Ross Greiner. 2000. "Making Youth Violence Visible: The News Media and the Summer of Violence." *Denver University Law Review* 77:661–88.

Colomy, Paul, and Martin Kretzmann. 1995. "Projects and Institution Building: Judge Ben B. Lindsey and the Juvenile Court." *Social Problems* 42:191–215.

Colorado Criminal Justice Reform Coalition. http://www.ccjrc.org.

Colorado Department of Education. 2003. "Teacher Count by Gender and Race/Ethnicity." Fall. http://www.cde.state.co.us/index_stats.htm.

Cromley, Ellen K. 1999. "Mapping Spatial Data." In *Mapping Social Networks, Spatial Data, and Hidden Populations*, edited by J. Schensul, M. D. LeCompte, R. T. Trotter, E. K. Cromley, and M. Singer, 51–124. Walnut Creek, Calif.: AltaMira Press.

Cuch, Forrest S. 2000. *A History of Utah's American Indians*. Salt Lake City: Utah State Division of Indians Affairs, Utah State Division of History.

Cureton, Steven R. 2008. *Hoover Crips: When Cripin' Becomes a Way of Life*. Lanham, Md.: University Press of America.

Curry, G. David, Richard A. Ball, and Scott H. Decker. 1996. "Estimating the National Scope of Gang Crime from Law Enforcement Data." *Research in Brief*. Washington, D.C.: U.S. Department of Justice, Office of Justice Programs, National Institute of Justice. NCJ 161477.

Davis, James Harlan. 1963. "Ku Klux Klan Interviews." Western History/Genealogy Department, Denver Public Library.

Dawley, David. 1973 (repr. 1992). *A Nation of Lords: The Autobiography of the Vice Lords*. Prospect Heights, Ill.: Waveland Press.

Decker, Scott. 1996. "Collective and Normative Features of Gang Violence." *Justice Quarterly* 13 (2): 243–64.

Decker, Scott H., and Barrik Van Winkle. 1996. *Life in the Gang: Family, Friends, and Violence*. New York: Cambridge University Press.

Decker, Scott H., and Frank W. Weerman. 2005. *European Street Gangs and Troublesome Youth Groups*. New York: AltaMira Press.

Deegan, Mary Jo. 2001. "The Chicago School of Ethnography." In *Handbook of Ethnography*, edited by P. Atkinson, A. Coffey, S. Delamont, J. Lofland, and L. Lofland, 11–25 . Thousand Oaks, Calif.: Sage.

Defa, Dennis R. "The Goshute Indians of Utah." In *A History of Utah's American Indians*, edited by F. S. Cuch, 73–122. Salt Lake City: Utah State Division of Indian Affairs, Utah State Division of History.

Delgado, Richard. 1995. *The Rodrigo Chronicles: Conversations about America and Race*. New York: New York University Press.

———. 1996. *The Coming Race War? And Other Apocalyptic Tales of America After Affirmative Action and Welfare*. New York: New York University Press.

———. 1999. *When Equality Ends: Stories About Race and Resistance*. Boulder: Westview Press.

Delgado, Richard, and Jean Stefancic. 1999. "Home-grown Racism: Colorado's Historic Embrace—and Denial—of Equal Opportunity in Higher Education." *University of Colorado Law Review* 70.

———. 2001. *Critical Race Theory: An Introduction*. New York: New York University Press.

———. 2003. *Justice at War: Civil Liberties and Civil Rights During Times of Crisis*. New York: New York University Press.

———. 2005. *The Derrick Bell Reader*. New York: New York University Press.

Delgado-Gaitan, Concha. 1988. "The Value of Conformity: Learning to Stay in School." *Anthropology & Education Quarterly* 19:354–81.

Denver Commission on Human Relations. 1947. *A Report on Minorities in Denver, with Recommendations by the Mayor's Interim Survey Committee on Human Resources*. Box 1.

Denzin, Norman K. 1970 (repr. 1989). *The Research Act: A Theoretical Introduction to Sociological Methods*. Englewood Cliffs, N.J.: Prentice Hall.

———. 1989. *Interpretive Interactionism*. Newbury Park, Calif.: Sage.

Department of Planning and Research. 2003. "Summary Report of Student Membership by Ethnicity." October 1. City and County of Denver.

Diaz, Tom. 2009. *No Boundaries: Transnational Latino Gangs and American Law Enforcement*. Ann Arbor: University of Michigan Press.

Donner, Frank J. 1980. *The Age of Surveillance: The Aims and Methods of America's Political Intelligence System*. New York: Knopf.

Dorsett, Lyle, and Michael McCarthy. 1986. *The Queen City: a History of Denver*. Boulder: Pruett.

Douglas, Jack D. 1976. *Investigative Social Research: Individual and Team Field Research*. Beverly Hills, Calif.: Sage.

Dunn, Timothy J. 1996. *The Militarization of the U.S.-Mexico Border 1978–1992: Low-Intensity Conflict Doctrine Comes Home*. Austin: University of Texas Press.

———. 2009. *Blockading the Border and Human Rights: The El Paso Operation That Remade Immigration Enforcement*. Austin: University of Texas Press.

Dunworth, Terence, and Gregory Mills. 1999. "National Evaluation of Weed and Seed." U.S. Department of Justice, Office of Justice Programs, National Institute of Justice.

Durán, Robert J. 2010. "Gang Organization: Slangin,' Gang Bangin,' and Dividin' a Generation." *Latino Studies* 8 (3): 373–98.

———. 2011. "An Attempt to Change Disproportionate Minority Contact by Working in Youth Corrections." In *Experiencing Corrections: Lessons from the Field*, edited by M. Johnson, 149–64. Thousand Oaks, Calif: Sage.

———. Forthcoming a. "Policing the Barrios: Exposing the Shadows to the Brightness of a New Day." In *Latinos and Latinas (Hispanics) in the US Criminal Justice System: The New American Demography*, edited by M. G. Urbina. Springfield, Ill.: Charles C. Thomas.

———. Forthcoming b. "Immigration, Border Concerns, and Youth Gangs." In *Encyclopedia of Criminology and Criminal Justice*, edited by G. Bruinsma and D. Weisburd. New York: Springer.

Durkheim, Emile. 1951. *Suicide*. New York: Free Press.

———. 1984. *The Division of Labor in Society*. New York: Free Press.

Earl, Jennifer, Andrew Martin, John D. McCarthy, and Sarah A. Soule. 2004. "The Use of Newspaper Data in the Study of Collective Action." *Annual Review of Sociology* 30:65–80.

Ehrenreich, Barbara. 1997. *Blood Rites: Origins and History of the Passions of War*. New York: Metropolitan Books.

Erikson, Kai T. 1966. *Wayward Puritans: A Study in the Sociology of Deviance*. New York: John Wiley & Sons.

Esbensen, Finn-Aage, and David Huizinga. 1993. "Gangs, Drugs, and Delinquency in a Survey of Urban Youth." *Criminology* 31:565–89.

Esbensen, Finn-Aage, and D. Wayne Osgood. 1997. "National Evaluation of G.R.E.A.T. Research in Brief." Washington, D.C.: U.S. Department of Justice, Office of Justice Programs, National Institute of Justice. NCJ 167264.

Escobar, Edward J. 1999. *Race, Police, and the Making of a Political Identity: Mexican Americans and the Los Angeles Police Department 1900–1945*. Los Angeles: University of California Press.

Espinoza-Herold, Mariella. 2003. *Issues in Latino Education: Race, School Culture, and the Politics of Academic Success*. Boston: Pearson Education Group.

Esteva Martínez, Juan Francisco. 2003. "Urban Street Activists: Gang and Community Efforts to Bring Peace and Justice to Los Angeles Neighborhoods." In *Gangs and Society: Alternative Perspectives*, edited by L. Kontos, D. Brotherton, and L. Barrios, 95–115. New York: Columbia University Press.

Fagan, Jeffrey, and Garth Davies. 2000. "Street Stops and Broken Windows: Terry, Race and Disorder in New York City." *Fordham Urban Law Journal* 28:457–504.

Fanon, Frantz. 1963. *The Wretched of the Earth*. New York: Grove Press.

Farkas, George, Robert P. Grobe, Daniel Sheehan, and Yuan Shuan. 1990. "Cultural Resources and School Success: Gender, Ethnicity, and Poverty Groups Within an Urban School District." *American Sociological Review* 55:127–42.

Feagin, Joe R. 2010. *The White Racial Frame: Centuries of Racial Framing and Counter-Framing*. New York: Routledge.

Feagin, Joe R. and Melvin P. Sikes. 1994. *Living with Racism: The Black Middle-Class Experience*. Boston: Beacon.

Felson, Richard B., and Henry J. Steadman. 1983. "Situational Factors in Disputes Leading to Criminal Violence." *Criminology* 21:59–74.

Fine, Michelle, Nick Freudenberg, Yasser Payne, Tiffany Perkins, Kersha Smith, and Katya Wanzer. 2003. "Anything Can Happen with Police Around': Urban Youth Evaluate Strategies of Surveillance in Public Places." *Journal of Social Issues* 59:141–58.

Fischer, Constance. 1984. "A Phenomenological Study of Being Criminally Victimized: Contributions and Constraints of Qualitative Research." *Journal of Social Issues* 40:161–78.

Fishman, Laura T. 1995. "The Vice Queens: An Ethnographic Study of Black Female Gang Behavior." In *The Modern Gang Reader*, edited by M. W. Klein, C. L. Maxson, and J. Miller, 83–92 . Los Angeles: Roxbury.

Fleisher, Mark S. 1998. *Dead End Kids: Gang Girls and the Boys They Know*. Madison: University of Wisconsin Press.

Franklin, John Hope, and Alfred A. Moss. 2000. *From Slavery to Freedom: A History of African Americans*. New York: Knopf.

Freire, Paulo. 1970 (repr. 2000). *Pedagogy of the Oppressed*. New York: Continuum.

Fremon, Celeste. 1995. *Father Greg and the Homeboys: The Extraordinary Journey of Father Boyle and His Work with the Latino Gangs of East L.A.* New York: Hyperion.

Delgado-Gaitan, Concha. 1988. "The Value of Conformity: Learning to Stay in School." *Anthropology & Education Quarterly* 19:354–81.

Garcia, Mario T. 1981. *Desert Immigrants: The Mexicans of El Paso, 1880–1920*. New Haven: Yale University Press.

Garot, Robert. 2010. *Who You Claim: Performing Gang Identity in School and on the Streets*. New York: New York University Press.

Garza-Caballero, Azenett. 2005. "Weed and Seed: Final Report." Ms.

Geary, William R. 2000. "The Creation of RICO: Law as a Knowledge Diffusion Process." *Crime, Law, and Social Change* 33:329–67.

Geertz, Clifford. 1973. *The Interpretation of Cultures*. New York: Basic Books.

Gemert, Frank V., and Mark S. Fleisher. 2005. "In the Grip of the Group." In *European Street Gang and Troublesome Youth Groups*, edited by S. H. Decker and F. M. Weerman, 11–29. New York: AltaMira Press.

George, Hermon, Jr. 2004. "Community Development as the Politics of Deracialization: The Case of Denver, Colorado, 1991–2003." *ANNALS of the American Academy of Political and Social Science* 594:143–57.

Gilliam, Philip B. 1943. *Report on the Delinquency Situation in Denver. From January 1, 1943 to September 1, 1943*. Juvenile Court.

——. 1950. "Youngsters in Trouble." *Juvenile Family Court Journal* 1 (3): 16–17.

Goffman, Erving. 1959. *The Presentation of Self in Everyday Society*. New York: Doubleday Anchor Books.

——. 1961. *Asylums: Essays on the Social Situation of Mental Patients and Other Inmates*. Anchor.

——. 1963. *Behavior in Public Places: Notes on the Social Organization of Gatherings*. New York: Free Press of Glencoe.

Goldberg, Robert Alan. 1975. *Hooded Empire: The Ku Klux Klan in Denver*. Illinois: University of Illinois Press.

——. 1981. Papers, WH649, Western History Collection, Denver Public Library.

Gómez, Laura E. 2007. *Manifest Destinies: The Making of the Mexican American Race*. New York: New York University Press.

Gorman-Smith, Deborah, and Patrick Tolan. 1998. "The Role of Exposure to Community Violence and Developmental Problems among Inner-City Youth." *Developmental and Psychopathology* 10 (1): 101–16.

Greenfeld, Lawrence A., Patrick A. Langan, and Steven K. Smith. 1999. "Police Use of Force: Collection of National Data." Washington, D.C.: U.S. Department of Justice, Bureau of Justice Statistics and National Institute of Justice. NCJ 165040.

Gutierrez, Jose Angel. 1996. "Tracking King Tiger: The Political Surveillance of Reies Lopez Tijerina by the Federal Bureau of Investigation." Paper presented at the Twenty-third National Association for Chicana and Chicano Studies (NACCS) Annual Conference, Chicago, March 20–23.

———. N.d. "Illegal Border Crossings: The FBI's Border Coverage Program." Ms.

Hagedorn, John M. 1988 (repr. 1998). *People and Folks: Gangs, Crime and the Underclass in a Rustbelt City.* Chicago: Lakeview Press.

———. 1990. "Back in the Field Again: Gang Research in the Nineties." In *Gangs in America*, edited by C. R. Huff, 240–59. Newbury Park, Calif.: Sage.

———. 2008. *A World of Gangs: Armed Young Men and Gangsta Culture.* Minneapolis: University of Minnesota Press.

Haley, Alex. 1964. *The Autobiography of Malcolm X.* New York: Ballantine.

Hall, Daniel E. 1996. *Criminal Law and Procedure.* New York: Delmar.

Haney-López, Ian F. 1996. *White by Law: The Legal Construction of Race.* New York: New York University Press.

———. 2003. *Racism on Trial: The Chicano Fight for Justice.* Cambridge: Belknap Press of Harvard University.

Hayden, Tom. 2004. *Street Wars.* New York: New Press.

Hechter, Michael. 1975. *Internal Colonialism: The Celtic Fringe in British National Development, 1536–1966.* Berkeley: University of California Press.

Hemmens, Craig, and Daniel Levin. 2000. "Resistance Is Futile: The Right to Resist Unlawful Arrest in an Era of Aggressive Policing." *Crime and Delinquency* 46:472–96.

Hentig, Hans von. 1940. "The Colorado Crime Survey." Archives. University of Colorado Boulder. April 1.

Hertz, Rosanna. 1997. *Reflexivity and Voice.* Thousand Oaks, Calif.: Sage.

Hispanic Oral Histories. 1984–87. Salt Lake City: Special Collections, J. Willard Marriott Library, University of Utah.

Holmes, Malcolm D. 2000. "Minority Threat and Police Brutality: Determinants of Civil Rights Criminal Complaints in U.S. Municipalities." *Criminology* 38:343–67.

Horowitz, Ruth. 1983. *Honor and the American Dream: Culture and Identity in a Chicano Community.* New Brunswick, N.J.: Rutgers University Press.

Howell, James C. 1998. "Youth Gangs: An Overview." Washington, DC: Office of Juvenile Justice and Delinquency Prevention.

———. 2008. "Youth Gang Bibliography." National Youth Gang Center.

———. 2012. *Gangs in America's Communities.* Thousand Oaks, Calif.: Sage.

Howell, James C. and Debra K. Gleason. 1999. "Youth Gang Trafficking." Research in Brief. Washington, DC: U.S. Department of Justice, Office of Justice Programs, National Institute of Justice.

Hughes, Everett C. 1945. "Dilemmas and Contradictions of Status." *American Journal of Sociology* 50 (5): 353–59.

Hughes, Lorine A., and James F. Short. 2005. "Disputes Involving Youth Street Gang Members: Micro-social Contexts." *Criminology* 43:43–76.

Huizinga, David, Anne Wylie Wiher, Scott Menard, Rachele Espiritu, and Finn Esbensen. 1998. "Some Not So Boring Findings from the Denver Youth Survey." National Criminal Justice Reference Service.

Human Rights Watch. 1998. *Shielded from Justice: Police Brutality and Accountability in the United States.* New York: Human Rights Watch.

Hunt, Geoffrey P., Karen Joe-Laidler, and Kristy Evans. 2002. "The Meaning and Gendered Culture of Getting High: Gang Girls and Drug Use Issues." *Contemporary Drug Problems* 29:375–416

Hutchison, Ray, and Charles Kyle. 1987. "Hispanic Street Gangs in Chicago's Public Schools." n *Gangs: The Origins and Impact of Contemporary Youth Gangs in the United States,* edited by S. Cummings, and D. J. Monti, 113–36. Albany: State University of New York Press.

Iber, Jorge. 2000. *Hispanics in the Mormon Zion: 1912–1999.* College Station: Texas A&M University Press.

Jackson, Pamela Irving. 1989. *Minority Group Threat, Crime, and Policing: Social Context and Social Control.* New York: Praeger.

Jacobs, David, and Robert M. O'Brien. 1998. "The Determinants of Deadly Force: A Structural Analysis of Police Violence." *American Journal of Sociology* 103:837–62.

Jones, Nikki. 2004. " 'It's Not Where You Live, It's How You Live': How Young Women Negotiate Conflict and Violence in the Inner City." *ANNALS of the American Academy* 595:49–62.

Jones, Sondra. 2000. *The Trial of Don Pedro León Luján: The Attack Against Indian Slavery and Mexican Traders in Utah.* Salt Lake City: University of Utah Press.

Jorgensen, Danny L. 1989. *Participant Observation: A Methodology for Human Studies.* Thousand Oaks, Calif.: Sage.

Juvenile Hall: A Division of Denver's Famous Juvenile Court. 1960. Denver Juvenile Court Cases and Hearings 1941–1959.

Kane, Robert J. 2002. "The Social Ecology of Police Misconduct." *Criminology* 40:867–96.

Kaplan, Paul J. 2009. "Looking Through the Gaps: A Critical Approach to the LAPD's Rampart Scandal." *Social Justice* 36:61–81.

Kelen, Leslie G., and Eileen Hallet Stone. 1996. *Missing Stories: An Oral History of Ethnic and Minority Groups in Utah.* Salt Lake City: University of Utah Press.

Kennedy, Randall. 1997. *Race, Crime, and the Law.* New York: Vintage Books.

Katz, Charles M., and Vincent J. Webb. 2006. *Policing Gangs in America.* New York: Cambridge University.

Kaufman, Phillip, Martha Naomi Alt, and Christopher D. Chapman. 2001. "Dropout Rates in the United States: 2000" (NCES 2002–114). U.S. Department of Education, NCES. Washington, D.C.: U.S. Government Printing Office.

Keefe, Susan E. 1979. "Urbanization, Acculturation, and Extended Family Ties: Mexican Americans in Cities." *American Ethnologist* 6:349–65.

King, Martin Luther, Jr. 1967. *Where Do We Go From Here: Chaos or Community?* Boston: Beacon Press.

Kirk, Jerome, and Marc L. Miller. 1986. *Reliability and Validity in Qualitative Research.* Beverly Hills, Calif.: Sage.

Klein, Malcolm. W. 1968. *From Association to Guilt: The Group Guidance Project in Juvenile Gang Intervention.* Los Angeles: Youth Studies Center, University of Southern California, and Los Angeles County Probation Department.

———. 1971. *Street Gangs and Street Workers.* Englewood Cliffs, N.J.: Prentice-Hall.

———. 1995. *The American Street Gang: Its Nature, Prevalence, and Control.* New York: Oxford University Press.

———. 2004. *Gang Cop: The Words and Ways of Officer Paco Domingo.* Walnut Creek, Calif.: AltaMira.

———. 2005. "The Value of Comparisons in Street Gang Research." *Journal of Contemporary Criminal Justice* 21 (2): 135–52.

———. 2007. *Chasing After Street Gangs: A Forty-Year Journey.* Upper Saddle River, N.J.: Prentice Hall.

Klein, Malcolm W., and Cheryl L. Maxson. 2006. *Street Gang Patterns and Policies.* New York: Oxford University Press.

Krisberg, Barry. 1975. *Crime and Privilege: Toward a New Criminology.* Englewood Cliffs, N.J.: Prentice Hall.

Krivo, Lauren J., and Ruth D. Peterson. 1996. "Extremely Disadvantaged Neighborhoods and Urban Crime." *Social Forces* 75:619–48.

Krivo, Lauren J., Ruth D. Peterson, and Danielle C. Kuhl. 2009. "Segregation, Racial Structure, and Neighborhood Violent Crime." *American Journal of Sociology* 114 (6): 1765–1802.

Ku Klux Klan Tapes. 1962. Collaborative Digitization Project. Western History and Genealogy, Denver Public Library.

Kubrin, Charis E., and Ronald Weitzer. 2003. "Retaliatory Homicide: Concentrated Disadvantage and Neighborhood Culture." *Social Problems* 50: 157–80.

Ladner, Joyce A. 1973. *The Death of White Sociology.* New York: Random House.

Larson, Gustive O. 1971. *The Americanization of Utah for Statehood.* San Marino, Calif.: Huntington Library.

Leonard, Stephen J., and Thomas J. Noel. 1990. *Denver: Mining Camp to Metropolis.* Niwot: University Press of Colorado.

Lofland, John, and Lyn H. Lofland. 1995. *Analyzing Social Settings: A Guide to Qualitative Observation and Analysis.* New York: Wadsworth.

Logan, John R., and Brian J. Stults. 2010. "Racial and Ethnic Separation in the Neighborhoods: Progress at a Standstill." *US 2010, Discover America in a New Century.* American Communities Project. Russell Sage Foundation. http://www.s4.brown.edu/us2010/Data/Report/report1.pdf.

Lopez, Edward M., Alison Wishard, Ronald Gallimore, and Wendy Rivera. 2006. "Latino High School Students' Perceptions of Gangs and Crews." *Journal of Adolescent Research* 21 (3): 299–318.

Luckenbill, David F., and Daniel P. Doyle. 1989. "Structural Position and Violence: Developing a Cultural Explanation." *Criminology* 27:419–36.

Macey, David. 2000. *Frantz Fanon: A Biography.* New York: Picador.

MacKinnon, William P. 2008. *At Sword's Point, Part I: A Documentary History of the Utah War to 1858.* Norman, Okla.: Arthur H. Clark Company.

MacMillan, Ross. 2001. "Violence and the Life Course: The Consequences of Victimization for Personal and Social Development." *Annual Review of Sociology* 27:1–22.

Madsen, Brigham. 1980. *Corinne: The Gentile Capital of Utah.* Salt Lake City: Utah State Historical Society.

Marx, Karl. 1994. *The Eighteenth Brumaire of Louis Bonaparte.* In *Karl Marx: Selected Writings,* edited by L. H. Simon, 187–208. Indianapolis: Hackett.

Mastrofski, Stephen D., Michael D. Resig, and John D. McCluskey. 2002. "Police Disrespect Toward the Public: An Encounter-based Analysis." *Criminology* 40:519–52.

Mauck, Laura M. 2001. *Five Points Neighborhood of Denver.* Chicago: Arcadia Publishing.

Mauer, Marc. 1999. *Race to Incarcerate.* New York: New Press.

Maxson, Cheryl L. 1998. "Gang Members on the Move." *Juvenile Justice Bulletin.* U.S. Department of Justice, Office of Justice Programs, Office of Juvenile Justice and Delinquency Prevention.

May, Dean L. 1987. *Utah: A People's History.* Salt Lake City: University of Utah Press.

Mazón, Mauricio. 1984. *The Zoot-Suit Riots: The Psychology of Symbolic Annihilation.* Austin: University of Texas Press.

McConkie, Bruce R. 1979. *Mormon Doctrine.* Salt Lake City: Bookcraft.

McCorkle, Richard C., and Terance D. Miethe. 2002. *Panic: The Social Construction of the Street Gang Problem.* Upper Saddle River, N.J.: Prentice Hall.

McPherson, Robert S. 2000. "Setting the Stage: Native America Revisited." In *A History of Utah's American Indians,* edited by F. S. Cuch, 3–24. Logan: Utah State University Press.

McWilliams, Carey. 1948 (repr. 1990). *North From Mexico: The Spanish-Speaking People of the United States.* Westport, Conn.: Praeger.

Meehan, Albert J., and Michael C. Ponder. 2002. "Race and Place: The Ecology of Racial Profiling African American Motorists." *Justice Quarterly* 19:399–430.

Meier, Matt S., and Feliciano Ribera. 1996. *Mexican Americans/American Mexicans: From Conquistadors to Chicanos* .New York: Hill and Wang.

Memmi, Albert. 1965. *The Colonizer and the Colonized.* Translated by Howard Greenfield. New York: Orion Press.

Merton, Robert K. 1968. *Social Theory and Social Structure.* New York: The Free Press.

———. 1972. "Insiders and Outsiders: A Chapter in the Sociology of Knowledge." *American Journal of Sociology* 78:9–47.

Miller, Jody. 2001. *One of the Guys: Girls, Gangs, and Gender.* New York: Oxford University Press.

Miller, Walter B. 1958. "Lower Class Culture as a Generating Milieu of Gang Delinquency." *Journal of Social Issues* 14:5–19.

———. 1982 (repr. 1992). *Crime by Youth Gangs and Groups in the United States*. Washington, D.C: U.S. Department of Justice, Office of Justice Programs, Office of Juvenile Justice and Delinquency Prevention. NCJ 156221.

Mills, C. Wright. 1959 (repr. 2000). *The Sociological Imagination*. New York: Oxford University Press.

Mirandé, Alfredo. 1977. "The Chicano Family: A Reanalysis of Conflicting Views." *Journal of Marriage and the Family* 39:747–56.

———. 1985. *The Chicano Experience: An Alternative Perspective*. Notre Dame: University of Notre Dame Press.

———. 1987. *Gringo Justice*. Notre Dame: University of Notre Dame Press.

Moloney, Molly, Kathleen MacKenzie, Geoffrey Hunt, and Karen Joe-Laidler. 2009. "The Path and Promise of Fatherhood for Gang Members." *British Journal of Criminology* 49:305–25.

Montejano, David. 2010. *Quixote's Soldiers: A Local History of the Chicano Movement, 1966–1981*. Austin: University of Texas Press.

Montgomery, Charles. 2002. *The Spanish Redemption: Heritage, Power, and Loss of New Mexico's Upper Rio Grande*. Los Angeles: University of California Press.

Mooney, Bernice M., and J. Terrence Fitzgerald. 2008. *Salt of the Earth: The History of the Catholic Church in Utah, 1776–2007*. Salt Lake City: University of Utah Press.

Moore, Joan W. 1978. *Homeboys: Gangs, Drugs and Prison in the Barrios of Los Angeles*. Philadelphia: Temple University Press.

———. 1991. *Going Down to the Barrio: Homeboys and Homegirls in Change*. Philadelphia: Temple University Press.

Moore, Joan W., and John Hagedorn. 2001. "Female Gangs: A Focus on Research." Juvenile Justice Bulletin, March. Office of Juvenile Justice and Delinquency Prevention, U.S. Department of Justice, Washington, D.C..

Morales, Armando. 1972. *Ando Sangrando: A Study of Mexican American-Police Conflict*. La Puenta, Calif.: Perspectiva Publications.

Moses, Anne. 1999. "Exposure to Violence, Depression, and Hostility in a Sample of Inner City High School Youth." *Journal of Adolescence* 22 (1): 21–32.

Muñoz, Carlos. 1989. *Youth, Identity, Power: The Chicano Movement*. New York: Verso.

Murguía, Edward. 1975. *Assimilation, Colonialism, and the Mexican American People*. Austin: University of Texas Press.

National Change Database CD. 1970–2000. Geolytics.

National Committee Against Discrimination in Housing. 1951. *Report*. In Denver Public Library Western History Collection. March.

National Youth Gang Center. 2009. Demographics: Race/Ethnicity of Gang Members. http://www.nationalgangcenter.gov/Survey-Analysis/Demographics#anchorregm

Nephi 2, 5:20–21. Pp. 66 in *The Book of Mormon: Another Testament of Jesus Christ*. Salt Lake City, UT: The Church of Jesus Christ of Latter-day Saints.

Newman, Katherine S. 2004. *Rampage: The Social Roots of School Shootings.* New York: Basic Books.

Obregón Pagán, Eduardo. 2003. *Murder at the Sleepy Lagoon: Zoot Suits, Race, and Riot in Wartime L.A.* Chapel Hill: University of North Carolina Press.

Ogden's Enterprise Community. 1997. "An Overview."

———. 1999. "Executive Report."

Ogden Police Department Gang Statistics. 1994–2005.

Ogden/Weber Metro Gang Unit. 1997. Northern Utah Gang Conference.

———. 1998. Northern Utah Gang Update.

———. 1999. Working Together for a Safer Community, Northern Utah Gang Conference.

Olguin, Ben V. 1997. "Tattoos, Abjection, and the Political Unconscious: Toward a Semiotics of the Pinto Visual Vernacular." *Cultural Critique* 37:159–213.

Omi, Michael and Howard Winant. 1994. *Racial Formation in the United States: From the 1960s to the 1990s.* New York: Routledge.

Padilla, Felix M. 1992. *The Gang as an American Enterprise.* New Brunswick, N.J.: Rutgers University Press.

Page, J. Bryan. 1997. "Vulcans and Jutes: Cuban Fraternities and Their Disappearance. *Free Inquiry* 25 (1): 65–73.

Parker, Robert N., and Kathleen Auerhahn. 1998. "Alcohol, Drugs, and Violence." *Annual Review of Sociology* 24:291–311.

Parks and Recreation Department. 1958. City of Denver.

Pate, Anthony M., and Lori A. Fridell. 1993. "Police Use of Force." Washington, D.C.: Police Foundation.

Peguero, Anthony, and Zahra Shekarkhar. 2011. "Latino/a Student Misbehavior and School Punishment." *Hispanic Journal of Behavioral Sciences* 33 (1): 54–70.

Pelto, Gretel H., and Pertti J. Pelto. 1979. *The Cultural Dimension of Human Adventure.* New York: Macmillan.

Perkins, Useni Eugene. 1987. *Explosion of Chicago's Black Street Gangs: 1900 to Present.* Chicago: Third World Press.

Peterson, Ross F., and Robert E. Parson. 2001. *Ogden City: Its Governmental Legacy.* Ogden, UT: Chapelle.

Peterson, Ruth D., and Lauren J. Krivo. 2009. "Race, Residence, and Violent Crime: A Structure of Inequality." *Kansas Law Review* 57 (4): 903–33.

Phillips, Julie A. 2002. "White, Black, and Latino Homicide Rates: Why the Difference?" *Social Problems* 49:349–73.

Poremba, Chester D. 1955. "Group Probation: An Experiment." *Federal Probation* 19:22.

Portillos, Edwardo L. 1999. "Women, Men and Gangs: The Social Construction of Gender in the Barrio. In *Female Gangs in America: Essays on Girls, Gangs, and Gender,* edited by M. Chesney-Lind and J. M. Hagedorn, 232–44. Chicago: Lake View Press.

Quinney, Richard. 1975. *Criminology.* Boston: Little, Brown.

Rebellon, Cesar J., and Michelle Manasse. 2004. "Do 'Bad Boys' Really Get the Girls? Delinquency as a Cause and Consequence of Dating Behavior Among Adolescents." *Justice Quarterly* 21:355–89.

Reimer, Jeffrey W. 1977. "Varieties of Opportunistic Research." *Urban Life* 5:467–77.

Reinarman, Craig. 2001. "The Social Construction of Drug Scares." In *Constructions of Deviance: Social Power, Context, and Interaction*, edited by P. A. Adler and P. Adler, 147–68 . Belmont, Calif.: Wadsworth.

Rios, Victor M. 2011. *Punished: Policing the Lives of Black and Latino Boys.* New York: New York University Press.

Ritter, Bill. 1997. "Investigation of the Shooting Death of Manuel Moreno-Delgado." April 7.

———. 2003. "Investigation of the Shooting Death of Anthony Ray Jefferson." March 7. http://www.denverda.org/Decision_Letters/02Jefferson.htm.

Roberts, Richard C., and Richard W. Sadler. 1985. *Ogden: Junction City.* Northridge, Calif.: Windsor Publications.

Rodgers, Frederic B. 1976. "Judge Ben B. Lindsey and the Colorado Ku Klux Klan." *Colorado Lawyer.*

Rodriguez, Luis. 1994. *Always Running: La Vida Loca: Gang Days in L.A.* New York: Touchstone.

———. 2003. *Hearts and Hands: Creating Community in Violent Times.* Seven Stories Press.

Rodriguez, Roberto. 2002. Presentation given at University of Colorado-Boulder.

Roediger, David R. 1991. *The Wages of Whiteness: Race and the Making of the American Working Class.* New York: Verso.

Romney, Thomas Cottam. 2005. *The Mormon Colonies in Mexico.* Salt Lake City: University of Utah Press.

Romo, Ricardo. 1983. *East Los Angeles: History of a Barrio.* Austin: University of Texas Press.

Rosenbaum, Robert J. 1981 (repr. 1998). *Mexicano Resistance in the Southwest.* Dallas: Southern Methodist University Press.

Rosenbloom, Susan, and Niobe Way. 2004. "Experiences of Discrimination Among African American, Asian American, and Latino Adolescents in an Urban High School." *Youth and Society* 35:420–51.

Ruiz, Mona, and Geoff Boucher. 1997. *Two Badges: The Lives of Mona Ruiz.* Houston: Arte Público Press.

Russell, Katheryn K. 1998. *The Color of Crime: Racial Hoaxes, White Fear, Black Protectionism, Police Harassment, and Other Macroaggressions.* New York: New York University Press.

Sadler, Richard W., and Richard C. Roberts. 2000. *Weber County's History.* Ogden, Utah: Weber County Commission.

Salt Lake Area Gang Project. 1996. Building Bridges of Hope: 6th Annual Utah Gang Conference, April 18–19, Salt Lake City, Utah.

———. 1997. "The Writing Is on the Wall: 1997 Utah Gang Update."

———. 1999. "If a Community Works Together It Stays Together: Utah Gang Update 1999."

———. 2000. "Working Together Toward a Gang-Free Community: Utah Gang Update 2000."

———. 2001. "Gangs—Drugs and Violence: Utah Gang Update 2001."

Sampson, Robert J., and John H. Laub. 2003. "Life-Course Desisters? Trajectories of Crime Among Delinquent Boys Followed to Age 70." *Criminology* 41:555–92.

Sampson, Robert J., and William Julius Wilson. 1995. "Toward a Theory of Race, Crime, and Urban Inequality." In *Crime and Inequality*, edited by J. Hagan and R. Peterson, 37–54. Stanford: Stanford University Press.

Sánchez-Jankowski, Martin. 1991. *Islands in the Street: Gangs and American Urban Society*. Los Angeles: University of California.

———. 2008. *Cracks in the Pavement: Social Change and Resilience in Poor Neighborhoods*. Berkeley. University of California Press.

Sanders, William B. 1994. *Gangbangs and Drive-bys: Grounded Culture and Juvenile Gang Violence*. New York: Aldine De Gruyter.

Scott, Greg. 2004. " 'It's a Sucker's Outfit' How Urban Gangs Enable and Impede the Reintegration of Ex-convicts." *Ethnography* 5:107–40.

Segura, Denise. 2003. "Navigating Between Two Worlds: The Labryinth of Chicana Intellectual Production in the Academy." *Journal of Black Studies* 34 (1): 28–51.

Sena-Rivera, Jaime. 1979. "Extended Kinship in the United States: Competing Models and the Case of la Familia Chicana." *Journal of Marriage and the Family* 41:121–29.

Shakur, Sanyika. 1993. *Monster: The Autobiography of an L.A. Gang Member.* New York: Atlantic Monthly Press.

Sheets, Rosa H. 2002. " 'You're Just a Kid That's There'—Chicano Perception of Disciplinary Events." *Journal of Latinos and Education* 1:105–22.

Shelden, Randall G. 2001. *Controlling the Dangerous Classes: A Critical Introduction to the History of Criminal Justice*. Needham Heights, Mass.: Allyn and Bacon.

Sherman, Lawrence W., Patrick R. Gartin, and Michael E. Buerger. 1989. "Hot Spots of Predatory Crime: Routine Activities and the Criminology of Place." *Criminology* 27:27–55.

Short, James F. 1997. *Poverty, Ethnicity, and Violent Crime*. Boulder: Westview Press.

Short, James F., and Fred L. Strodtbeck. 1965 (repr. 1974). *Group Process and Gang Delinquency*. Chicago: University of Chicago Press.

Sitkoff, Harvard. 1978. *A New Deal for Blacks: The Emergence of Civil Rights as a National Issue: The Depression Decade*. New York: Oxford University Press.

Solórzano, Daniel G. 1998. "Struggle Over Memory: The Roots of the Mexican Americans in Utah, 1776 Through the 1850s." *Aztlán* 23 (2): 81–117.

Souryal, Sam S. 2005. "The Role of Police in Nation Building." A paper presented at the ACJS annual meeting, Chicago, Illinois.

Spanish Speaking Peoples in Utah Oral Histories. 1970–75. Salt Lake City: Special Collections, J. Willard Marriott Library, University of Utah.

Spann, Girardeau A. 1993. *Race against the Court: The Court and Minorities in Contemporary America*. New York: New York University Press.

Spergel, Irving A. 1995. *The Youth Gang Problem: A Community Approach.* New York: Oxford University Press.

Spergel, Irving A., and G. Davidy Curry. 1993. "The National Youth Gang Survey: A Research and Development Process. In *The Gang Intervention Handbook*, edited by A. P. Goldstein and C. R. Huff, 359–400. Champaign, Ill.: Research Press.

Stacey, Judith. 1988. "Can There Be a Feminist Ethnography?" *Women's Studies International Forum* 11:21–27.

Stallworth, Ron. 1995. "Criminal Street Gangs of Utah: A 1995 Year End Status Report." http://judiciary.house.gov/legacy/353.htm.

Stansbury, Howard. 1966. *An Expedition to the Valley of the Great Salt Lake.* Readex Microprint.

State of Utah. 1999. *Annual Report: Edward Byrne Memorial State and Local Law Enforcement Assistance Grant Program.* Salt Lake City: Commission on Crime and Juvenile Justice.

———. 2000. *Annual Report: Edward Byrne Memorial State and Local Law Enforcement Assistance Grant Program.* Salt Lake City: Commission on Crime and Juvenile Justice.

———. 2001. *State of Utah: Drug and Violent Crime Enforcement Control Plan: 2001 Strategy Update.* Salt Lake City: Commission on Crime and Juvenile Justice.

Sun Tzu. 1963. *The Art of War.* New York: Oxford University Press.

Sutton, John R. 2000. "Imprisonment and Social Classification in Five Common-Law Democracies, 1955–1985." *American Journal of Sociology* 106:350–86.

Tannenbaum, Frank. 1938. *Crime and the Community.* New York: Ginn and Company.

Taylor, Carl S. 1990. *Dangerous Society.* East Lansing: Michigan State University Press.

Terrill, William, and Michael D. Resig. 2003. "Neighborhood Context and Police Use of Force." *Journal of Research in Crime and Delinquency* 40:291–321.

Thomas, Deborah. 2002. "1st Annual Report: Denver Police Department Contact Card Data Analysis, June 1, 2001 through May 31, 2002." Report for the Denver Police Department on Racial Profiling Data.

Thomas, Deborah, and Richard Hansen. 2004. "2nd Annual Report: Denver Police Department Contact Card Data Analysis, June 1, 2002 through May 31, 2003." Report for the Denver Police Department on Racial Profiling Data.

Thornberry, Terence P. 1998. "Membership in Youth Gangs and Involvement in Serious and Violent Offending." In *Serious and Violent Offenders: Risk Factors and Successful Interventions*, edited by R. Loeber and D. P. Farrington, 147–66. Thousand Oaks, Calif.: Sage Publications.

Thornberry, Terence P., Marvin D. Krohn, Alan J. Lizotte, Carolyn A. Smith, and Kimberly Tobin. 2003. *Gangs and Delinquency in Developmental Perspective.* New York: Cambridge University Press.

Thrasher, Frederic M. 1927 (repr. 1963). *The Gang: A Study of 1,313 gangs in Chicago.* University of Chicago.

Tuggle, Justin L., and Malcolm D. Holmes. 1997. "Blowing Smoke: Status Politics and the Smoking Ban." In *Deviant Behavior*, edited by C. D. Bryant, 53–66. New York: Worth.

United States Census. 1940–2010.

United States Commission on Civil Rights. 1970. *Mexican Americans and the Administration of Justice in the Southwest.* Washington, D.C.: U.S. Government Printing Office.

———. 1977. "School Desegregation in Ogden, Utah." Staff Report of the U.S. Commission on Civil Rights.

United States Senate. 1976. *Supplementary Detailed Staff Reports on Intelligence Activities and the Rights of Americans.* Book 3. Washington, D.C.: U.S. Government Printing Office.

Utah Commission on Criminal and Juvenile Justice. 2006. *Annual Report.*

Valdez, Avelardo. 2007. *Mexican American Girls and Gang Violence.* New York: Palgrave Macmillan.

Valdez, Avelardo, Alice Cepeda, and Charles Kaplan. 2009. "Homicidal Events Among Mexican American Street Gangs: A Situational Analysis." *Homicide Studies* 13 (3): 288–306.

Valencia, Richard R. 1991. "The Plight of Chicano Students: An Overview of Schooling Conditions and Outcomes." In *Chicano School Failure and Success: Research and Policy Agendas for the 1990s,* edited by R. Valencia, 3–26. New York: Falmer Press.

Valencia, Richard R., and Mary S. Black. 2002. "'Mexican Americans Don't Value Education!'—On the Basis of the Myth, Mythmaking, and Debunking." *Journal of Latinos and Education* 1:81–103.

Vélez, María B. 2001. "The Role of Public Social Control in Urban Neighborhoods: A Multi-Level Analysis of Victimization Risk." *Criminology* 39:837–63.

Venkatesh, Sudhir. 2000. *American Project: The Rise and Fall of a Modern Ghetto.* Cambridge: Harvard University Press.

———. 2008. *Gang Leader for a Day: A Rogue Sociologist Takes to the Streets.* New York: Penguin.

Verdoia, Ken, and Richard Firmage. 1996. *Utah: The Struggle for Statehood.* Salt Lake City: University of Utah Press.

Vigil, Ernesto B. 1996. "Eagle Eyes: The Early FBI Surveillance of Denver's Crusade for Justice." Paper presented at the Twenty-third National Association for Chicano or Chicana Studies (NACCS), Annual Conference, Chicago.

———. 1999. *The Crusade for Justice: Chicano Militancy and the Government's War on Dissent.* Madison: University of Wisconsin Press.

Vigil, James Diego. 1988. *Barrio Gangs: Street Life and Identity in Southern California.* Austin: University of Texas Press.

———. 2002. *A Rainbow of Gangs: Street Cultures in the Mega-City.* Austin: University of Texas Press.

———.2007. *The Projects: Gang and Non-gang Families in East Los Angeles.* Austin: University of Texas Press.

Walker, Ronald W., Richard E. Turley, and Glen M. Leonard. 2008. *Massacre at Mountain Meadows.* New York: Oxford University Press.

Wallace, Irving. 1961. *The Twenty-Seventh Wife.* Simon and Schuster.

Walsh, James Patrick. 1995. "Young and Latino in a Cold War Barrio; Survival, the Search for Identity, and the Formation of Street Gangs in Denver, 1945–1955." Master's thesis, University of Colorado at Denver.

Wax, R. 1971. *Doing Fieldwork: Warnings and Advice.* Chicago: University of Chicago Press.

Weitzer, Ronald. 1999. "Citizen Perceptions of Police Misconduct: Race and Neighborhood Context." *Justice Quarterly* 16:819–46.

Werner, Oswald, and Mark G. Schoepfle. 1987. *Systematic Fieldwork.* Beverly Hills, Calif.: Sage.

Westley, William A. 1953. "Violence and the Police." *The American Journal of Sociology* 59:34–41.

White, Richard. 1991. *It's Your Misfortune and None of My Own: A New History of the American West.* Norman: University of Oklahoma Press.

Whyte, William F. 1943 (repr. 1993). *Street Corner Society: The Social Structure of an Italian Slum.* Chicago: University of Chicago Press.

Wilderson, Frank B. 2003. "The Prison Slave as Hegemony's (Silent) Scandal." *Social Justice* 30 (2): 18–27.

Williams, Stanley. 2007. *Blue Rage, Black Redemption: A Memoir.* New York: Touchstone.

Wilson, William J. 1996. *When Work Disappears: The World of the New Urban Poor.* New York: Vintage.

Winfree, Thomas L., Frances P. Bernat, and Finn-Aage Esbensen. 2001. "Hispanic and Anglo Gang Membership in Two Southwestern Cities." *Social Science Journal* 38:105–17.

Yablonsky, Lewis. 1962 (repr. 1970). *The Violent Gang.* Baltimore: Penguin.

———. 1997. *Gangsters: Fifty Years of Madness, Drugs, and Death on the Streets of America.* New York: New York University Press.

Yorgason, Ethan R. 2003. *Transformation of the Mormon Culture Region.* Urbana: University of Illinois Press.

Zatz, Marjorie S. 1987. "Chicano Youth Gangs and Crime: the Creation of a Moral Panic." *Contemporary Crises* 11:129–158.

Zatz, Marjorie S., and Edwardo L. Portillos. 2000. "Voices from the Barrio: Chicano/a Gangs, Families, and Communities." *Criminology* 38 (2): 369–402.

Newspapers

Denver Post (DP)
April 4, 1936. "Deportation Plans Protested by Group."
September 8, 1946. James T. Burke. "Grand Jury Probe Background Reviewed by District Attorney."
March 11, 1950. "Hoodlum Gang Here Joins Side of Law."
November 12, 1950. Bernard Beckwith. "Knives Promote Crime: Teen-age Stabbing Menace Grows."
December 10, 1950. Charles Little. "Girl Gangs: A Civic Problem."

June 3, 1952. Bernard Beckwith. "City Police Open Drive Against Teen-Age Gangs."

April 5, 1959. Lawrence G. Weiss. "How Good is Denver's Police Force?: A Report on the Skill and Quality of the City's Finest."

November 29, 1959. Lawrence G. Weiss. "Kids With the Odds Against Them: Why Spanish-American Children Get in Trouble."

1960. "The Spanish American in Denver."

November 10, 1982. Tom Coakley. "Students Forbidden to Use Alley: North High Principal Trying to Prevent Mexican-Hispanic Violence."

April 25, 1983. Jim Kirksey. "Park Sweep Nets Guns, Tire Irons."

June 20, 1983. Jim Kirksey. "Denver DA Backs Gangs Crackdown."

December 12, 1983. Tom Coakley. "Gangs' Graffiti, Fighting Help Spread Reputations."

May 12, 1988. Sebastian Sinisi. "Crips-Bloods Gang Warfare Leaves 2 Shot."

July 15, 1988. "Juvenile Arrested in Slaying."

September 4, 1988. Bill Briggs and Ginny McKibben. "Violence Eases, but Gang Ranks Up: Some Groups Have Spread into Suburbs, other Counties."

November 5, 1988. Bill Briggs and Jennifer Gavin. "Peña Hits Back: 'We Won't Put Up with It.'"

November 6, 1988. Brice Finley. "Cops Nab Crips Gang Member in Shootings."

November 10, 1988. Jim Kirksey. "Drive Against Gangs, Crack Dealing Beefed Up."

November 10, 1988. Jim Kirksey. "N.E. Denver 'Police State,' Black Leader Says."

December 9, 1988. Jim Kirksey and Bruce Finley. "Gang Link Suspected in Chase, Shooting."

December 17, 1988. "Ministers Will Ride with Police: Clerics Hope to Defuse Tensions, Make Contact with Gangs."

January 7, 1989. Bruce Finley. "Police Seek $1.5 Million for Gang Crackdown."

December 5, 1993. Christopher Lopez. "List Brands 2 of 3 Young Black Men."

July 18, 2004. Sean Kelly, John Ingold, and David Migoya. "Deadly Pace in Police Gun Use 18 People Died Out of 26 Shot by Officers Since '01."

Denver Weekly News

January 29, 2004. K. Muhammad. "Police Brutality Concerns Addressed on MLK Holiday," 32 (47).

Deseret News (DN)

October 1, 1981. "L.A.-Style Gangs Plague Ogden Now, Police Say."

April 23, 1989a. "Salt Lake Gang History." By Brent Israelsen.

April 23, 1989b. Brent Israelsen. "Writings on the Walls: Gangs from Coast Come to Utah Toting Guns, Drugs and Trouble."

April 13, 1990. "Job Corps Officials Deny L.A. Gangs are Infiltrating Campus."

Los Angeles Times

September 21, 1999. S. Glover and M. Lait. "Ex-Officer Calls Corruption a Chronic Cancer."

February 14, 2000. S. Glover and M. Lait. "Beatings Alleged to be Routine at Rampart."

February 27, 2003. M. Lait and S. Glover. "Secret LAPD Testimony Implicated Nine Officers."

August 23, 2003. S. Glover and M. Lait. "Ex-Chief Refuses to Discuss Rampart."

Metropolitan

March 11, 2004. T. Nguyen. "Activists Attack Gang Database."

New York Times

December 11, 1993. Dirk Johnson. "2 Out of 3 Young Black Men in Denver Are on Gang Suspect List."

April 4, 2003. Nick Madigan. "North Utah Faces Influx Of Racists: Prison-Bred Gangs Take Root in Ogden."

Rocky Mountain News (RMN)

1936. "Armed Force Acting Under Martial Law to Stop All: Entire Southern Border of Colorado Will Be Patrolled by Soldiers to Halt Aliens, Needy."

October 23, 1936. "Vigilance Holds Crime at Low Ebb in Denver: 28 Men Patrol Downtown with Bulk of Arrests for Drunkenness."

December 19, 1942. "Hoodlums Watched by Police."

December 21, 1942. "Zoot Suit Gang: Companion Unmasks Youth, Five Arrested."

June 8, 1943. "Mexicans Warned Off Streets in L.A. as Zoot Rioting Overwhelms Police."

June 19, 1943. "No Coast Zoot Suiters Can Alight in Denver."

August 31, 1943. "'Wolf Order' Zootists Sought in Auto Death."

May 8, 1944. "Outbreaks of Violence; 7 are Held."

May 9, 1944. "High Officials Probe City's Zoot Flareup."

May 9, 1944. "A Terrible Denver Tragedy."

May 10, 1944. "Curfew Revision Planned to Curb Hoodlums."

May 11, 1944. "Sentences up to $300 or 90 Days Given 11 Youths in War on Gangs."

May 13, 1944. "Warrants for Arrest of 19 Accused Zooters are Issued in Denver."

May 14, 1944. "8 Youths, 6 Girls Are Arrested as Part of Gang of Zooters."

October 8, 1944. "Problems of Spanish-Americans Will Be Studied at Regis Seminar."

October 18, 1944. "Urge Community Councils to Aid Spanish-Americans."

April 8, 1946. "Two Youths Wounded in East Side Gang War."

August 12, 1946. Sam Lusky. "Kirschwing Charges Burke Never Asked for Help As Political Dispute Breaks over Police Probe."

1946. "Grand Jury Returns Indictments on Three Denver Police Officers."

January 11, 1947. Edward Lehman II. "Steele Upholds Hanebuth Refusal To Answer Grand Jury Questions."

October 23, 1949. Sam Lusky. "Kids Form Gangs, Send Juvenile Crime Rate Soaring."

October 24, 1949. Sam Lusky. "Rich and Poor Kids Alike Want to Be 'Tough Guys.'"

October 26, 1949. Sam Lusky. "Gang Kids Get Choice: Work, School or Jail."

January 23, 1950. Zuckerman, Leo. "Teen Gang Wary Flares Again; 2 Boys Stabbed."

March 12, 1950. "Gilliam Joins Hoodlum Gang to Help Them Out."

March 15, 1950. "Youthful Gang, the Heads, Tell Judge Gilliam, 'We'll Go Straight."

March 30, 1950. Jack Gaskie. "Judge Gilliam Lays Down Law To Teenage Gang He Joined."

March 31, 1950. Jack Castel. "Encourage These Boys to Succeed."

May 4, 1950. "Girl Gangs in Denver Wage Worse Battles Than Boys, Police Say."

May 9, 1950. Kelly, George V. "Adult Reds Guiding Kid Gangs, Belief of Denver Judge."

February 22, 1953. "Organized Denver Gangs Few, But Juvenile Crime Increasing."

March 29, 1953. Bill Bardsley. "40 Teeners Stage Melee After Drinking at Dance."

May 31, 1953. Bill Bardsley. "Lovers Lane Terrorism Ends With Gang's Arrest."

January 31, 1954. Robert Perkin. "Study of Critical Denver Problem."

February 2, 1954. Robert Perkin. "Underpaid, Ill Fed, Badly Housed: Can We Blame the Poor After Half-Century of This?"

February 4, 1954. Robert Perkin. "High Infant Death Rate."

February 5, 1954. Robert Perkin. "No Running Water, No Heat: It's Home to Denver's Poorest of the Poor."

February 6, 1954. Robert Perkin. "What Are the Solutions To This Denver Problem?"

February 20, 1954. "New Gang Organized."

March 16, 1954. "Teen-Age Gangs in Denver Cited by Probe Report."

April 4, 1954. Jack Gaskie. "Perkin Series Hailed as Delinquency Drops in Denver."

January 27, 1955. Robert Perkin. "Denver's Spanish Americans—a Year Later: New Finds Indications of Progress."

1957. "Police Put Clamps on Teenage Battle."

1957. "White Delinquents Are Found Worst-Adjusted."

October 9, 1957. "Spanish-Americans Show Social Gains."

October 10, 1957. "Spanish-Americans Move Onward."

January 10, 1959. Al Nakkula. "Police Department's Grown, But Stickup Detail Hasn't."

December 9, 1959. "Police Move to Smash Youthful Gangs."

March 15, 1960. Jack Gaskie. "Denver Girls Forming Gangs at Shocking Rate."

April 26, 1960. Gene Wortsman. "Congress Told About Hoods."

April 27, 1960. Al Nakkula. "Work Gangs Start As War on Teen Hoods Continues."

December 30, 1982. Chance Conner. "Member of Gang Killed: Police Warning Preceded Shooting of Two Teens."

June 18, 1983. Chance Conner. "New Law Termed Tool Against Gang Violence."

June 7, 1986. Stacey Burling. "City Plans Crackdown on New Gang."
July 15, 1988a. Mark Brown and Tony Pugh. "Kelly Fears 'Open Season' on Police."
July 15, 1988b. Karen Bowers. "Juvenile Arrested in Slaying; Alleged Bloods Member Sought."
November 5, 1988. Karen Bowers. "Slain Teen in 'Wrong Place at Wrong Time.'"
November 10, 1988. Karen Bowers. "Slain Teen was Shot Five Times."
February 23, 1989.
November 18, 1989. Robert Jackson. "Anti-gang Effort Inaugurated."
November 19, 1989. Fawn Germer. "Parents Tackle Gang Conflict."
December 2, 1989. Robert Jackson. "Teamwork Mounts Against Gangs: Police, Athletes Try to Show Youths a Better Way."
October 10, 1990. J. C. Ensslin. "Denver Schools Ban Gang Apparel."
October 14, 1990. T. Amole. "ACLU to Help if Color Ban is Challenged."
November 18, 1993. Bill Scanlon. "Colorado Teen Slayings Soar, Report Says."
March 27, 1994. Burt Hubbard. "How Gangs Took Hold in Denver."
July 20, 2000. K. Vaughan. "Charges Filed Against Two Cops Veteran Gang Officers Accused of Destroying Evidence in 'At least' 80 Criminal Cases." Local, p. 4A.
November 24, 2001. P. Lowe. "Panel, Police See Different Theories in Glass Shards: Glass, Gun and Blood Focus 'Forensic Battle.'"
January 26, 2002. J. Kass. "Portrait of O'Shea: a Cop with Conviction."
March 18, 2004. H. Gutierrez. "Denver Cops Get an Earful."
April 21, 2004. S. Lindsay. "Police Acted 'Inappropriately.'"
June 14, 2009. B. Hubbard and F. Cardona. "Denver's Original Gangsters: 1986 Rolling 30 Crips."
Standard Examiner (SE)
May 1, 1992. Ralph Wakley. "Conference Looks at Gang Control."
July 19, 1999. J. Haws. "Meeting on Gangs Seeks Zero Tolerance."
April 5, 2003. Mark Gray. "N.Y. Times: Weber Co. Is a Racism Hotbed."
October 23, 2003. T. Gurrister. "Police Tactics Queried: Union Station Case Builds."
February 22, 2004. T. Gurrister. "FBI Probing Ogden incident."
April 1, 2004. T. Gurrister. "Officer Accused of Payback Arrest."
July 19, 2007. Scott Schwebke. "Gang Issues Turn Political."
August 12, 2007. "Spotlight on Gangs."
August 13, 2007a. "Suppression Versus Prevention."
August 13, 2007b. "Too Many Parents in Denial, Police Say."
January 2, 2010. Scott Schwebke. "Garcia Pledges to Remain Advocate for Minorities."
September 14, 2010. "Ogden Trece Injunction Opens Door to Legalized Harassment."
September 15, 2010. T. Gurrister. "Judge: No to ACLU Bid to Join Gang Case."
Westword
June 3, 2004a. Laura Bond. "The Gang Is All Here: What's in a Name?"

June 3, 2004b. Laura Bond. "Street Wise: Robert Duran Got Jacked Up. Then He Grew Up."

February 25, 1999. Steve Jackson. "Dealing with the Devil."

February 22, 2007. Luke Turf. "The Transformers: They Created Denver's Gang Life. A Generation Later, Can They Break Free?"

July 20, 2000. K. Vaughan. "Charges Filed Against Two Cops Veteran Gang Officers Accused of Destroying Evidence in 'At Least' 80 Criminal Cases."

Index

education/schools (*continued*)
—gangs in: higher-achieving students and, 137–39; schools as recruiting grounds for, 134–37, 139–40; strength of, 138
Ehrenreich, Barbara, 156
El Paso, Texas, 10
emergent gang cities. *See* Ogden, Utah
employment and incarceration, 126
entrenched solidarity, 154
Erikson, Kai T., 196
Escobar, Edward J., 82
ethnicity. *See* race/ethnicity
ethnography: about, 6; advantages, 9; location focus, 9–10; multiple forms of membership roles, 28; and race, 28; summary of studies, 7–8 (table); techniques, 21, 22, 34
Eurogang, 4
excessive regulation, 206–207, 208, 210, 212

families: and decision to join gang, 140, 152; and education, 132; goals of Latino, 123; importance of extended, 127–28; involvement with gangs, 124–25, 127; profiling of, of gang members, 50–51; social exclusion of, outside barrios, 124; structure of Latino, 125
Fanon, Frantz, 175, 205; on colonization, 27, 149
fatalism, 154, 206
Father of Juvenile Court, 68
Federal Bureau of Investigation (FBI), 57, 179–80, 181
federal government: counterintelligence programs, 85–86; funding for gang suppression, 110, 111; funding for policing, 66; investigations of police brutality, 57; joint operations with state and local agencies, 42, 90; and Mormons, 100; neighborhood revitalization funds, 113–15; racketeering laws,

42, 90, 115, 216n1(ch2); surveillance of organizations, 179–80, 181
Felson, Richard B., 157
female gangs, 78, 84, 144
field studies, 6, 7–8 (table), 9–10, 23
Fine, Michelle, 48
fractured gangs, 142–44, 152
Fresques, James, 73
Fridell, Lori A., 59–60
Frieire, Paulo, 27
friendships, 140–41, 142, 144

gang associates: and members, 137–39; membership of, as choice, 141–42; profiling of, 50–51; women as, 151
Gang Group, 32–33
gang ideals, core: development of, 203–204; functions of, 18, 149, 150; and gender inequality, 150; incarceration as strengthening, 160–61; overview of, 18. *See also* courageous response to threats; loyalty; status; stoicism
gang injunctions, 115–16
gang lists: effect of being on, 49, 52–53; nourish deviant behavior, 196; validity of, 49–51, 188–92
gang members: academics as, 4, 218n4; and associates, 137–38, 141–42; attraction of women to, 129; contribution to group's subordination, 204; cost and benefits to, 150; as criminals, 3–5, 41–42, 111–12, 167, 168; defining, 112; drug dealing by, 108–109, 161–62; duration of involvement, 89, 166–67, 169–70; effect of police underprotection on, 13, 63; elevated status of, 75, 137, 166, 167, 203–204; and family involvement, 124–25, 127, 152; family structure of, 125; and fatherhood, 24; informal code of behavior of, 169,

179; initiation of, 1–2, 151–52, 153, 218n1; media portrayal of, 1, 2, 74, 92; OGs, 164; responsibilities of, 23, 142; risk-taking behavior of, 130–31; rivalries in prison, 159; as socially constructed identity, 24; victimization of communities by, 130–31, 155–56, 167, 204, 212; as victims, 63–64. *See also* gang lists; white gangs

—demographics: during civil rights movement, 13; of girl gangs, 78, 84, 143; in Ogden, 112, 113; police inflation of number of, 188–92; race/ethnicity of, 11, 54; undercounting of white, 189–90; whites in nonwhite gangs, 141; women, 77–78, 131, 143, 150; youth, 119

—former: as academics, 215n2; as co-opters, 183; as professional ex-s, 28; role in gang suppression, 174–75, 194, 195

—recruitment of: associates, 141–42; of friends, 140; schools as grounds for, 134–37, 139–40

Gang Reduction Initiative in Denver (GRID), 66

gangs, definitions of, 4, 5

gangsters. *See* gang members

gang suppression model, 15, 16, 41, 42, 202

gang symbols: status and display of, 162–65; tattoos, 164, 218n3

—clothing: and gender, 164; as reason for police stops, 43, 44, 48; in schools, 134; zoot suits, 70–73

Garot, Robert, 162–63

gender: and Aryan supremacy groups, 145; breakdown of gang members, 131; and courageous response to threats, 158–59; and duration of gang involvement, 169–70; equality promotion, 186–87, 195; and gang symbols, 164; and incarcera-

tion, 159; inequality and gang ideals, 150; and informal gang code of behavior, 169, 179; profiling by, 47–48; socialization of, roles, 128–31; and violence, 158–59. *See also* women

getting jumped: into gangs, 1–2, 151; out of gangs, 24

ghettos, 62–63, 120–21. *See also* colonization

Gilliam, Philip B.: gang feuds, 77; overview of, 92; programs to combat gangs, 80–81; use of guns by gangs, 74; and work gangs, 84

girl gangs, 78, 84, 143

Gleason, Debra K., 161

gloried selves, 75, 137, 166, 167

Godfrey, Mathew, 114

Goldberg, Robert Alan, 68–69

Gómez, Laura E., 27, 175

Gonzalez, Corky, 85–86, 179–80, 181

grandfathering into gangs, 151–52

grassroots empowerment: and alteration of gangs, 13–14; ASAP, 31, 67, 172–73, 174, 175; challenging predominant view of gangs, 188–92; and civil rights movement, 13–14, 85–86, 202; Crusade for Justice, 177–80, 181; cultural empowerment as decolonization, 184–86; evolution of gangs into community organizations, 174, 176; examples of, 18, 175–76, 211; FBI investigations of organizations, 179–81; and gang development, 13; and inability to enter dominant group organizations, 211; POP, 32, 61; post World War II, 85; SOCIO, 106–107, 181–82; through gender equality, 186–87, 195; transforming gangs for, 213; violence reduction strategy, 192–96

Greiner, Laura Ross, 88–89

Guevara, Che, 176, 186, 205

predominant view of gangs of,
188–92; federal funding, 66; and
media, 83, 191; minority officers,
43, 217n1(ch5); as perpetua-
tors of gangs, 153; police stops,
40–41, 43, 46, 51–52, 112; racial
oppression by, 55–59; status and
response to, 154, 157–58; treatment of gang associates, 142;
underprotection from, 62–64,
73, 107; view of entire communities as criminal, 196; view
of gangs, 3–5, 54; violence by,
53, 55–59, 62, 74, 216n2(ch2),
216n3; and white gangs, 54–55;
zero tolerance policy, 66. *See also*
profiling; suppression of gangs;
war on gangs
Levin, Daniel, 62
Lindsey, Ben B., 68
locotes, 23, 216n1(ch1)
Lofland, John, 23
Lofland, Lyn H., 23
Lopez, Edward A., 137
loyalty, 151–54, 204
lumpen proletariat, 175–76
Lusky, Sam, 74

MacKinnon, William P., 98, 100
Malcolm X, 27, 205
Manasse, Michelle, 130–31, 166
marginalized neighborhoods, 119–22
Martínez, Esteva, 13–14, 183
Marx, Karl, 67
Mastrofski, Stephen D., 51, 52
Maxson, Cheryl, 4, 143–44
McPherson, Robert S., 98
media: focus on race, 109; and
police, 83, 191; portrayal of gang
members, 1, 2, 74, 92; portrayal of
Summer of Violence, 88–89; and
public perception of violence, 89
Memmi, Albert, 27
Mendelsohn, Harold, 60
Merton, Robert K., 27, 29
Mexican Americans. *See* Latinos

Miller, Walter, 171
Mills, C. Wright, 9
Mirandé, Alfredo: disrespect by
police, 52; and racialized oppression theory, 205; socialization of
gender roles, 128; undocumented
immigrants, 58
*Missing Stories: An Oral History of
Ethnic Minority Groups in Utah*
(Kelen and Stone), 102
Moloney, Molly, 24
Monster Kody, 5
Montgomery, Charles, 27
Moore, Joan W., 120, 127, 129, 200
Morales, Armando, 59
Mormonism: and African Americans, 99; early years, 96–98,
217n2(ch4); evolution into
mainstream organization, 176;
ideological changes, 101; Latino
converts to, 104; Mormons as
undocumented immigrants, 97,
217n2(ch4); and Native Americans, 98–100; in Ogden, 101; and
white supremacy, 201
Movimiento Estudiantil Chicano de
Aztlán (MEChA), 186–87

Native Americans: and Mormons,
98–100; in nineteenth-century
Denver, 68; racial oppression of, in
Utah, 106; tribes in Utah, 97
neighborhood revitalization, 113–15
neighborhoods. *See* barrios; communities; ghettos
Newton, James Quigg, 73–74

Ogden, Utah: community advocacy
organizations, 14; disrespect/
violence by police, 56–57; early
history, 100–101; education in,
132, 133; Latinos in, 43, 117, 120;
overview of, 2; population, 35, 66,
101–102, 120, 216n4; profiling in,
43–49; research time period, 39;
segregation in, 102, 106